# ZERO
# SIX
# BRAVO

Also by Damien Lewis:

*Operation Certain Death*
*Bloody Heroes*
*Apache Dawn*
*Cobra 405*
*Fire Strike 7/9* (with Paul Bomber Graham)
*Sergeant Rex* (With Mike Dowling)
*It's All About Treo* (with Dave Heyhoe)

# ZERO
# SIX
# BRAVO

*60 Special Forces. 100,000 Enemy.*
*The Explosive True Story.*

# DAMIEN LEWIS

Quercus

First published in Great Britain in 2013 by
Quercus
55 Baker Street
7<sup>th</sup> Floor, South Block
W1U 8EW

A CIP catalogue record for this book is available
from the British Library

HB ISBN 978 1 78206 080 2
TPB ISBN 978 1 78206 081 9
Ebook ISBN 978 1 78206 082 6

Maps © 2013 William Donohoe

Text designed and typeset by Ellipsis
Printed and bound in Great Britain by Clays Ltd. St Ives plc

For
Roger Hammond
*Semper fidelis*

A brother and a true friend
Gone but not forgotten

# AUTHOR'S NOTE

For reasons of operational security I have changed the names of the men who appear in this book, and for similar reasons I have, where necessary, appropriately disguised certain operational details and elements.

Rarely are two soldiers' recollections of a mission such as the one related in these pages the same, and individual written records compiled after the event also tend to differ. I have spoken to many different sources from all ranks, and I have done my best to paint a true picture of what took place during the mission. British publishers practice a voluntary code of conduct with relation to books about British military operations. Under this, such books are submitted to the MOD for checking on Operational Security (OPSEC) and Personal Security (PERSEC) grounds. Changes required by the MOD on OPSEC and PERSEC grounds, and agreed as justified under such grounds by the author and publisher, were made to this book. At no stage did the author seek the MOD's official approval for this book, nor did author or publishers desire or request such, and author and publisher sought no verification from MOD of the factual accuracy or otherwise of events portrayed herein.

This book is an impartial, independent and unbiased rendering of the events as they took place in Iraq in 2003. Factual accuracy of the events portrayed remains the responsibility of the author solely, and the author takes full responsibility for any errors that may inadvertently have been made. Any such mistakes are entirely of the author's own making and he will be happy to correct them in future editions.

Over the past decade I have written several books about contemporary British and allied Special Forces missions, featuring operations by the SAS and the SBS. The manuscripts for those books were submitted to the Ministry of Defence before publication, for clearance for OPSEC and PERSEC reasons. Those books have been well received by key individuals within the military, and they portrayed British forces operating in a professional and dedicated manner.

The servicemen portrayed here displayed the ultimate professionalism and can-do attitude of our elite military and Special Forces operators, putting their own personal danger second to the success of the mission they had been tasked to undertake. At the time the mission portrayed in these pages took place, those who participated in it were largely denigrated in the world's media – a condemnation fuelled in part by the capture of some of the Squadron's vehicles, which the Iraqi regime paraded before the world's press. These men deserve a far better, more balanced portrayal of what took place, and my purpose in writing this book is largely to set the record straight.

The operation was extremely high-risk. Rather than being the failure that was portrayed at the time, this elite unit performed to the maximum of its ability and training, both on the ground and in supporting roles. Operating far behind enemy lines against a force by which they were vastly outnumbered and outgunned, they brought every man out alive. This book, written with the benefit of hindsight, should go some way towards setting the record straight – to the benefit of all those involved. The SBS motto is 'By Strength and by Guile'; that of the SAS, 'Who Dares Wins'. This mission demonstrated how, in seemingly impossible and unwinnable situations, these mottoes were put into effect.

# ACKNOWLEDGEMENTS

Thanks to the following: my literary agent Annabel Merullo and her assistant Laura Williams; my film agent Luke Speed, and associates; all those individuals who helped with the research and writing of this story; photographer Andy Chittock, for some of the fantastic images; Philip Campion, for casting an appraising eye over the drafts. Special thanks to Richard Milner, David North, Josh Ireland, Patrick Carpenter, Caroline Proud, Dave Murphy, Ron Beard and all at my publisher, Quercus, for recognizing from the get-go what an extraordinary story this is, and why it had to be told. Special thanks also to my very good friend Mike Mawhinney for all the help, and to Lt Col Crispin Lockhart, of the MOD, for his efforts to clear this book for publication.

Out of the night that covers me,
Black as the Pit from pole to pole,
I thank whatever gods may be
For my unconquerable soul.

In the fell clutch of circumstance
I have not winced nor cried aloud.
Under the bludgeonings of chance
My head is bloody, but unbowed.

Beyond this place of wrath and tears
Looms but the Horror of the shade,
And yet the menace of the years
Finds, and shall find, me unafraid.

It matters not how strait the gate,
How charged with punishments the scroll,
I am the master of my fate:
I am the captain of my soul.

'Invictus' William Ernest Henley

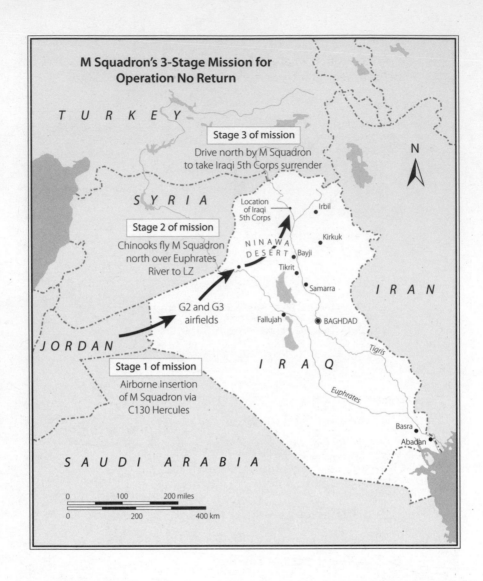

M Squadron's 3-Stage Mission for Operation No Return

TURKEY

SYRIA

**Stage 3 of mission**

Drive north by M Squadron to take Iraqi 5th Corps surrender

Location of Iraqi 5th Corps

Irbil

**Stage 2 of mission**

Chinooks fly M Squadron north over Euphrates River to LZ

NINAWA DESERT

Bayji

Kirkuk

Tikrit

G2 and G3 airfields

Fallujah

Samarra

BAGHDAD

IRAN

JORDAN

IRAQ

Tigris

**Stage 1 of mission**

Airborne insertion of M Squadron via C130 Hercules

Euphrates

Basra

Abadan

SAUDI ARABIA

N

0    100    200 miles

0    200    400 km

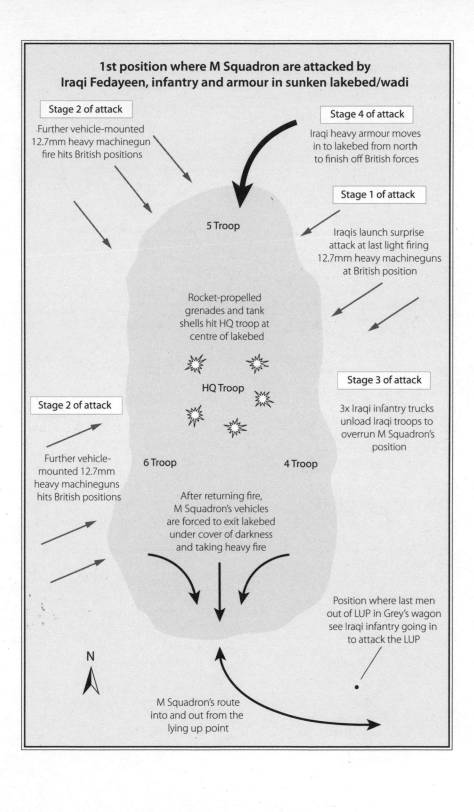

**1st position where M Squadron are attacked by
Iraqi Fedayeen, infantry and armour in sunken lakebed/wadi**

Stage 2 of attack

Further vehicle-mounted
12.7mm heavy machinegun
fire hits British positions

Stage 4 of attack

Iraqi heavy armour moves
in to lakebed from north
to finish off British forces

Stage 1 of attack

Iraqis launch surprise
attack at last light firing
12.7mm heavy machineguns
at British position

5 Troop

Rocket-propelled
grenades and tank
shells hit HQ troop at
centre of lakebed

HQ Troop

Stage 3 of attack

3x Iraqi infantry trucks
unload Iraqi troops to
overrun M Squadron's
position

Stage 2 of attack

Further vehicle-
mounted 12.7mm
heavy machineguns
hits British positions

6 Troop                    4 Troop

After returning fire,
M Squadron's vehicles
are forced to exit lakebed
under cover of darkness
and taking heavy fire

Position where last men
out of LUP in Grey's wagon
see Iraqi infantry going in
to attack the LUP

N

M Squadron's route
into and out from the
lying up point

# Escape route from LUP where ambushed to Wadi of Death where vehicles bogged-in

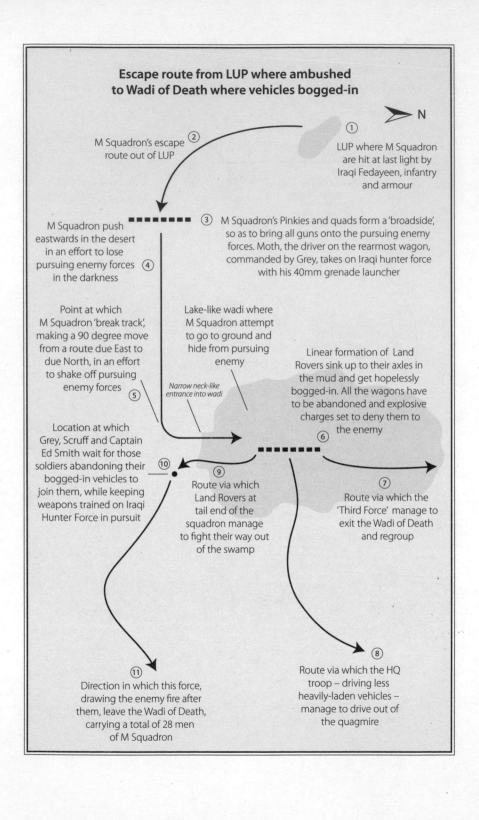

N

① LUP where M Squadron are hit at last light by Iraqi Fedayeen, infantry and armour

② M Squadron's escape route out of LUP

③ M Squadron's Pinkies and quads form a 'broadside', so as to bring all guns onto the pursuing enemy forces. Moth, the driver on the rearmost wagon, commanded by Grey, takes on Iraqi hunter force with his 40mm grenade launcher

④ M Squadron push eastwards in the desert in an effort to lose pursuing enemy forces in the darkness

⑤ Point at which M Squadron 'break track', making a 90 degree move from a route due East to due North, in an effort to shake off pursuing enemy forces

Lake-like wadi where M Squadron attempt to go to ground and hide from pursuing enemy

*Narrow neck-like entrance into wadi*

⑥ Linear formation of Land Rovers sink up to their axles in the mud and get hopelessly bogged-in. All the wagons have to be abandoned and explosive charges set to deny them to the enemy

⑩ Location at which Grey, Scruff and Captain Ed Smith wait for those soldiers abandoning their bogged-in vehicles to join them, while keeping weapons trained on Iraqi Hunter Force in pursuit

⑨ Route via which Land Rovers at tail end of the squadron manage to fight their way out of the swamp

⑦ Route via which the 'Third Force' manage to exit the Wadi of Death and regroup

⑪ Direction in which this force, drawing the enemy fire after them, leave the Wadi of Death, carrying a total of 28 men of M Squadron

⑧ Route via which the HQ troop – driving less heavily-laden vehicles – manage to drive out of the quagmire

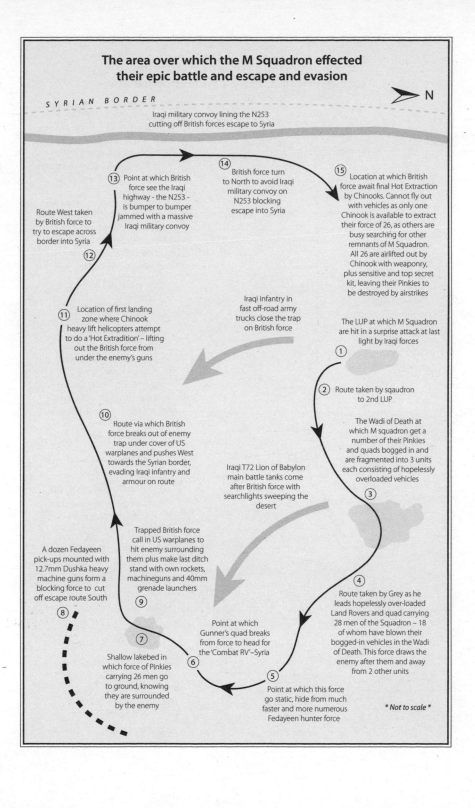

# The area over which the M Squadron effected their epic battle and escape and evasion

*SYRIAN BORDER*

N

Iraqi military convoy lining the N253
cutting off British forces escape to Syria

⑬ Point at which British
force see the Iraqi
highway - the N253 -
is bumper to bumper
jammed with a massive
Iraqi military convoy

⑭ British force turn
to North to avoid Iraqi
military convoy on
N253 blocking
escape into Syria

⑮ Location at which British
force await final Hot Extraction
by Chinooks. Cannot fly out
with vehicles as only one
Chinook is available to extract
their force of 26, as others are
busy searching for other
remnants of M Squadron.
All 26 are airlifted out by
Chinook with weaponry,
plus sensitive and top secret
kit, leaving their Pinkies to
be destroyed by airstrikes

Route West taken
by British force to
try to escape across
border into Syria

⑫

⑪ Location of first landing
zone where Chinook
heavy lift helicopters attempt
to do a 'Hot Extradition' – lifting
out the British force from
under the enemy's guns

Iraqi infantry in
fast off-road army
trucks close the trap
on British force

The LUP at which M Squadron
are hit in a surprise attack at last
light by Iraqi forces

① 

② Route taken by sqaudron
to 2nd LUP

The Wadi of Death at
which M squadron get a
number of their Pinkies
and quads bogged in and
are fragmented into 3 units
each consisting of hopelessly
overloaded vehicles

③

⑩ Route via which British
force breaks out of enemy
trap under cover of US
warplanes and pushes West
towards the Syrian border,
evading Iraqi infantry and
armour on route

Iraqi T72 Lion of Babylon
main battle tanks come
after British force with
searchlights sweeping the
desert

④ Route taken by Grey as he
leads hopelessly over-loaded
Land Rovers and quad carrying
28 men of the Squadron – 18
of whom have blown their
bogged-in vehicles in the Wadi
of Death. This force draws the
enemy after them and away
from 2 other units

A dozen Fedayeen
pick-ups mounted with
12.7mm Dushka heavy
machine guns form a
blocking force to cut
off escape route South

Trapped British force
call in US warplanes to
hit enemy surrounding
them plus make last ditch
stand with own rockets,
machineguns and 40mm
grenade launchers

⑨

⑧

⑦ 

Shallow lakebed in
which force of Pinkies
carrying 26 men go
to ground, knowing
they are surrounded
by the enemy

Point at which
Gunner's quad breaks
from force to head for
the 'Combat RV'–Syria

⑥

⑤ Point at which this force
go static, hide from much
faster and more numerous
Fedayeen hunter force

*Not to scale*

# CHAPTER ONE

Steve Grayling was crouched in a hidden position, the ink-black desert night deathly quiet all around him. Or at least it had been until the last few minutes of his sentry duty, which was scheduled to last from 0400 hours until first light. But then the first of the animals had appeared.

In the open, empty quiet of the Iraqi desert his senses had been heightened, his hearing tuned in to the utter absence of life. The slightest noise would signify movement, which meant something living was out there, which in turn might signal danger. But the bone-dry rock and sand had offered little to remind him that he was still on earth and not on some barren, lifeless moonscape.

That was how it had been for the first ninety minutes of his watch – until, from out of nowhere, the herd of goats had appeared. The hollow tinkling of the animal's bell sounded alien and alarming as it beat out an eerie rhythm across the bare stillness. It seemed impossible that any four-legged creature could survive in a place so empty of water and vegetation – yet here the goats were. And with the scraggly creatures had come the inevitable two-legged escort.

ZERO SIX BRAVO

Everything about the desert night was black. The moon was hanging low on the horizon, and above it the stars formed a skein of brightness that stretched across the heavens, but still the light intensity at ground level had to be no more than 10 millilux. Under such illumination the terrain all around him was so devoid of features as to form a flat, uniform void.

It was only the goats that stood out, their erect forms casting long, leggy moon-shadows. The white splotches on their coats glowed silvery bright, like patches of polished chain mail set into a suit of dark armour. As for the goat-herder, he appeared giant-like, casting mighty distorted shadows as he walked, using a long stick to steer the herd to wherever it was he was heading.

Steve Grayling hunched over the hulking great form of a .50-calibre heavy machine-gun, its barrel tracing the herd's every move. He'd long lost the feeling in his hands. Come nightfall, the temperature plummeted in the desert, and he was stiff from the cold. Ice had seeped into his every joint and limb, yet still his frozen fingers gripped resolutely the twin handles of his weapon. He was minutely adjusting his aim, and poised to unleash a barrage of rounds onto the target – that's if the goat-herder made the fatal mistake of stumbling onto their position.

He hoped to hell that moment never came, for then he'd have to decide whether or not to open fire. Steve faced a horrible dilemma; if he were to open fire it would be against all the rules of engagement and he might well face the full force of law for doing so – for the goat-herder was no more than an adolescent kid.

Killing kids: that wasn't what he had imagined doing when he'd gone for selection into Special Forces. Back then he'd fancied joining the elite, the few who dare, so he could take the fight to the bad guys, Britain's foremost terrorist enemies. Steve was one

2

of the veterans of the Squadron, one of the 'old and the bold'. Back when he'd joined, Britain's chief enemy had been the IRA, and he'd never for one moment imagined himself preparing to unleash a barrage of armour-piercing rounds against a kid.

But if that goat-herder did blunder into their position and Steve didn't open fire, then he had few doubts about the consequences. They'd have to consider their mission well and truly blown, and to expect the enemy to come after them relentlessly and in massive and deadly strength. After all, one of their units had already got shot up and hunted by Iraqi forces across miles of trackless desert – prompting a series of battles from which its men had been very lucky to escape with their lives.

The Squadron was a good 150 kilometres into Iraq by now. Although their route northwards lay through the empty wastes of the Ninawa Desert, due east lay the heavily populated area of Bayji, one of Saddam Hussein's key strongholds. During the pre-mission briefings they'd been warned that the population of Bayji – both the military based there and the militias – were fanatically loyal to the 'Great Leader' Saddam. No doubt about it – if Goat Boy saw them and raised the alarm, the Squadron was going to be in a whole world of trouble.

The nearest animals had to be a good hundred yards away, but with every second they seemed to be drawing closer. With Grayling's open-topped vehicle shrouded in camouflage netting, and his face caked in several days' worth of camouflage cream mixed with dried sweat and dirt, he figured the goat-herder would have to be right on top of their position before he noticed anything. He'd likely have to peer long and hard into the bed of the wadi before the indistinct blobs might resolve themselves into the recognizable shapes of more than twenty four-wheel-drive vehicles and quad bikes. By that time Goat Boy would be just yards away from the gaping muzzle of Steve's weapon. He'd be opening fire at point-blank range.

A round unleashed from the .50-cal would leave the muzzle at a velocity of 2,910 feet per second. It would rip a cigar-sized hole where it hit, but exit leaving a gaping wound the size of a giant frying-pan. It was bad enough thinking of it doing that to a fully grown man, let alone to the body of an Iraqi kid, and Steve wanted nothing more than for those goats to piss right off out of there.

Momentarily, he flicked his eyes away from the approaching threat, to do a visual check on their position. As the sentry for Six Troop of M Squadron, he had the northwestern segment of their position to keep watch over. His arc of responsibility ran from 12 o'clock around to 4 o'clock, 12 o'clock being due north.

To either side and humped along the jagged rim of the wadi he could just make out the silhouettes of two of the other sentries, the blokes from Four and Five Troop. Like him, they were hunched motionless over their vehicle-mounted weapons, the body of each of their wagons hidden in the cover of the dry riverbed.

He had to assume the other sentries had heard, if not seen, the goats from where they were positioned. But it was towards his arc of fire that the foremost animals were heading, wandering across the flat desert and taking the occasional nibble at God only knew what. Over the three days that the Squadron had been pushing through the Iraqi wilderness, Steve had started to think that nothing could grow in this sun-blasted wasteland.

Clearly, the goats knew otherwise.

Steve shifted his gaze further east, towards the centre of the sheer-sided wadi. There sat the vehicles of their Headquarters Troop, the distinctive whippy antennae marking out the signals wagon. The HQ Troop was surrounded by the protective firepower of the sixty-odd men of the Squadron – though all apart from the handful on sentry were sleeping the sleep of the dead right now.

Steve had to assume that Reggie, their Squadron OC, was oblivious to the threat, but there was little point in alerting him to the goat-herder's presence, for the decision to pull the trigger would be Steve's and Steve's alone. If the herd kept its distance, the shepherd would live. If the animals came too close and the goat-herder got wise to M Squadron's presence, Steve would have to decide in that split second whether to open fire and kill him.

There was no chance of trying to capture the little blighter. By the time Steve had made it out of the wagon – fighting his way through the camo-netting as he went – and clambered up the steep, rocky side of the wadi, the kid would be long gone.

Regular soldiers in the British Army tended to be told when to eat, sleep or take a piss. Often, only the senior ranks carried a map, and the riflemen knew little about where they were going or what the bigger picture might be. Special Forces soldiering was a whole different ball game. Operators like Grayling were given the entire sketch of the mission, and they were sent out to find their own way and achieve the objective using their own drive and initiative.

Decisions were based on intuition and past operational experience, and Steve had plenty of that to draw on. He'd done several missions serving in joint SAS–SBS units, and on many of those they'd been outnumbered and outgunned. Those ops had given men like Grayling a baptism of fire at the hard and brutal end of soldiering.

But the trouble was, Grayling had no experience to draw on whatsoever when it came to killing kids.

He had no idea exactly how long he'd spent on stag. He couldn't risk a glance at his watch. The slightest movement might draw the goat-herder's eye, plus the faintly luminous dial would shine out like a beacon in the dark. All he knew was that the horizon to the east was brightening slightly, which had to mean that first light – 0600 – couldn't be that far away.

Steve noticed a figure moving silently through the shadows of the dry riverbed. It was the Six Troop Sergeant Major. He paused to wake one of Steve's fellow Six Troop operatives. Dave Saddler was scheduled to take over from him on watch. He was lying comatose on the dirt next to one of the 'Pinkies', as they called their open-topped desert-adapted Land Rovers.

You always woke the next guy a good fifteen minutes early, so he had time to get some food and liquid on board before taking over sentry. He could hardly set his watch to wake himself at the right time – for even the faintest bleep-bleep-bleep or the brrrr of an alarm's vibrations could travel a great distance on the still desert air. So one bloke had to stay alert and organize the sentry rotation, waking the others at their allotted times.

With Dave being wakened, Grayling figured it had to be around 0545, which meant that he had fifteen minutes in which to make the call. He didn't want to leave that decision to Dave, one of the youngest and least experienced operators in the Squadron. Steve had got him on his team in part so he could mentor him through the coming mission.

Killing kids definitely wasn't the way to get him started.

Steve flicked his pale ice-blue eyes back to scrutinize the herd. He had a horrible suspicion that their destination was the wadi in which M Squadron had made its lying-up position. Just after last light their vehicles had crawled into this patch of cover, hoping the darkness would shield their hiding-place from any watchful eyes. If any terrain in this vast and empty wilderness was likely to nurture vegetation suitable for hungry goats, then the wadi was it. On the rare occasion that it rained, this dry gully would be transformed into a raging torrent driving all before it, and much of that moisture would soak deep into the riverbed.

Here and there a stubborn shrub still clung tenaciously to life, roots penetrating deep into the desert sands and leaves sheltering in the shadows of the wadi wall. Steve felt increasingly certain the goat-herder was steering his animals towards the location of such greenery, which meant that sooner or later he was bound to blunder into M Squadron's place of hiding.

His hands tightened around the spade-handle-like grips on either side of the .50 cal, his thumbs poised over the V-shaped butterfly trigger and minutely adjusting his aim. As long as he kept still and in cover, Grayling knew that Goat Boy had almost zero chance of seeing him. But no amount of immobility would hide an entire Special Forces squadron.

Over the past few days the sun had cooked off the cam-cream that had been smeared across Grayling's features. It felt as if he had an old, dried mud mask plastered across his face. Growing up in London's East End, he'd loved getting covered in mud as a kid. His family had lived next to the Lea Valley, a great place for messing about in muddy canals. But that was then and this was now – and right now he wished he could scratch the driest, itchiest patches, which were driving him close to insane.

Patience was a Special Forces virtue, but it was one that many of the blokes weren't exactly blessed with. They'd joined the military elite thirsting for action, not for long, freezing hours waiting to see if some unfortunate kid blundered onto their place of hiding. It was hard to acquire the patience necessary for such covert, stealthy operations. Luckily, Steve had been in the Squadron longer than just about anyone, and with age had come the ability to watch and to wait.

He was willing the kid to steer his herd in any direction but east, so as to avoid the coming confrontation. He hadn't seen a weapon on the kid, but he was certain he'd be armed. Firing from a place of hiding and at such close range, Steve had no doubts he'd get the drop on Goat Boy. His real worry – hell, his only worry – was whether he had it in him to shoot an Iraqi kid in cold blood.

Almost as if it could sense the murderous direction Steve's thoughts were taking, the nearest of the goats – a stubborn-looking billy with a wispy beard – raised its head and stared in Grayling's direction. Its curved horns gleamed eerily in the moonlight as it pawed the earth a good few times, eyeing him. Then it began to wander over, seemingly making a beeline for his place of hiding. Steve felt the adrenalin kicking in now. His heart began to hammer away like a football ricocheting around in his rib cage. His mouth felt dry and he found it hard to swallow.

A voice was screaming inside his head: *Fuck off back the way you came. Fuck off right out of here.*

The billy-goat turned and bleated at the rest of the herd. *Bleaaahhhh.*

Oddly, Steve felt as if he knew what it was saying: *Come on, girls, I've found the wadi. Let's get feasting. Oh, and ignore the guy with the weird face paint. I've got his number.*

8

The billy turned back to Steve, stepped forward and kept coming. The other goats formed up in a ragged line and began to follow after, the herder bringing up the rear. The billy-goat came to a halt at the very lip of the wadi, practically in spitting distance of the muzzle of Steve's weapon. It fixed him with the kind of half-demented look only a goat is able to give. Its bulging eyes shone golden-amber in the moonlight, as it stared down at him with dumb curiosity. There was no doubt whatsoever that it had somehow seen or sensed him.

Steve could hear the animal chewing on its cud, the lower jaw moving weirdly from side to side as it worked its way up and down, making a powerful grinding motion to pulp whatever greenery it had found. The acrid stench of a billy-goat in rut, mixed with the sweet-sickly scent of half-chewed and semi-digested vegetation, drifted across to him on the still night air.

Steve's thumbs tensed on the butterfly trigger, but he realized he faced a new problem now – the goat was standing directly in front of the barrel of the .50-cal and blocking his line of fire. He couldn't just open up and blast the animal apart, much as he was tempted to. With it and the rest of the herd blocking his line of fire, the kid goat-herder might well escape, and then the entire mission would be blown.

A memory of the Bravo Two Zero mission of the First Gulf War flashed through Steve's mind at warp speed. An eight-man SAS patrol – call-sign *Bravo Two Zero* – had been forced to go on the run in Iraq. Three men died, four were captured and only one escaped. They had been compromised when a flock of curious goats had stumbled across their hiding-place.

*Steve had a horrible feeling that M Squadron was about to suffer a similar fate right here and right now.*

As the billy-goat gave Steve the evil eye, an idea suddenly came to him. With the animal blocking the line of sight between him and the goat-herder, he figured he could risk making the move. He took his right hand off the weapon and brought it around to the left chest pouch on his webbing. He flipped it open and felt around inside. His fingers made contact with the hard cylindrical form of his infrared laser torch. An IR laser torch provides a beam of light that's invisible to the naked eye. But when using a light amplifier such as night-vision goggles (NVG) the beam becomes visible and acts like a flashlight. Deployed in conjunction with night-vision equipment, it was the perfect covert means by which to see in the dark.

The IR laser was harmless to both humans and animals unless shone at a hypersensitive body part, like the retina. If the beam was concentrated on the eyeball for several seconds it would start to burn the retina, causing severe pain – which was just the kind of thing that Steve had in mind right now.

He pulled out the torch, flicked it on and levelled it at the head of the billy-goat. Sighting along its length, he aimed the beam at the goat's eyes. For several seconds it stared back at him, and he began to wonder if the animal was so brainless as to not feel any pain. All the while the rest of the herd was backing up behind it, and he guessed the Iraqi boy was no more than thirty yards away by now.

Steve was just about to give up when the goat began to shake its head irritably, as if something was troubling it. It blinked several times, big heavy eyelids flicking rapidly up and down, and then it let out a low goaty moan. The head-shaking became more and more vigorous, as it tried to wrestle the pain out of its skull. Again, Steve heard the sound that had first alerted him to the herd's presence – the jangling of an ancient-looking bell worn on the animal's collar.

He kept the laser focused directly on the eyes, willing the billy-goat to piss off out of there before the beam sent it totally blind. With a final violent shaking of the head and a clanging of the bell the goat turned and stumbled away, legs quivering in shock as it went. Steve heard it emit a few pained and panicked bleats, and then the rest of the herd turned as one and followed. Their progress became close to a stampede as the billy led them away from this unseen but terrible and agonizing danger. As the herd beat a hasty retreat from the rim of the wadi, Steve slipped the laser torch back into its pouch and swung his weapon back onto target.

His line of sight cleared momentarily, and there was the goat-herder staring hard in his direction. He was bound to know that something had spooked his animals, and he looked torn between coming forward to investigate and hurrying after them. For a second or so the boy seemed rooted to the spot, staring in Steve's direction, and then he took a few careful steps towards him.

From thirty-odd paces away Steve sensed that the herder's eyes and his own had suddenly connected. He felt as if the kid was staring right into his hiding-place and right at him. For an instant his thumbs pressed harder on the trigger mechanism, as he tensed to blow Goat Boy away. One second's worth of pressure, and all that would be left of the kid would be a faint pink mist on the cool desert air.

But an instant later the boy herder turned and hurried after his animals, and the moment had passed.

He was maybe a hundred and fifty yards away when Steve noticed that his line of flight was taking him eastwards, in the direction of Bayji. He was darting this way and that, using his

stick to round up his scattered herd. For an instant he turned and
threw a fearful glance over his shoulder in Steve's direction. Grayling
figured the Iraqi kid had sensed that some danger – something
that could kill – lurked in the wadi. The only thing that he couldn't
be sure of was whether Goat Boy had identified the true nature
of the threat.

Now the tiny figure was running and running, driving his herd
further into the distance across the empty expanse of the desert.
He was maybe three hundred yards away when Steve saw him
pause momentarily, and an indistinct voice rang out across the
night.

'*Feringhi! Feringhi!*'

The word echoing across to Steve sounded like the Arabic for
'foreigner'.

The .50-cal has an accurate range of some two thousand yards.
A few hundred yards was a snip. Steve leaned his weight onto the
hand-grips, bringing the muzzle up a fraction, and got the herder
pinned in his sights. It would be an easy kill. A few seconds, a
few dozen rounds, and it would be done. He'd blast the herd apart,
and Goat Boy with it.

His thumbs hovered over the trigger, poised to punch out the
rounds.

But was it really 'Foreigner!' that the boy had been yelling?
Steve's Arabic was pretty basic. He could have been shouting pretty
much anything, and maybe Steve's mind was playing tricks on
him? Maybe Goat Boy was simply yelling at his herd, trying to
get it under control again?

How could he have shouted 'Foreigner!'? There was no one else
out here that he could be calling to. Goat Boy had to be shouting
at his bloody goats. *Nothing else made any sense.*

Either way, Steve just didn't know for certain. He couldn't be *sure*. And for that reason he eased off the pressure, and decided not to pull the trigger.

# CHAPTER TWO

Two months prior to the start of their Iraq mission, M Squadron had been sent to Kenya in East Africa, to prepare for war. It was January 2003, and over the preceding months the Iraqi leader Saddam Hussein had been given a series of ultimatums by the United Nations to force him to reveal whether his country had developed weapons of mass destruction. United Nations weapons inspectors were trying to check his WMD arsenal, but they were being blocked and obstructed at every turn.

Over the years Saddam had spent a staggering amount of the nation's oil wealth on armaments, and the country had long had an active nuclear, biological and chemical warfare programme. Saddam's forces had used chemical weapons in the war against Iran, and he'd unleashed them on his own peoples, most notably the Kurds. In one terrible incident he'd rained chemical shells onto the Kurdish town of Halabja, causing horrific deaths and injuries, not to mention deformities that would recur over generations.

But while the media were full of stories of the struggle to get Saddam to comply with United Nations resolutions, the men of M Squadron were pretty damn certain they were heading to Iraq.

The drums of war were beating fiercely and, as had been the case in the First Gulf War, it would be British Special Forces who led the way. Small teams of determined British and allied elite operators would be first onto the ground, to prepare the way for conventional troops.

It was a little over a year since the 9/11 terror attacks on America, and British Special Forces had already fought one war in the intervening months – to liberate Afghanistan from Taliban (and al-Qaeda) control. Like its sister Special Forces unit the SAS, the Special Boat Service (SBS) had spent months deep in the Afghan mountains, working closely with a loose-knit coalition of Afghan warlords called the Northern Alliance.

In rapid order the Taliban had been driven out of the Afghan capital Kabul, and their forces routed across the wider country. That done, M Squadron had been re-tasked to baby-sit powerful Afghan warlords based in some of the more remote and lawless outposts. The men of the Squadron had lived for weeks on end in decrepit shepherd huts, trying to make sense of the archaic rules that governed the Afghan wildlands.

The Afghan warlords had loved having the M Squadron blokes with them, as had the locals, but it had been exhausting work. They'd returned from Afghanistan hoping for a proper break from operations, but they'd had no such luck. Following the 9/11 terror attacks the world had changed, perhaps for ever, and British Special Forces – like their US and other allies – were facing serious overstretch.

The men of the Special Boat Service had no equals when fighting on, in or under water, as recent operations had so powerfully shown. Immediately following 9/11 the men of M Squadron had been called upon to launch a top-secret mission off the British coast, one that epitomized what these specialist warriors had trained for.

Intelligence had uncovered what appeared to be a terrorist plot to attack London with a devastating chemical weapon, and M Squadron – with a troop of SAS operators in support – had been called into action. The MV *Nisha*, an unremarkable-looking cargo ship, was fast steaming up the English Channel towards the Thames estuary. In the vessel's hold was believed to be a poor-man's chemical weapon – a makeshift nerve agent. Intelligence feared the ship was intending to dock on the approaches to London, whereupon the device would be triggered and a cloud of gas would drift over the city – with catastrophic consequences.

That is, unless she could be stopped.

On a bleak and storm-torn December night in 2001 the Chinooks carrying M Squadron had swept in low over the wind-whipped seas. The men had burst out of the hovering aircraft and plummeted towards the ship via fast-ropes – thick nylon cords that had been thrown out of the helo's open ramp. They slid down them using their gloved hands to slow themselves, before hitting the vessel's wildly pitching deck.

Recovering from the jarring impact, they raised their weapons and sprinted for the ship's bridge, engine room and cargo hold. At the same instant a sister force raised hook-and-pole assault ladders, clambering up from their rigid inflatable boats and surging over the vessel's sides. Attacking from both sea and air the elite operators swarmed the ship, blasting in doors using pump-action shotguns and hurling flash-bang stun-grenades inside. The bridge was seized immediately and the captain and crew overpowered, leaving the ship firmly in the elite operators' hands. In a textbook operation, the entire vessel was cleared from bow to stern – a perfect marine counter-terrorism takedown on the high seas.

That was exactly the kind of mission the men of M Squadron had trained for so relentlessly over the years. But now they were headed for Africa and the sweeping, scorched plains of Kenya, where they would learn a completely new way of going to war. In Kenya, they would have to master the use of specialist vehicles to cross hundreds of miles of dry, waterless terrain, so as to penetrate well beyond enemy lines.

It was going to be one hell of a challenge.

During the First Gulf War in 1991, the SAS had led the way, highly mobile units roaming the Western Desert of Iraq hunting for Scud missiles and other targets of opportunity. One SAS unit had gone in on foot and got badly shot up, then captured – the Bravo Two Zero patrol. But other teams had gone in by vehicle, and they had largely achieved their mission objectives and come out unscathed.

Special Forces patrols sent in on foot were deprived of the heavy firepower the vehicles could offer, and lacked any means of rapid mobility. The lessons from the First Gulf War were well learned: in 2003 elite units would be heading into Iraq on vehicle-borne missions. And so it was that M Squadron was off to Kenya, tasked with learning the intricate craft of vehicle-based mobility operations.

Fortunately, a great deal of expertise was on hand to help with their training. Recently Major Reginald 'Reggie' Field had been brought in from the SAS to command M Squadron. Though the Squadron was an SBS unit, it was made up of operators from both outfits. Nowadays, ancient rivalries had largely been put aside so the SBS and SAS could better serve as one united fighting force, and the unit even included a sprinkling of blokes from foreign Special Forces outfits.

In spite of his somewhat grandfatherly appearance – he liked mooching around in a cardigan back at the Squadron lines – Reggie, the OC, was rumoured to be a closet dagger-between-the-teeth type of a bloke. Steve, for one, was glad to have him commanding the Squadron, for he brought bags of operational experience into the unit. Captain Andy Smith, Reggie's second in command, was a veteran operator with the SAS.

M Squadron had also secured the assistance of a four-man SAS team, plus a unit from the equivalent American Special Forces outfit, for the Kenyan training.

The four American operators on loan to the Squadron were in their mid-thirties, and bore all the appearance of grizzled veterans of operations. Likewise, the four-man SAS unit embedded in the Squadron was made up of some of the Regiment's best. With six weeks of intensive 'beat-up' training ahead of them – full-immersion exercises in preparation for war – the men of M Squadron couldn't have wished for a better group of soldiers from which to learn vehicle-based combat.

There was one other factor that served to ease the Squadron's transition from a maritime counter-terrorism force to one of land-based mobility ops. There were a handful of veterans in the Squadron who had fought side by side with the SAS, during which time they'd learned their vehicle mobility skills well. They would act as mentors to the younger blokes, and guide them through the coming land-based missions.

One of those 'old and bold' was Steve Grayling. Many in the Squadron viewed Grayling as a cantankerous and cynical old bastard. He was tall and lean but with a rock-hard muscular physique, one honed by years of training for ship and oilrig assaults – which required clambering out of the freezing sea in full scuba gear and laden with weaponry, to scale the decks high above and launch an attack. In his early forties, Grayling was too old to worry about promotion, and he had zero interest in rising above the rank of sergeant. Unsurprisingly, he took no shit from anyone, regardless of rank. Renowned for speaking his mind, he wasn't a particular favourite with the SBS's top management. At one point in the past they'd shunted him sideways into the SAS, which had got him well out of the way for a couple of years.

But now that the Squadron was preparing for war in Iraq, having Grayling in their number had an unexpected upside: he was one of the most experienced at vehicle-borne ops, and so could take the less experienced under his wing. While he was renowned for not suffering fools gladly, he was also known as a safe pair of hands to handle the younger blokes, which was something of a relief if you were placed on his team.

Grayling was known to all simply as 'Grey' – a nickname that suited his no-shit kind of persona. A while back he'd suffered a bad accident while on an SBS deep-water mission, and he was still using painkillers to deal with the long-term effects of the injuries. Many argued that that accounted for his up-front, devil-may-care attitude.

M Squadron deployed to Kenya as three Troops – Four, Five and Six Troop – and Grayling was a vehicle commander in Six Troop. Each Troop consisted of teams driving specially adapted, open-topped Land Rovers designed for penetration missions deep behind enemy lines. In addition to those, each Troop had a similar number of powerful quad-bikes, ones that acted as an outrider force to scout for the enemy.

The Land Rovers were nicknamed 'Pinkies', for they were painted the same light shade of desert pink that had proved such an effective camouflage for David Stirling's Special Forces during the North African campaign of the Second World War. In fact, the Pinkies were pretty much the same kind of vehicle that Stirling's SAS had used to attack German and Italian forces some sixty years before.

Penetrating hundreds of miles into the empty wastes of the Sahara Desert, Stirling's SAS had used light jeeps to mount lightning raids on enemy targets, hitting especially hard at their airfields. Many argued that Stirling's SAS – plus its sister force, the Long Range Desert Group – had managed to destroy more enemy aircraft in North Africa than the entire RAF. The commander of the German Afrika Korps, Field Marshal Erwin Rommel, admitted their forces had caused him 'more damage than any other British unit of equal strength', and the Pinkies had certainly proved their worth.

The driver on Grey's Pinkie was Dave Saddler, otherwise known as 'Moth'. Moth had pale skin through which you could see the blue of his veins, and there was an air of silent mystery about him. With his near-albino features and his watery-eyed, unblinking stare, he had a distinctly alien look. Moth was in his early twenties and he'd not long been with M Squadron. He'd transferred across from the SBS's swimmer delivery vehicle (SDV) unit, and he was a specialist at underwater missions.

The swimmer delivery vehicle is a top-secret midget sub-mersible, designed to transport combat divers over long distances to target. Needless to say, such underwater missions were a far cry from desert mobility ops, and Moth had the appearance of one who would be far more at home under water than under a burning Iraqi sun.

In terms of land-based combat ops Moth was a complete virgin, and Grey worried how he'd handle the forthcoming deployment to war. Grayling was a far more experienced vehicle operator, and he knew that he was going to have to force himself to hold back in Iraq if Moth was going to find his way as the driver on his team. Grey sat in the vehicle commander's – the passenger – seat, behind a general-purpose machine-gun (GPMG) mounted on a pivot on the bonnet. In sharp contrast to himself and Moth – the former grim-faced, the latter decidedly spooky – the gunner positioned behind them in the wagon's open rear was a cheerful breath of fresh air.

Chris McGreavy was an open-faced young American who'd somehow found his way into British Special Forces. He was one of the newest guys in the Squadron, and one of the tallest to boot. At six-foot-four he towered over most of them. He'd earned the nickname 'Dude' for the simple reason that he was seriously laid back, and he peppered his every sentence with that word. McGreavy never seemed to tire of nattering on, and it was all 'Dude this' and 'Dude that'.

Grey didn't particularly mind the Dude's easy-going talkative ways. With Moth and Phil – the fourth member of his team – he'd got a couple of right still-waters-run-deep types, and McGreavy was good for filling in the long silences. In fact, the Dude was the odd one out in a lot of ways. No matter how hard they might try to smarten themselves up, both Moth and Phil were far from easy on the eye, not to mention hopelessly scruffy. And as for Grey, with his hooked and broken nose he was one ugly, scary-looking bastard. By contrast, the Dude sat tall and proud astride his perch on the rear of their wagon, like an advert for Rip Curl.

M Squadron being Special Forces, McGreavy was allowed to wear his beach-blond hair shaggy and long, framing his rugged good looks. But what really set the Dude apart as far as Grey was concerned was his family background. McGreavy was highly educated and he hailed from a mega-wealthy dynasty based in Houston, Texas, the oil-rich capital of the USA.

None of the others in Grey's team – himself included – had more than scraped together a few O-levels. Grey couldn't imagine what on earth had brought the Dude into British Special Forces, but he was determined to find out. During the weeks ahead he'd catch a quiet moment with him, fix him with his killer stare and get the full story out of him . . . that's if McGreavy survived their coming Iraq missions.

The Dude was the least-practised operator in the Squadron, having been with the SBS for less than a year. He'd only just finished his probationary period – the months after selection during which a new operator has to learn and assimilate dozens of specialist skills. He was also bloody tall for a rear gunner. The .50-cal operator sat high on the vehicle's rear, and Grey worried that having McGreavy perched up there was like an invitation to getting his head blown off.

Dude and Moth had been part of the M Squadron assault force that had hit the MV *Nisha* over those storm-swept December seas, but that was about the entirety of the action they'd seen. It had all been over in a couple of hours max, and it was very much a maritime operation. Once the Squadron deployed to Iraq Grey felt certain they'd be seeing combat, and he was determined to bring every man on his team out alive.

Phil Birch was the fourth member of Grey's team. He operated outside the Pinkie on their dedicated quad bike. By contrast with Dude, Birch was definitely not the sharpest tool in the box, or over-easy on the eye. A slow-talking northerner, he always looked like a sack of shit – hence his nickname, 'Mucker'.

Mucker's grumpy persona turned a lot of blokes off, and that's why Grey figured he'd got him on his team. But Grey actually valued his presence. He was hard as nails and a superlative soldier, plus he was totally and utterly reliable. No matter what shit went down, Grey knew that Mucker would always be there on his shoulder, his weapon at the ready.

Grey's team had been bolted together at the start of their Kenya training. Grey was conscious of the lack of battle experience on his vehicle, and especially for the kind of missions they were likely to be tasked with once they were at war. Having Phil on his team helped balance things out a little – with a safe pair of hands being only ever a blast on the quad bike away.

Each team member had skills that he might well be called upon to use if the Squadron landed itself in the shit. Moth doubled as their communications specialist, and would be the one to call in any air strikes. He had recently qualified as a joint terminal attack controller (JTAC), which meant he could call in warplanes to drop precision-guided weapons onto targets. Small elite units such as theirs were almost inevitably going to face a larger, better-armed enemy force, and air power was one of the few ways they had in which to even up the odds a little. Grey was the team's demolitions and sniper specialist, plus its medic.

Dude was the new kid on the block and he hadn't yet secured any adquals (additional qualifications), but in the .50-cal he controlled one of the heaviest pieces of firepower in their Troop.

M Squadron established their training camp in a remote patch of Kenyan bush and set about learning to know and love their Pinkies. Each open-topped wagon was fitted with a .50-cal heavy machine-gun or a 40mm grenade launcher, plus a GPMG up front. As a result they packed some fearsome firepower, but when loaded with ammo, water, food, fuel and associated kit they were badly overweight. There was no spare capacity for armour or ballistic matting, which meant that the vehicle's occupants had zero protection from enemy rounds – other than speed, manoeuvrability and firepower.

At first the Pinkies seemed to suffer an alarming design fault. When out doing the Squadron's first driving exercises in the bush, the driveshafts broke on two of the Pinkies, including Grey's wagon. Fortunately, their Land Rover had been crawling at dead slow over a dry, boulder-strewn riverbed. Even so, the noise the driveshaft had made as it sheared in two and smacked into the rocks below had sounded pretty close to terminal.

As he was the wagon's driver, vehicle maintenance was Moth's baby. It had taken him just a few moments to slip out of his seat and slide under the Pinkie to diagnose the problem. Mucker had roared up on his Honda quad bike to check what was wrong, and upon Moth's announcing that the driveshaft had sheared he was quick to give vent to his feelings.

'Fucking wagons are a fucking pile of shit,' Mucker grunted.

'Not normally, mate, they're not,' Grey remarked. 'The Pinkie's about as good as it gets for desert ops.'

'Well, what kind of a wanker thinks we can take them to Iraq?' Mucker continued. 'Two days in and we're two cranks down. They're shit.'

'Like I said, normally they're not,' Grey replied, with infinite patience. 'I did six weeks in the Omani desert and never had a problem. Normally, they're pretty much bullet-proof. I reckon we got a Friday afternoon batch with this lot.'

'Should have been driving a Hummer, dude,' McGreavy remarked, in his signature Texan drawl. 'Man, those things are freakin' unstoppable.'

The problem with the Pinkies only worsened. The crankshafts on six of the vehicles went down in as many days. It was hugely worrying. No way could the Squadron afford to carry spare drive-shafts with them in Iraq, let alone risk the time required to replace a broken one when moving covertly behind enemy lines.

Finally, the Squadron's mechanics diagnosed the root cause of the problem: the Land Rovers had been fitted with a dodgy set of drive-shafts. The drive-shafts were replaced, and that seemed to solve the issue – which meant that the Squadron could get back to readying itself to drive and fight at war.

One of the US Special Forces operators was a Brit, an ex-Parachute Regiment bloke called Jim Smith. A few years back he'd married an American girl and joined the US military, progressing by stages into the ranks of the elite. Predictably, the men of the Squadron had nicknamed him 'Delta Jim'. It was fascinating to hear him talk them through US Special Forces procedures for vehicle operations behind enemy lines.

Delta Jim talked about what it was like to deploy and to fight behind enemy lines when facing a far superior enemy force that was hell-bent on hunting you down. He described the means via which vehicle-mounted SF troops could evade enemy tracking and tracing techniques, and the kind of escape options that were available. The golden rule of such operations was always to try to avoid a fight against a far larger enemy force, but if you had to stand and fight, then to do so at a time and place of your choosing.

As Grey listened to the briefing and chipped in the odd remark, he figured this would all be very new to Moth, Dude and the Squadron's other youngsters. This was the hard reality of what it meant to play hide-and-seek with a far superior enemy force in terrain that more often than not offered little or no cover. This was what they would be heading into in Iraq, and he was keen to see how the new guys on his team would face up to the coming challenge.

Their unit-specific call-sign for Iraq was *Zero Six Bravo*, which Moth would use when calling in the warplanes. Grey couldn't help noticing how much their call-sign echoed that of *Bravo Two Zero*.

And although he wasn't the superstitious kind, he couldn't shake off the feeling that all hell awaited them in the deserts of Iraq.

# CHAPTER THREE

The vehicle mobility training was as rigorous as they could make it – but getting slick at such ops was still going to be a massive challenge in the time available. A few years back Grey had spent six weeks traversing the Omani desert with the SAS, living and breathing the reality of a simulated patrol deep behind enemy lines, and before that he'd spent months learning the standard operating procedures of desert mobility work.

Here in Kenya, all of that had to be telescoped into a fraction of the time. The Squadron would spend fourteen days learning the basics of vehicle-borne mobility work, after which they'd run a makeshift 'test week'. The eight blokes from the SAS and US Special Forces would act as informal 'examiners', as they put the men through an extended desert exercise. The training programme was designed to squeeze as much rigour into the time available, and to extract as much as possible from the expertise on hand.

Those first two weeks covered the A–Z of vehicle mobility ops: how to live from a wagon over extended periods; how to manage all the food, water, fuel, ammo, weaponry and personal kit, and to maximize ease of access in a cramped, open-topped vehicle;

how to refuel from jerry-cans in a burning-hot and dust-ridden environment; how to free a vehicle bogged to its axles in sand, using shovels, sand-ladders and winches; how to keep the vehicle-mounted weapons clean during endless days spent driving through a dust cloud thrown up by the wagon in front.

Moving as a squadron meant orchestrating close to thirty Pinkies plus quad bikes on the move. It meant operating in a strict formation within which each vehicle commander understood his place in relation to the others, while keeping a good distance between Pinkies so as to avoid making an easy target. It meant doing so in conditions akin to a massive sandstorm, and while keeping complete radio silence so that the Squadron's movements couldn't be traced by an enemy using electronic tracking.

It meant learning to do so under the permanent threat of attack, and always being ready to use vehicle fire-and-manoeuvre drills to extract from an enemy ambush. It meant learning what amount of fuel the wagons burned over what type of ground, how much water a man needed in what conditions, and what type of driving techniques various terrains required. But most challenging of all was learning how to do all of this at night, when driving with no lights – on 'black light' – and using night-vision aids to render the desert into a fluorescent green video-game daylight.

Jim Smith and his fellow American operators had been given a Pinkie and a quad between them, so they could muck in with the Squadron's training. They'd deployed to Kenya complete with rakes of top-notch Gucci kit, including state-of-the-art weaponry, body armour and GPS. They were used to driving hulking great Humvees, which like everything else American were built extra-large. Now they had to squeeze themselves, plus all of their gleaming kit, into the cramped confines of a jeep that was completely open to the elements.

For an ex-Para like Delta Jim, being in a Land Rover again was like coming home. But the rest of Jim's team were seriously non-plussed. They were used to their Humvees. A 4WD on steroids, a Humvee is 'up-armoured' – encased in an armoured shell which provides substantial protection for the vehicle's occupants from enemy fire or mine strikes. By comparison, M Squadron's Pinkies were open to sun, rain and bullets alike – like throwbacks to the Second World War.

Yet over the days in Kenya the rest of Jim's team warmed to the Pinkies. They weren't low, claustrophobic or cramped, which was how the interior of a Humvee felt. They had better all-round vision, and vastly superior arcs of fire. There was a real sense of freedom when working from an open-topped vehicle, one that imbued the operators with something of a Lawrence of Arabia devil-may-care attitude. And on a practical level the Land Rovers were far more frugal with the diesel, which gave them a much greater range.

There was one other serious advantage to operating from an open vehicle: it made for easier navigation. On top of everything else, the lads of M Squadron had to learn how to find their way across hundreds of miles of trackless bush, more often than not at night. Under such conditions the stars provided an invaluable 'map' from which to keep track of progress, and a wagon open to the elements offered all-round vision of the moon and stars.

The final week of mobility training was a blur of desert-driving exercises, ones that were scrutinized by Jim and his team, some of the best at vehicle-borne mobility operations that the Americans have, plus the SAS team. By now the men of M Squadron had acclimatized well, growing seriously unshaven and sporting a thick film of dust and dirt over any exposed skin. As their bodies adjusted to the searing heat, they were sweating and drinking less than they had been during the first few days.

This last week wasn't so much about being tested as about getting the men to work as a team in such conditions. The Squadron headed out one evening at last light. The men were tasked with spending the entire night pushing through the dry bush and scrub. They had a distant objective to reach by first light, and they had to navigate their way using the stars and compass alone. Grey's wagon took the lead, for he was a shrewd and skilful navigator when moving during the hours of darkness.

When doing such a night drive the Squadron moved in such a fashion that vehicles had to basically play follow-my-leader. It was the best way to ensure they didn't lose each other in the dark. Grey was using night-vision goggles that flipped down over the eyes on twin leather cups. They looked like a small pair of binoculars, weighed about the same and worked by amplifying the ambient light given off by the moon and stars.

There was little cloud cover and the wide expanse of the African sky was star-bright. The NVG functioned exceptionally well under such conditions. Every way Grey looked the desert was illuminated in a weird, foggy-green glow, which was almost as good as driving in daylight. In an effort not to lose his natural night vision he kept flicking the NVG up and down as their wagon pushed ahead. Every now and then he'd catch the twin glow of a big cat's eyes staring out from the darkened bush.

They had been making good progress when, almost without warning, the sandstorm hit. They heard it before they saw it, a strange hollow roaring sound whipping through the night. As the storm bore down upon them Grey flipped up his NVG and pulled on his sand goggles – plastic eyewear a bit like a welder's glasses – to keep the cloud of driving grit out of his eyes. Above the deafening snarl of the storm he yelled for Moth and Dude to do likewise.

The sandstorm was a monster, piling up like a thundercloud on the horizon and dumping half the desert on their heads. The standard operating procedure was to go firm when hit by such a storm. You'd wrap a *shemagh* – an Arab headscarf – tightly around your face to shield it from the stinging sand, and wait for it to pass. But tonight's mission was a time-specific tasking, and if they held still for too long they'd fail to reach their objective.

The thick, howling storm blanked everything out, cutting off the Pinkies from the heavens – which meant that Grey couldn't use the stars to navigate any more. But there was one upside. The storm having reduced visibility to a matter of tens of metres, no watching 'enemy' would be able to see them, and that in turn meant that Grey could risk using a GPS. The faint glow thrown off by the gizmo's screen was invisible in such conditions.

Earlier that day Grey had studied the maps closely, and inputted a way-marked route into his military-issue GPS, one that would lead them to their objective. He punched in the relevant instructions and the GPS spun up to speed, mapping out the route ahead. Using that, and keeping a close watch on his compass as a backstop, he was able to press onwards. But the wagons following behind had to bunch up much closer together to maintain visual contact.

One of the golden rules of mobility driving is that you should never enter a patch of difficult terrain or try to move across an obstacle before the vehicle in front has cleared it. Otherwise, several wagons could get trapped at the point of greatest difficulty.

Grey navigated them into a steep-sided wadi, and Moth found himself trying to exit via a near-vertical track that led out of the far side. With all the food, water, fuel and ammo aboard, even in four-wheel drive the wagon got only two-thirds of the way out before it slipped and skidded its way back down, its engine howling like a thing possessed and its wheels spinning horribly. Within seconds the dry riverbed was filled with the acrid smell of burning rubber, and then the second and the third wagon came rumbling in behind them. It was only by chance that a major pile-up was avoided.

Moth only managed to find a way out of the wadi when he stumbled across an easier exit point, and at least by then the worst of the sandstorm had blown over. They pushed onwards and Grey navigated the Squadron right to its very objective. They had made it through the heart of the raging storm, and there was a massive sense of achievement to have done so.

The men ended that exercise with a Chinese parliament – a Squadron-wide heads-up to which all could contribute ideas and suggestions. They'd toyed with the idea of driving in two-wheel drive when in Iraq, because it reduced fuel consumption and increased range. On firm, flat terrain 2WD was all that was needed. But the experience of that night's exercise had proved that you never knew when you might hit trouble, and keeping the wagons in 4WD was vital.

But that in turn meant that the weight the Pinkies were carrying had to be cut, so as to be able to carry more fuel – and about the only thing they could possibly consider losing was ammo. Yet less ammo meant less firepower, which increased the risk of getting caught and smashed by the enemy. This was the eternal conundrum of vehicle mobility operations: how to maximize range, mobility and firepower on a small 4WD vehicle.

The Squadron rounded off their time in Kenya with a week's high-altitude training, just in case they did end up heading into the more mountainous parts of Iraq. While no one doubted they were going to war – President Bush had already approved the deployment of 200,000 American troops to the Gulf – they didn't have the faintest idea what their mission might be, or over what kind of terrain they'd be operating. It made sense to prepare for every eventuality, especially when the Squadron had such limited experience of overland operations.

There was only one place to do mountain training in Kenya, and that was Mount Kenya itself – a 17,000-foot peak high enough to be permanently snowcapped even though it lies bang on the equator. The blokes drew specialist mountaineering kit from the stores, including ropes, cold-weather gear and rigid-soled rock-climbing boots. The ascent was done in four stages under crushing loads, each stage taking them to a higher altitude, then dropping lower overnight. This was in line with the concept of 'climb-high, sleep low'– designed to help the body adjust to altitude. The lower slopes were clad in a dense tropical jungle, but the higher reaches were fields of bare rock and massive boulders, interspersed with ice fields.

The first three days of the climb were rain-lashed and sodden, and after the blistering heat of the savanna it was truly miserable. The final ascent was done overnight, so as to reach the high point at sunrise. But en route the wind blew up and flurries of snow began to whirl around their frozen ears. By the time Grey, Moth, Dude and Mucker reached the summit they were chilled to the core, and gasping for breath due to the lack of oxygen.

As they crouched in the howling gale the weather miraculously cleared, and a view opened before them that took their breath away. They were sitting on the roof of the world, while two thousand feet below them a carpet of fluffy white clouds stretched into the distance. And at the very limit of the horizon the cloud cover burned off over the golden-brown expanse of the African plains.

During the last stages of the summit climb Grey had been leading his team, and he'd kept calling to the youngsters: 'Moth! Dude! Come on! I got something to show you!' They'd only managed to catch up with him when the summit itself was reached, and Dude for one was curious as to what Grey had been going on about.

'Say, boss, so what you got to show us?' he gasped, fighting to breathe in the thin, oxygen-deprived atmosphere.

'You what?' Grey replied, feigning ignorance.

'During the last few minutes of the climb – something you wanted to show us?'

'So there is, mate.' Grey stretched his arm out into the far distance. 'See where I'm pointing?'

'Kind of. Yeah.'

'Well, I can see your house from here.' Grey swung his arm around a bit and repositioned it. 'And you know what, Moth? I can see yours 'n' all. Fucking marvellous, eh?'

Moth eyed him silently for a few moments, as if it just didn't compute. As for the young American, it took a few seconds for the penny to drop – the lack of oxygen was seriously fogging his brain. The Dude cracked up laughing, although at such high altitude it petered out into a strangled gasp and a wheeze.

'Don't worry about Grey,' a figure remarked from behind. 'Full of more shit than a Christmas goose.'

'Christmas goose?' Moth queried.

'Christmas goose,' the figure confirmed. 'Got to be full of shit. When was the last time you ate goose for Christmas?'

It was Andy 'Scruff' McGruff making the comment, a fellow veteran of Six Troop. As his name suggested, Scruff was hardly the most organized or smartest-looking of soldiers, but he was a first-class Special Forces operator. A few months back he and Grey had fought side by side in the epic siege of Qala Janghi, the battle to secure an ancient mud-walled fortress in northern Afghanistan. Eight SBS and SEAL operators had put down a savage uprising by six hundred Taliban and al-Qaeda fighters.

Grey and Scruff had bonded during that die-hard encounter, and if Grey had a confidant in M Squadron, Scruff was it. The two of them gazed out over the dramatic scenery for a good few moments, before the chilling cold and the lack of oxygen finally got the better of them.

'Seen enough to last a lifetime,' Grey announced. 'Anyone care to join me going down?'

Grey and Scruff fell into an easy step, as the rough, worn path wound away below them. Shortly, they caught up with the distinctive figure of Delta Jim, who was also heading down. Jim was a super-fit bloke, and a hugely experienced soldier: before joining US Special Forces he'd been in the US Rangers, the nearest American equivalent to the Paras. He had chiselled features and close-cropped blond hair, and he spoke with a weird half-British half-American accent.

'So, how d'you reckon the Squadron's done?' Scruff ventured, as they caught up with Delta Jim.

'Six weeks' beat-up training,' Grey panted. 'Could've done with six months.'

'You've been taught by the best,' Jim remarked, with a wide smile. Then, more seriously: 'We couldn't have done more in the time available. It's been relentless, for you and for us.'

'Yeah, but we could have done with more time,' Grey repeated. 'For a lot of the blokes this is all the mobility work they've ever done. And a lot of us were in rag order, threaders, and that was before Kenya. We'd gone from the MV *Nisha* to months of Afghan ops, now Kenya and soon Iraq. It's been non-stop.'

Delta Jim eyed Grey for a long second. 'So, you'd rather not be going to Iraq?'

Grey held his look. 'There's not a bloke isn't dying to get deployed, and that includes the new lads. It's just that the Squadron's washed up. Who wouldn't be, after six months in the Afghan mountains surviving on British Army rations, plus hot air and bullshit?'

Jim laughed. 'All routes to war right now lead to Iraq. It's the only place to be.'

'It's route, not *rowt*,' Grey needled him. 'Ever heard yourself? A scouser with a Texan accent. Dunno how your lovely young American wife puts up with it.'

'In our outfit, we even get the Padre to bless our weapons,' Jim retorted, 'and my wife sure is blessed to be married to a regular Mr Nice Guy like me.'

This was partly true. Jim's unit did get their main weapon – invariably the superlative Diemaco Colt 7.62mm assault rifle – blessed by their priest, before going into battle.

'Mate, you've seen us over the weeks,' Scruff remarked to Delta Jim. 'How d'you reckon the Squadron's shaping up for Iraq?'

'Way I see it, you're like one big football team,' Jim replied. 'There are a lot of characters, a lot of star strikers who don't always rub along that well together. But come Iraq you're gonna have to knit together as one team at war. Those strikers are gonna have to learn to put rivalries aside and pass the ball, so as to score. That's the only way you'll ever get through whatever's coming.'

'Thanks,' Grey grunted. 'That sounds like an easy way of telling us bugger all.'

'You're only as good as your weakest link, obviously,' Jim continued. 'And like any dogs of war you're gonna need to pull those new guys through. But if you want my opinion – yeah, I figure the Squadron'll do fine out there.'

For a moment Grey pondered his weakest links – Moth and the Dude. He ran them through the on-the-run test. It was one that he often used to gauge the measure of a man. If they got badly whacked in Iraq and were forced to go on the run, who would he choose to be with, Moth or Dude? He figured it had to be the Dude. At least with him you'd have a laugh as the enemy hunted you down, plus he was sharp as a pin and you could bounce ideas off him. There was no way to read Moth, and after a few days alone together Grey figured he'd want to murder the young operator, even if the Iraqis failed to nail him.

But in truth there were no limp-wristed belly-dancers among any of his men. The last few weeks of training had revealed a real mental toughness, and when push came to shove it was that that mattered most. Psychological strength had got them through SBS selection, which was designed to make even the most physically fit and hardened crack. It was when the mind told a bloke that he couldn't go on that most failed selection, not when the body broke.

As they continued down the mountain, Grey threw Delta Jim a shrewd, appraising look. He figured Jim had ended up in US Special Forces – as opposed to the SBS or SAS – by a simple twist of fate: his marriage to an American. But he clearly missed the camaraderie and easy piss-taking of a predominantly British unit. During the coming Iraq conflict there was no telling who the Squadron might be paired up with, and either the SEALs or Delta Force were their natural partners.

Having spent several weeks training together, there was every chance that Jim's unit might join M Squadron on joint-ops. While Jim had witnessed the Squadron's lack of expertise in vehicle mobility work, Grey had sensed a hunger in the guy to go in alongside them. It was well known within Special Forces circles that the Brits – along with their Kiwi and Aussie counterparts – tended to get the most extreme and out-there kind of missions.

'You'd like to be coming with us, wouldn't you, mate?' Grey asked him. 'All that apple pie and godliness you get in your outfit – not really your thing, is it?'

Jim paused for a second. 'Honestly, mate, I'd jump at the chance, even if it meant driving one of those rat-shit Pinkies all the way to Baghdad.'

It was a matter of a few weeks and a whirlwind of activity before M Squadron found itself heading to a forward mounting base before deploying to Iraq. But by then – and unbeknown to all but the military's top commanders – the scenario for the coming war had shifted beyond all recognition.

On 1 March 2003 the Turkish parliament had rejected a resolution allowing US and allied forces to deploy via their territory. In one fell swoop, the opening of a northern front for the coming war had been scuppered – for the only other nations that have borders with northern Iraq are Syria and Iran, and neither is a particular friend of the West. Turkey's refusal to provide access constituted a massive blow to the American and British war plans, and came as a major shock. Turkey was a fellow NATO member, and she had enjoyed a long strategic alliance with the US. Over protracted negotiations, the American government had agreed to a six-billion-dollar aid package, plus preferential treatment for Turkish companies doing business with America – all in return for the use of the nation's territory.

But at the last moment the powerful Turkish military – not to mention the overwhelming opposition of the Turkish public – had halted the bill's passage through parliament. On its southern border Turkey had long been fighting a rebellion by the thirty-million-strong Kurdish people. The Kurds are spread across a mountainous region that straddles Turkey and Iraq, which they call Kurdistan. Various Kurdish armed-resistance movements had been fighting against both Turkish and Iraqi rule, seeking to carve out their Kurdish homeland.

Over the years Saddam had suppressed such insurrections with an unbelievable savagery, and the Turkish military had also launched brutal crackdowns. The Turks feared that invading Iraq and toppling Saddam would give the Kurds their chance, not to mention risk destabilizing the entire region. Saddam was no particular friend of Turkey, but he was at least the devil they knew, and his iron rule had kept the Kurds in hand.

In the final analysis the risks of doing a deal with the Americans had outweighed the possible benefits, as far as the Turkish military – and the nation's people – were concerned, and no NATO forces were going to be allowed into Iraq via their territory.

The surprise rejection by Turkey had caught the Americans on the hop. Tens of thousands of troops from the US 4th Army had already been dispatched, en route to military bases in Turkey. The massive force that had planned to mass on Iraq's northern border now had no way of doing so. Any push into Iraq would have to go in from one front alone now – Kuwait, to the far south of Iraq.

And in the aftermath of Turkey's shock decision, M Squadron was about to be given the mission of a lifetime.

# CHAPTER FOUR

Grey could hardly believe it when first he laid eyes on the bloke. He was in the stores tent, part of a makeshift camp under canvas tucked away in a discreet corner of the Forward Mounting Base. M Squadron had deployed here complete with weapons, ammo, vehicles and all the communications and other kit they would need for war. This was the last stop before Iraq, and here was this bloke straight from central casting drawing a brand-new set of kit from the stores.

The bloke was tall, lanky and distinctly well-bred in appearance, lacking the weather-beaten, grizzled look of an SF soldier. But what really singled him out was his snowy-white complexion, in contrast to the rest of the Squadron – Moth included – who had managed to get something of a Kenyan tan. Grey watched as Stores handed him a set of ironed and pressed combats, a pair of shiny boots, plus a mess tin with the cellophane packaging still wrapped round it.

'All right, mate?' Grey greeted the stranger, as he loaded up his pile of gleaming kit.

The bloke's face lit up. 'Good morning. Yes, I'm absolutely fine, thanks.'

The voice confirmed it. The guy spoke with the kind of crisp upper-class accent that only long years of the finest schools and the coldest showers could nurture. He looked to be in his mid-twenties, no older, and he was springing about like an eager puppy. What on earth was this guy doing in a camp set aside for M Squadron – a Special Forces unit in lockdown that was screened and sanitized for war?

'So erm – who exactly are you, then, mate?' Grey asked.

'Oh, sorry.' A hand was extended. 'Sebastian. Seb to my friends. Seb March-Phillips. I'm your Iraq terp.'

'Terp' was military slang for interpreter. Grey took the proffered hand – which was noticeably smooth and uncallused – and shook it. 'Glad to have you with us, mate.' What else was there to say?

Grey watched in fascination as the new bloke unpacked the uniform, which was several sizes too big for him. For some reason, Stores only had extra-large. The combat jacket would reach to the guy's knees, while the trousers would need six-inch turn-ups. Next, the guy unwrapped his clomping great Army boots. He stared at them in horror for several seconds.

'You know, I've got this pair of civvie boots,' he remarked to Grey. 'I did my Prince of Wales Silver Warder in them. Do I really have to wear these? I hope I don't get blisters. Will we be doing much walking, do you think?'

Grey was lost for words. This guy had just pitched up to join a Special Forces squadron heading to war, yet he appeared to be completely and utterly blasé about whatever might lie ahead. He struck Grey as being one of those classic English eccentrics who love an adventure, and whose innocent enthusiasm seems to trump everything – and a part of Grey just couldn't help liking him for it.

In quick time Grey got the guy's story from him. Until a few days ago he'd been working for an investment banking firm in London. Some months back he'd joined a specialist unit – so he could learn some soldiering in his spare time. It was there that someone had realized he was fluent in Arabic. He'd been brought up on a military base in the Middle East, hence the language skills. And from there it had apparently been a short step to him being recruited as the terp for M Squadron's coming deployment to Iraq.

A few minutes chatting to the bloke, and Grey could tell that he was phenomenally intelligent. It seemed that he could mention just about anything – a geranium maybe – and Sebastian would start going: 'Okay-yah, the geranium – more commonly known as cranesbills, due to the fruit looking like the beak of a crane. Take *Geranium maginificum*, for example …' Compared to most of the men in the Squadron – a dose of doughnuts who'd fallen out of school and into the military – Sebastian was a rocket scientist.

As Grey and Sebastian left the stores, they bumped into Mick 'Gunner' McGrath, the commander of the Squadron's quad bikes. While each quad formed part of a single-vehicle team, the quad-operators also had a bloke in overall charge of them as a distinct force. In that way they could work as one coordinated unit when scouting out the Squadron's route and searching for the enemy.

Gunner was a shaven-headed, solid chunk of fighting man – a real soldier's soldier. He was a supremely capable Special Forces operator, but he was also known to be fiery and impulsive. He'd been with the Squadron for an age – he was another of the old and the bold. Gunner was also a real gym queen, always pumping iron. By contrast, Grey put in only the odd appearance on the weights, whenever he felt age was getting the better of him.

Grey and Gunner had a certain respect for each other, one forged over long years of elite soldiering. Grey did the introductions with Sebastian, stood back and waited for the sparks to fly. Sebastian launched into a long welcome speech, delivered in his best public schoolboy accent and peppered with lots of syllables. Once he was done, Gunner stared at him in silence for several seconds.

'Terp?' he finally grunted. 'What the hell do we need a terp for? We don't want to *talk* to the fuckers.' Then: 'You do weights?'

In his long-winded way Sebastian explained that pumping iron wasn't really his thing. Gunner had not another word to say to him.

Before Grey and the Squadron's New Bloke parted company, Sebastian pulled out a mobile phone. He waved it in Grey's direction. 'If you need to speak to anyone, feel free to use mine. I know it can be terribly tough getting comms home, but I've got this super-duper new mobile provider.'

'Not really supposed to, mate,' Grey told him. 'Didn't anyone warn you? We're supposed to be in lockdown. Isolation. No comms to anyone, family included.'

'No. No one's mentioned a thing. My parents are actually very concerned about me. I've been phoning home every day.'

A little later that morning the Squadron was called together for a special briefing. There was a distinct tension in the air, for they were about to be addressed by the Director of Special Forces (DSF), Brigadier Graeme Lamb, known to the men as 'Lamby'. They gathered in the cookhouse tent, which was about the one space large enough to house the entire Squadron. If Lamby was about to address them all then something momentous had to be afoot, and the men sensed they were about to learn the nature of their coming mission.

The Brigadier had just stepped up to speak when this dishevelled figure wandered in. It was Clive 'Raggy' Clarke – the guy who regularly won first prize for being the scruffiest bloke in the entire Squadron. Raggy was actually super-hard and super-fit, but he was always the last to arrive for any training session or briefing. He'd drift in wearing his trademark black trench-coat, mug of tea in hand, then realize that everyone was waiting.

'Oh, yeah, I was just checking all the buildings, and there's no one else,' he'd remark. 'I'm the last.' He'd carry on like that until he had the entire Squadron in stitches.

Brigadier Lamb did his best to ignore Raggy's late entry and began speaking. His address was delivered in his typically laid-back yet überconfident manner. In simple terms he outlined the key developments regarding the coming conflict, the most notable of which was the decision by Turkey to deny US and British forces the ability to open a northern front in the coming war. Little if any news of the wider war effort or its planning had filtered through to the men of M Squadron. But now, in this one instant, they understood that no forces were going into Iraq via the north of the country – or at least so they thought – which changed the entire roadmap for the coming war.

'The United Nations has more than had its chance in Iraq,' the Brigadier told the assembled men. 'It's clear that Saddam is not going to comply. That's obvious, and that means it's time to get you men in to do the job properly. It's true that the north of Iraq is now closed to conventional forces, but I want you to know that it has just been assigned as M Squadron territory. It will be the Squadron's area of operations for the coming conflict, and pretty much yours alone.

'Your mission is to move into the area where the Iraqi 5th Corps is situated,' he continued, 'which is up around the northern city of Salah. The 5th Corps is tasked with the defence of the whole of the north of Iraq. They have recently moved location at night and under complete radio silence, although we understand them to be demoralized and we are expecting them not to put up any significant resistance. You are to find the Corps and make contact with them. Your task is to go in and take their surrender, as they capitulate en masse.'

The Brigadier paused and eyed the room. 'You should know that the Turks have 130,000 of their own troops massed on the border. They are believed to be preparing to enter northern Iraq and to occupy Kurdistan, the territory of the Kurdish rebels. Needless to say, their presence would complicate your mission somewhat, but they are being offered several carrots to keep them out of the war – most notably European Union membership.

'Rest assured that Turkey will not be sending in troops, which gives you a free rein to achieve your mission.' The Brigadier was speaking with a reassuring degree of confidence. 'Make no mistake, whilst northern Iraq may be closed to conventional forces, it is not closed to us. Yours is a mission that may well change the entire course of the war. I have every confidence in M Squadron, and I am expecting the extraordinary from you in Iraq. Good luck.'

As the briefing came to an end, Grey reflected on what he'd just heard. A corps usually consists of two divisions or more, plus support units, each division being 10,000-plus men-at-arms. At a minimum the Iraqi 5th Corps would be some 20,000-strong. Grey wondered how the sixty operators of M Squadron were supposed to take the surrender of such a massive force. Moreover, a corps would be made up of infantry, artillery and light and heavy armour, and M Squadron was going to be a few dozen men in thin-skinned

Pinkies sporting machine-guns. While Special Forces operators were used to being outnumbered and outgunned – it went with the territory – the odds on this one didn't exactly look promising.

Another thing struck Grey. To move an entire corps by radio silence and at night was a seriously impressive undertaking. It required phenomenal discipline, training, logistical support, management and control, not to mention extreme self-confidence on the part of the corps' commanders. It didn't sound to him like the behaviour of a demoralized and ill-motivated force, one that was poised to surrender.

The key question was *why* had they chosen to move under radio silence and at night? The only possible answer was to hide such movement from watchful eyes. The 5th Corps could fear surveillance from only two possible sources. One was Saddam Hussein, and perhaps the corps commanders were trying to hide their movements from him, in preparation for their surrender. But the other source of surveillance was clearly the Americans, who owned the skies over Iraq. And if the 5th Corps was trying to hide its movement from the Yanks, that suggested the opposite of a desire to throw their hands in the air.

One thing did make very clear sense now, as Grey reflected on the mission they'd just been given. His eyes came to rest on the distinctive form of Sebastian March-Phillips. He was sitting with Reggie, the Squadron OC, and the rest of the men from the Head Shed (the Squadron's HQ Troop). It was blindingly obvious now why they needed a terp. How else were they to go and take the surrender of an entire Iraqi corps if they couldn't even speak to them?

The DSF's briefing was followed by one from the Army

Intelligence Corps bloke attached to the Squadron. Due to the unit's distinctive laurel-green beret they'd earned the affectionate nickname of 'the Green Slime'. He outlined the key background to the coming mission. The area of northwestern Iraq had been assessed as being 'relatively benign': in layman-speak, that meant that no hostile forces were known to be present in the region.

The main area of concern was Bayji, an Iraqi city situated on the main road to Salah. Bayji was an important industrial centre and the site of major oil refineries, chemical plants and weapons factories. It lay at one end of the 'Sunni Triangle', an area providing the bedrock of support for Saddam Hussein. M Squadron would need to give Bayji a wide berth, for neither the local inhabitants nor the military based there were reckoned to be friendlies.

'The Iraqi 5th Corps,' the briefer continued. 'During the 1991 Gulf War the 5th Corps fielded some 120,00 men-at-arms. In the aftermath of that conflict, dozens of senior 5th Corps commanders were executed by Saddam, for trying to topple him. There have been further attempted coups by senior 5th Corps commanders, the most recent being in 1998. From this and other intelligence we assess the Corps as being a hotbed of resistance to Saddam's rule, and ripe for capitulation. As of today, the 5th Corps is thought to number anything up to 100,000 men-at-arms, but we do not have absolute numbers.'

*One hundred thousand men-at-arms.* Grey did a quick flash of mental arithmetic: 100,000 divided by sixty equalled 1,666.66. Somehow, each bloke on the Squadron was supposed to take the surrender of over sixteen hundred Iraqi troops.

'The 5th Corps Commander is one Lt. General Yasin Al Maini,' the briefer continued. 'Normally, his forces are based at Salamieh,

Salah. However, as you know the entire Corps has recently moved under strict radio silence, and we are just now trying to tie down exactly where they are. We understand the men of the Corps to be underfed and not to have been paid for months. As a result, morale is low and there is little cohesive intent.

'The Corps consists of several infantry divisions and mechanized – armoured – divisions. In terms of weaponry, the Corps is equipped with the Iraqi-manufactured version of the Russian T-72 main battle tank – which the Iraqis call the Asad Babil, the "Lion of Babylon" – plus light armour, artillery and mortars. I'm sure you are all familiar with the specs of the T-72, and we'll be giving you a refresher on your AFV recognition drills before you deploy.'

AFV stood for 'armoured fighting vehicle', military-speak for tanks, armoured cars, armoured troop carriers, and whatever else the 5th Corps might boast in terms of heavy firepower.

'The weather window for your mission is prior to the end of March, by which time the short Iraqi winter will be coming to an end. Right now, daytime temperatures are just about bearable, and workable. There is a slight danger of rain, even in the deserts of northern Iraq, which brings the added risk of flash floods, especially in desert wadis. But we assess the risk as minimal, and more than compensated for by the lower temperatures during daylight hours.'

With the briefing from the Green Slime done, the men of the Squadron lined up to grab a brew. Grey found himself next to Scruff, and the two exchanged knowing glances.

'Us lot taking the surrender of an entire Iraqi corps,' Scruff snorted. 'They're having a laugh.'

'Yeah, sixty against a hundred thousand,' Grey remarked. 'Nice one.'

'Tell me, if you were tearing around the Iraqi desert in T-72s, would you want to surrender to a handful of scruffy tossers like us, driving Pinkies?'

'Not a chance.' Grey paused. 'What makes the Green Slime so sure they want to surrender, anyway? Remember Qala Janghi?'

'Fucking surrender? At Qala Janghi? Not a chance. Not a sniff of it. Not in Afghan, anyway. So why the hell should Iraq be any different?'

In late 2001 six hundred Afghan and foreign prisoners cooped up in the Qala Janghi fortress near the northern Afghan city of Mazar-i-Sharif had turned on their captors. They'd overpowered and killed Johnny Spann, an operative from the CIA's Special Activities Division (SAD), which was the trigger for an epic uprising. If there was one lesson Grey and Scruff had learned from Qala Janghi, it was that battle-hardened Muslim males weren't generally up for surrendering to the infidel.

That CIA operative was the first allied casualty of the post-9/11 war in Afghanistan. As the prisoners broke into the fort armoury, a lone SBS troop of eight blokes had been sent in to put down the uprising. A savage battle had followed, as the prisoners fought to the last man and the last round. They had resisted repeated air strikes called in by the SBS and their SEAL counterparts, not to mention sorties by T-55 main battle tanks operated by the Northern Alliance.

Scruff and Grey had fought a desperate battle from the fort's battlements, in which they'd used GPMGs and assault rifles to mow down waves of fighters attempting to rush their position. Many of the enemy sported suicide belts cobbled together from grenades, and they tried to blow themselves up right on top of the British operatives. Those repelling the assault – Scruff and

Grey amongst them – had believed they were going to die in that fort, so unwinnable had the battle seemed.

With a dozen ranged against six hundred, the odds had been horribly stacked against them. The brutal siege had lasted eight bloody days, at the end of which a rump of enemy fighters remained barricaded in the fort's dungeon. The only way to force them to surrender had been to pour diesel fuel into the underground chambers and burn them out, though British Special Forces played no role in that part of the assault. But even that wasn't enough to force the last to give up. Thousands of gallons of cold water had to be pumped below ground before the last few survivors had to surrender, or face death by drowning.

It had taken that level of base medieval brutality to force a few dozen survivors to surrender in Afghanistan: the grim reality of Qala Janghi was forever burned into Grey's and Scruff's minds. In light of that experience, the idea that a 100,000-strong Iraqi corps might choose to give themselves up to sixty lightly armed British soldiers seemed to stretch the bounds of credulity.

'Still, ours not to reason why, eh, mate?' Scruff remarked.

Grey forced a smile. 'Yeah, once more unto the breach and all that yada, yada, yada.'

In truth, Grey figured, there wasn't a man in that tent who didn't want to get on the ground in Iraq on this mission. Sure, Mucker, his quad-biker, looked his usual grumpy self. And Gunner – the quad commander – threw him a look that said: *This is all total bullshit*. But one glance at Moth and the Dude, and some of the other young guns, and he could tell they were right up for it. Even Sebastian – their high-born terp – had an expression on his face like Christmas had come early.

Grey knew he had a reputation for being a real grouch in the

Squadron, and he didn't always want to be the naysayer. He had to lead a number of the young blokes, which meant that he had to enthuse and inspire, and he couldn't forever be the downbeat voice. Plus there was a part of him that thrilled to the prospect of this mission. It was the kind of epic undertaking that he had trained for tirelessly over two decades of elite soldiering. Being in a Special Forces squadron was a little like being a boxer: you could hit the bag all your life, but there was nothing to beat getting into the ring to fight for real.

Yet once they got into the nitty-gritty of how to plan and execute the mission, he would at least air a note of caution and raise some of the key issues with Reggie, the Squadron OC. That was the least he owed himself and the rest of the blokes that he was leading into war.

The men gathered for a more informal mission-planning session. Reggie opened things, mug of coffee clutched in one hand. He started by outlining their mission in more detail: they were to cross the border from Jordan into Iraq at full Squadron strength, and drive north as one unit for several hundred kilometres. The plan when they finally reached the 5th Corps position was pretty loose: it was to drive up to them and ask to speak to their General.

The men scrutinized the maps, as the OC talked them through the options for their route in. The Squadron's passage into northern Iraq would take them through the Ninawa Desert, a vast area of sun-baked wasteland a good three hundred kilometres or more from end to end. It would offer them open driving in a terrain devoid of human presence and with little chance of being compromised.

But once the Squadron neared the Jabal Sinjar – the Mountain of Eagles – on the northern border of the Ninawa Desert, that bleak and impassable range of hills would serve to funnel the vehicles eastwards, whereupon they'd start to hit roads and more built-up farmland. By then the Squadron would still be a good hundred kilometres short of Salah and the Iraqi 5th Corps's positions, and they'd have to find a means to sneak through undetected. It was crucial that they did so.

The OC went on to stress the vital strategic importance of their mission to the entire Iraq war effort. If M Squadron could take the 5th Corps's surrender, it would constitute a major breakthrough in the coming conflict. In one fell swoop, the entire north of the country would have fallen into Coalition hands. Nothing of this scope and daring had been tried by UKSF for decades, and that, the OC argued, was all the more reason for M Squadron to grab the opportunity by the balls and to make it happen.

'Boss, I hear what you're saying,' Grey remarked, once the OC had finished his briefing. 'But still, several things trouble me. First, there's a hundred and thirty thousand Turkish troops massed on the border and poised to sweep south to take Kurdistan. Let's say they don't take the carrot of EU membership. At that moment, in their troops go, and they're going to brass up anything in their path, including us.'

Reggie gave his trademark easy-going nod: 'Okay, boy, I hear you.'

'Second, we've got a hundred thousand troops from the Iraqi 5th Corps to take the surrender of, and there's sixty of us in a handful of Pinkies. No way can us lot keep tabs on that number – that's supposing they do want to surrender, which is a big presumption to make.'

Reggie took a long slurp of his brew. 'Thanks, buddy. Got it. Good point.'

'Third, we're supposed to infiltrate into the area covertly overland. By my reckoning that's a seven-hundred-kilometre drive as the crow flies, so a lot further once we've navigated through, plus dodged around the enemy. From the maps it's clear that the further north we go the more heavily irrigated and vegetated it becomes, so we'll be channelled onto tracks and roads. That makes us highly visible.'

'Okay. Okay, boy. I hear you.' Reggie had a super-cool way of responding, and nothing ever seemed to ruffle him.

'For those reasons I'd question the feasibility of the mission, at least as it's presently constituted,' Grey concluded. 'I'm not saying I don't want us to get in there and do this, boss. I'm just saying there must be a better way to go about achieving our tasking.'

Reggie smiled. 'Thanks again, buddy, all points well made. I'll have a think on that one. We'll put our heads together in the Head Shed, and see where we get. But for now at least, boy, we've got to crack on.'

That pretty much silenced Grey's objections – although he did wonder whether the OC would be quite as laid back about things if the 5th Corps proved somewhat less than keen to surrender when they hit the deserts of northern Iraq.

Sixty against one hundred thousand: it would take a real Ice Man to maintain his cool with the odds so stacked against them.

# CHAPTER FIVE

Briefings followed briefings thick and fast now. The Americans had divvied up the territories in which each Special Forces unit could operate. The British, Aussie and Kiwi SAS had got the Western Desert, territory with which they were familiar from the First Gulf War. And in getting the north of the country the SBS had landed either the jackpot or the booby prize, depending on how you looked at it.

The more he learned, the more Grey reckoned that the mission they'd been given was actually a real peach. He knew his military history well, and the last time that British – hell, any – Special Forces had embarked upon anything like such a mission so deep behind enemy lines had been in the days of the Second World War.

Back then the SAS and the Long Range Desert Group (LRDG) had penetrated the North African desert driving Chevrolet trucks and Vickers jeeps, carrying out recce, capture and sabotage missions, hitting enemy supply lines, fuel dumps, airfields and ammunition stores. In September 1942 they had launched perhaps their best-known and most epic of missions – Operation Caravan.

Seventeen vehicles carrying forty-seven men had travelled 1,859 kilometres across the North African desert. On reaching their objective – the Italian-held Libyan town of Barce – the patrol had split up, one half attacking the enemy barracks and the other the airfield. During the airfield assault over thirty aircraft – mainly three-engined Italian Air Force bombers – had been damaged or destroyed.

If they could only pull it off, M Squadron's Iraq mission would be up there with such legendary exploits. And when in the entire course of military history had one squadron of elite operators ever taken the surrender of an entire corps? Sure, the mission feasibility left a bit to be desired, as did the intelligence picture, but this was the kind of operation that would get talked about in the officers' mess for years to come.

It was also going to be a massive personal test for each and every man on the Squadron. Sure, they were burned out after months of back-to-back operations. But equally, they were riding high on the success of the MV *Nisha* assault, not to mention their Afghan ops. So, while Grey had doubts about the specifics of the mission, he had every confidence in the individuals tasked to achieve it.

M Squadron also had an ideal opportunity to prove itself in Iraq. In the First Gulf War the SBS had never really got a look in, whereas the SAS had got decidedly down and dirty. This time around, the SAS was going to get similar taskings to the previous war – scouring the Western Desert for units that might be preparing to lob chemical weapons at US and British forces massing in Kuwait. By contrast, M Squadron had just landed a deep-penetration mission, one that would entail covering vast tracts of enemy territory to achieve an epic end.

As if to reinforce the hunger of the young guns to get going on this mission, Moth showed Grey a makeshift adaptation that he'd made to their Land Rover. Using bungee grips, gaffer tape and camouflage material, he'd cobbled together a cowboy-type sling for his Diemaco assault rifle. It lay to the right-hand side of the driver's wheel, so the weapon was held barrel downwards against the dash.

Moth demonstrated how he could reach for the weapon's butt, draw it one-handed, and aim and engage the enemy out of the front of the vehicle while keeping his other hand on the steering wheel. His Diemaco had an M203 grenade launcher attached beneath it, and in theory he could lob off 40mm grenade rounds single-handedly as he drove with the other.

Grey smiled indulgently. He appreciated Moth's keenness to engage with the enemy, but he reckoned the cowboy-style holster would be about as much use as an ashtray on a motorbike once they got going in Iraq.

'Mate, it looks super-cool,' Grey told him. 'But don't worry about it too much. Just concentrate on your driving.'

With each man in the Squadron tasked with taking the surrender of over sixteen hundred Iraqi troops, it made sense to get some basic Arabic into them. This was going to be Sebastian's baby. Trouble was, Sebastian had just been issued with a brand-new SBS beret, and no one seemed to have told him that you had to shape the distinctive headgear with hot – some argued boiling – water, so as to give it its distinctive, right-side-down skull-hugging profile.

When he walked in to the mess tent for the Squadron's first Arabic lesson, there was a chorus of 'Fuck me, I didn't know the chefs did Arabic!' Somehow, he seemed able to take all the piss-taking in his stride. It was like water off a duck's back, and he certainly didn't let it lessen his enthusiasm for banging some Arabic into the blokes of the Squadron.

He began by handing out some crib cards that he'd got printed up. They contained a list of common Arabic words and sentences, though oddly enough the phrase, 'Would you like to surrender?' appeared to be absent.

Sebastian was like a human dynamo as he talked the men through the basics of the language. He kept hopping about from foot to foot, and there was something about his boyish enthusiasm that was strangely infectious.

'Now, *here's* one you may have heard of – *Insh'Allah*, pronounced "Insha-a-lah"', he beamed. 'It means "God-willing", and absolutely everything is *Insh'Allah* in Arabic-speaking countries. Don't you just love the sound of it? – try it, all of you, now: *Insh'Al-lah*. *Insh'Allah* – really rolls off the tongue, don't you think?'

Seb was clearly playing to his audience, and playing up to the fact that all thought him to be some kind of mad, eccentric Englishman. 'Try it, Raggy, try it!' he enthused, as Raggy wandered in – his trademark five minutes late. '*Insh'Allah. Insh'Allah.* That's it. Fantastic, Raggy! Marvellous, isn't it?'

At the end of that first Arabic session Sebastian sidled up to Grey, as they joined the queue for a brew. 'So, erm, what do you think?' he ventured, a little self-consciously.

At first Grey figured he wanted some feedback on his Arabic teaching, but then he realized Seb was indicating the beret perched proudly atop his head. What on earth was there that he could say? He did some quick thinking. 'Mate, I dunno if you've noticed, but no one's wearing their berets much around here. OPSEC, mate. *Operational Security*. We don't want to risk anyone getting a photo of us, and rumour has it there are a few press types around the base. If they get a pic of any of us lot in the beret, well – they'll know SF types are off to Iraq, won't they?'

'Ahhh . . .' Seb looked a little crestfallen. He whipped the beret off his head, and folded it into one of his pockets. 'Oh well, waz-oh. Don't want to blow it that we're off on a spot of foreign adventure, do we?'

After acquiring some Arabic, the other key priority was getting the NBC (nuclear, biological and chemical) warfare defences sorted for the Squadron. Iraq had produced various chemical warfare agents over the years, including mustard, sarin, tabun and even VX – one of the most deadly nerve gases known to man – and the area the Squadron would be moving through was believed to harbour an underground chemical weapons plant.

Saddam had used chemical weapons extensively in the north of Iraq, both against both the Kurds and the Iranians, and the threat was seen as being very real. It was the avowed reason that the West was going to war. But it didn't make NBC defence any more of a popular a topic amongst the men. Compared to Sebastian's Arabic lessons, rehashing NBC drills was like watching paint dry.

The blokes had to learn the effects individual agents had on a victim, so as to recognize the symptoms and know when someone had been hit. They had to learn to suit up in all-enveloping gloves, suit and mask. They had to learn to use a special 'sniffer' device that sampled the air for deadly droplets, and how to employ fuller's earth – a talcum-powder-like decontaminant – to soak up and neutralize an agent. And, somehow, they had to work out how the overloaded Pinkies were going to carry the bulk of all the NBC defensive equipment.

The procedure that the Squadron hit upon for dealing with an NBC attack was designed to balance workability with defence. In truth, the British NBC suits made you look and feel like an oven-ready version of the Michelin Man. They were suffocatingly hot and impossibly bulky. Trying to operate vehicles or to move on foot was next to impossible while wearing one, let alone under a burning Iraqi sun. As to using a weapon, forget it.

The men would operate dressed as they saw fit, which meant T-shirts and combat trousers for the most part. The NBC suits and masks would be stowed on the wagons, ideally somewhere within reach. If a cloud of agent was spotted heading towards the Squadron, or if someone was seen going down with symptoms, the alarm would be raised via the radios. The first priority was to suit up and to save the lives of those not affected.

A chemical cloud would contaminate everything it touched, including the vehicles, and there was no way they could be decontaminated in the field. If the Squadron was hit, the entire mission would have to be aborted, and the wagons rigged with explosives and blown. The surviving men would radio for extraction by Chinooks, hopefully getting pulled off the ground and decontaminated safely at a forward mounting base.

The prospect of being hit by a chemical agent was not a pleasant one, and the men did their best to force it to the back of their minds – especially those who were going to be first onto the ground in Iraq.

It was 7 March 2003 when Reggie, the OC, decided on the Squadron's initial, probing insertion into Iraqi territory. Using satellite photographs the HQ Troop had identified a remote airfield at Al Sahara, way out in the Western Desert of Iraq. It looked to be largely deserted, and it offered an ideal forward mounting base – a stepping-stone – into the territory of northern Iraq.

The intel assessment on Al Sahara was that there were a couple of Iraqi Army trenches to either side of a dirt airstrip, but they were either unoccupied or ill-maintained by whatever force might be stationed there. The plan was to fly a lead element into the open desert some thirty klicks offset from the airfield, from where they would drive in under cover of darkness to recce and secure it. That done, the remainder of the Squadron would be ferried in by C130 Hercules transport aircraft, and the mission to take the 5th Corps's surrender would be well and truly under way.

If M Squadron were simply to drive across the Iraq border, the nearest point at which they could do so was from Jordan, to the west of Iraq. That would place them south of the main impediment to the Squadron's move into the north of the country – the mighty Euphrates River. The Euphrates runs from Syria southeast towards Baghdad, and the few bridges that crossed it would be heavily guarded. There was no easy way across the river, and it represented a major block to M Squadron's move overland.

But if they could seize Al Sahara, they could leap-frog the Euphrates and shave a good 250 kilometres off their journey. And in taking a working airstrip, they could get the big C130 transport aircraft to fly in the entire Squadron, as opposed to using the far smaller Chinooks. There weren't enough of the heavy-lift helicopters to ferry in an entire Squadron in one go, and Al Sahara offered them the only quick and covert way of getting onto the ground.

The team chosen to insert into Al Sahara consisted of Sean Timms, the Sergeant Major of Four Troop, with three highly experienced blokes under him. Like Grey, Timms had been attached to the SAS for two years, learning surveillance and recce ops, which made him an obvious choice for the job. All four men would be mounted on quad bikes, for maximum stealth, speed and manoeuvrability.

With the team going in on quads, a lone Chinook was able to ferry them all in. It dropped them in the open desert just over the Iraq side of the border, and under a night sky that was blissfully overcast and dark. Once the Chinook had disappeared in the direction from which it had come, the team bugged out from the dust-enshrouded drop zone. They searched for and found an LUP (lying-up point), and by first light they were safely hidden from prying eyes, their quads shielded by the rocky walls of a ravine and covered in camo-netting.

Back at their tented camp, the bulk of the Squadron were just finishing their breakfast. As he exited the cookhouse tent, Grey ran into the Squadron OC.

Reggie put out a hand to stop him. 'Okay, boy? All good?'

'Yeah, boss, it's all good.'

'I heard your concerns, buddy, and similar from the other OAB.' OAB was slang for 'the old and the bold'. 'The Al Sahara mission should answer some of 'em. It tests the waters. Probes the Iraqi defences. We'll see if there's any will to fight. Plus it shaves a good three hundred klicks off our infil, and should firm up the intel all round.'

'Nice one, boss,' Grey replied. 'They're a good team of blokes you've sent in. If anyone can do it, they can.'

All that day the four-man quad team remained in hiding, observing the desert terrain. Nothing seemed to be moving out there in the empty, barren landscape. By last light they were ready to move the two dozen kilometres to the outskirts of the airfield. The journey across the night-dark desert went without a hitch. They found the airfield easily – a clutter of decrepit buildings standing out like a dog's bollocks on the flat, featureless horizon. It looked to be long-abandoned. Even so, the four men probed the outskirts of the airbase first on foot, for maximum stealth.

Finding no sign of any hostile force, they mounted up their quad bikes to do a three-sixty-degree recce. They moved in to the airfield and were just about to turn across the airstrip itself when all hell let loose. A hidden force of Iraqis had spotted the small British force. Worse still, they were equipped with heavy machine-guns, plus vehicles.

The Squadron's Honda quad bikes could really shift, and one of the team had his machine airborne for several seconds as they powered out of there. But the Iraqis were no slouches. They chased the British vehicles with fierce tracer fire, hosing down the escape routes with long blasts from their heavy weapons. Others mounted up their vehicles and prepared to follow. They were using Toyota-type 4WDs – powerful, fast and highly manoeuvrable – and each was equipped with a mounted machine-gun.

A fast as the quad bikes were, right now they had a hunter force coming after them that was only marginally slower and by which they were heavily outgunned. The four M Squadron operators were armed only with their personal weapons – Diemaco Colt 7.62mm assault rifles, plus their pistols. They had no firepower to engage the Iraqis, let alone the range.

Timms led his team towards the open desert, where he planned to call in a Chinook to lift them out, but the Iraqis seemed well aware of the British soldier's intentions.

Each of M Squadron's Land Rovers was kitted out with a fixed radio antenna, one that resembled a horizontal crucifix and via which it was possible to call in a rescue force while on the move. But not the quads. The quad-borne force carried a satcom – an encrypted radio satellite communications system, one that the enemy would be hard-pressed to intercept. But the satcom worked on 'spider antennae', a Christmas-tree-like latticework that took time to erect and yet more time to find enough satellites to be serviceable. And each time the four-man force stopped to erect the kit and make a satcom call, the enemy were quickly onto them.

No sooner had they gone static and called through a set of coordinates for a hot extraction – a helo pick-up under threat of enemy attack – than the first bursts of enemy fire would come slamming into their position. Repeatedly, the four men were forced to mount up their quads and bug out, to try to get some distance between themselves and their pursuers, before repeating the process all over again.

They did this several times as they were hunted across the desert, and each time the hot-extraction point had to be abandoned. By the approach of first light the blokes were running low on fuel and ammo, not to mention options. By now they were pretty much surrounded by the Iraqi hunter force, and about to lose the cover of darkness. There was one upside. In the last few minutes they'd managed to get an American F15 warplane – call-sign *Irish* – flying top cover for them.

But the battle space below was so confusing, with vehicles charging about in all directions, that the F15 pilot refused to carry out any air strikes, for fear of hitting the quad-bike team. The one thing he could do in all safety was to get a laser onto the British force, so that the rescue Chinook could lock onto the hot point of the laser beam – the spot where it bounced back from the ground – and home in on that for the pick-up.

As the helo headed in with its tail ramp already lowered, it was audible from many miles out and the dust thrown up by its flight left a telltale trail. It powered across the desert towards the quad team's position, but so too did the Iraqi hunter force. They were drawn in by the Chinook's flight path, and were closing fast. Just as the giant helo put down, the enemy guns opened up, the Iraqis firing from their Toyotas as they wove at breakneck speed through the desert sands.

For a bare few seconds the Chinook held rock-steady while the quads tore up its ramp, and then it was airborne again and heading for cover. As it sped across the desert low and fast, the Iraqis unleashed hell, heavy bursts of fire chasing the helo through the night skies. But the enemy muzzle flashes gave the F15 aircrew an accurate fix on their position, and with the British force lifted out they were free to mount air strikes without fear of a friendly-fire incident.

The arrow-like form of the jet tore in, and the aircrew unloaded with the nose-mounted M61 six-barrel cannon, a storm of 20mm rounds raking the Iraqi positions. Under cover of that murderous fire the Chinook made it out of there, and M Squadron's lead element was able to return to their base, alive but decidedly shaken.

'What's the ground like?' Grey asked the Al Sahara airfield blokes, once they'd finished their mission debrief. 'What's it like to drive over?'

'Easy enough,' one replied. 'Hard compact gravel and grit, not soft sand dunes.'

'But it's bloody cold at night, especially when tearing about on a quad,' said another. 'Take your bloody thermals, your duvet jacket and everything in between.'

As they'd reported in on the outcome of their thirty-six-hour mission, the old and the bold within the Squadron had had a distinctly ominous feeling. If Sean Timms had got his tiny force compromised and badly shot up just as soon as they'd crossed the border, what hope was there of getting an entire Squadron inserted covertly hundreds of miles into Iraq?

They'd just put in one small, low-profile and highly-mobile team, only to get it seriously brassed-up. If it wasn't for the smart footwork by the US warplane, not to mention the RAF Chinook crew, the four-man team might well have never have made it out of there. The only advantage M Squadron would have was a greater degree of firepower, but it would be massively more visible to any watching Iraqi forces.

There was also little reason any more to assume that the 5th Corps was desperate to surrender, especially when the force stationed at Al Sahara airfield had proved so ready to fight. There were a hundred thousand 5th Corps soldiers, complete with light and heavy armour, and they might be just as aggressive and capable as the Al Sahara airfield defenders. If so, the sixty men of M Squadron were going to be toast.

As had been the case with the Bravo Two Zero mission, it looked as if M Squadron was being sent into Iraq on bugger-all usable intel. The only area they had tested for themselves was Al Sahara, and Al Sahara had proven far from 'relatively benign'. But in a sense, Special Forces soldiering was always like this. They were being sent in to prove the ground truth on what amounted to an offensive recce – and this way you risked a few good men, not an entire army.

Special Forces units only ever tended to trust the intel absolutely when it was delivered by one of their own – ideally a couple of their own blokes in a hide with eyes on the mission objective. And on this occasion the only possible way to get eyes on the Iraqi 5th Corps was to send the Squadron some seven hundred kilometres into Iraq, to find them.

The Al Sahara debrief over, Scruff turned to Grey: 'Mate, I've just thought of the operation codename: Mission Impossible Iraq'.

Grey shook his head and gave a wry smile. 'Nah, mate – more like Operation No Return.'

# CHAPTER SIX

Worryingly, the exact location of the Iraqi 5th Corps still hadn't been identified. It must have taken days, if not weeks, to move up to a hundred thousand men and arms at night into a place of hiding. But amazingly, that was exactly what the 5th Corps seemed to have done. They had managed to move an entire corps off the face of the earth, and M Squadron seemed to have no option but to go in and root them out.

There was no explicit Plan B, if the Squadron reached the 5th Corps's position only to find that the Iraqis were less than keen to surrender. If that was the case, every man knew he'd have to go on the run and fight his way out of there, however improbable that might seem.

In truth, most Special Forces operations were defined by such extreme risk and uncertainty. The kind of blokes who made up a force like M Squadron knew the hard realities of such missions. They'd rise to whatever challenges were placed before them, no matter what the uncertainties. That was the kind of mind-set the Squadron fostered, and that was why such soldiers had joined

Special Forces – to be part of a unit from which small groups of men went out to achieve the seemingly impossible.

Even so, from all that they had heard, the OAB of M Squadron figured there was a very different way of construing the Iraqi 5th Corps's make-up and intentions. Northern Iraq was Saddam's homeland. In Bayji and Tikrit – the cities just to the east of M Squadron's intended line of march – you had Saddam's tribal stronghold and his birthplace. If – when – Baghdad fell, Saddam would very likely retreat to this area, to make his last stand. That being the case, the 5th Corps – which made up as much as a third of Iraq's standing army – could well be Saddam's choice of men-at-arms for his last-ditch battle. Far from being ill-disciplined, ill-motivated, underfed and underpaid, these could be the boys that Saddam was relying on to fight to the last man.

There were two other significant forces in the area. First was the Iraqi Security Organization (ISO), Saddam's feared secret police. The ISO were fiercely loyal to the Great Leader, but they weren't considered a major combat unit. The second force – the Iraqi Fedayeen – was an entirely different matter. The Fedayeen was a combat militia that worked directly to Saddam's orders. They were recruited very young, and made to idolize Saddam and to show blind loyalty. The Fedayeen were equipped with fast, Toyota-type four-wheel-drive vehicles fitted with heavy machine-guns. They were constituted as a highly mobile, fluid, guerrilla-type army, and were probably the most feared of all fighters in the country.

The Iraqi Republican Guard – the nearest Saddam had to elite forces – would be better-trained, but they weren't manic, diehard lunatics like the Fedayeen.

M Squadron was shown a Fedayeen recruitment video. It

pictured these very young men and boys running around in robes and red-and-white checked headscarves, doing combat drills and yelling oaths of allegiance to Saddam and to the mother country. The highlight of the video was those young trainees slaughtering a goat with a knife, then drinking its blood and eating its flesh raw. It all looked very fanatical, hardcore and messed-up.

There were also some particularly gruesome stories of what the Fedayeen did to their own people if they ever suspected them of harbouring any resistance to Saddam's rule. Clearly, if M Squadron ran into any Fedayeen there was no way they would be taking their surrender. If they did come up against those brainwashed fanatics it would be a brutal fight to the death – on both sides.

As the Squadron began to load up the C130s for their onward deployment, Grey ran into Sebastian en route to the armoury. More or less everyone had been avoiding the Squadron's newest member, but not Grey. Grey had more than warmed to the bloke. He found him hilarious and oddly fascinating.

'How's it going then, mate?' he asked.

'Guess what?' Sebastian replied, excitedly. 'I'm going to be getting a gun! And guess what else? I'm going to be getting just a spot of training. From that chap you introduced me to – what's his name? Gunner. Yah, from him.'

Grey couldn't help but crack up laughing. Sebastian sounded like he was about to go on a pheasant shoot on the estate. It was priceless. For an instant he wondered if Seb was actually taking the piss. But he clearly wasn't. He was just a genuine, nice bloke who didn't try to hide who he was, or his lack of experience or his fallibilities.

Grey smiled. 'Well done, mate. I'm glad you're getting a gun. The Iraqis will be quaking in their boots.'

'Waz-oh! I say, d'you think I'll have to shoot anyone?'

Gunner was renowned for being a hard and merciless weapons instructor. He and Sebastian were the proverbial chalk and cheese. What Grey wouldn't give to sit in on that weapons-training session – but unfortunately, there was a mission to prepare for.

Following the failure to seize the Al Sahara airfield, the HQ Troop had rejigged M Squadron's operational plan. A combined force of British and Australian SAS had pushed into the far Western Desert of Iraq. There, they'd had far better success than M Squadron had achieved at Al Sahara. The British and Aussie force had seized the 'G2' and 'G3' airfields – Iraqi oil pumping stations that doubled as airstrips.

Under cover of darkness the SAS force had assaulted the deep desert locations – which lie just across the Jordanian border – using fleets of desert patrol vehicles and the Aussies' six-wheeled version of the standard open-topped Land Rovers. From out of the night they'd hit the guard towers like a whirlwind, then moved in to clear the large hangars and office buildings one by one.

*G2* lay to the north of the Iraqi settlement of Shab-al-Hiri and was the more northerly of the two airbases, but it was still the wrong side of the Euphrates River for M Squadron's purposes. Even so, it did offer the Squadron the ability to insert into Iraq via C130 Hercules, shaving a good hundred kilometres off their mission.

The strategy that had been adopted for the Squadron's insertion was complex, and a lot could go wrong, but if all went to plan it would get them over the Euphrates and well into northern Iraq. The entire Squadron was to be flown into *G2* over one night, using a fleet of C130 Hercules operated by highly trained Special Forces aircrew from a unit that specialized in dropping elite forces deep behind enemy lines. From there they would be airlifted north by Chinooks.

Due to the shortage of available helos, it would take three nights to ferry M Squadron into their remote LZ (landing zone). But crucially, that LZ was situated to the north of the Euphrates, so enabling the force to leapfrog that mighty river.

Grey and his team had scrutinized the intended LZ particularly closely, for they were scheduled to be first onto the ground. Using maps and aerial photos, a patch of terrain to the east of Sabkhat Abu Chars – a dry lake bed – had been indentified.

The Iraqi *sabkhats* – sand flats – were known to be treacherous, with subterranean water making them boggy and impassable. But the plateau to the east of Sabkhat Abu Chars seemed empty of human habitation and solid as a rock. It was a vast stretch of hard, barren land, with here and there the odd sprinkling of sand. As an added bonus, it was some seventy kilometres from end to end and at its northern extremity it merged into the Ninawa Desert – the bone-dry, lifeless wilderness that would take the Squadron most of the way to their objective. The LZ was about as far north as the Chinook pilots could afford to take them, bearing in mind the need to fly six runs with the helos over three nights so as to complete the infil.

But in spite of the rigorous planning, the risks involved in the coming insertion were legion. The *G2* airfield was a stretch of dirt runway surrounded by open desert. A fleet of Hercules would need to land during the hours of darkness and offload the Squadron vehicles, more than likely kicking up a violent dust storm. The wagons would somehow have to cross-deck from the C130s to the waiting Chinooks in next-to-zero visibility. That alone had all the makings of a disaster.

In 1980, US Special Forces had flown into deep trouble on a similar type of mission. Six helicopters had rendezvoused with a C130 Hercules in the depths of the Iranian desert. The helos were carrying US Delta Force operators, and their intent was to launch an assault on the US Embassy in Tehran so as to rescue fifty-two American hostages being held there. But one of the helicopters had crashed in a dust storm, and another had damaged its hydraulic systems.

The decision was made by the then US President, Jimmy Carter, to abort the mission, which was codenamed Eagle Claw. But as the aircraft prepared for take-off from their remote desert location, one of the helos crashed into a C130, which was loaded with men and fuel. A massive fire engulfed the two aircraft, in which eight US servicemen lost their lives. A further five helicopters had to be abandoned, and were subsequently captured by the Iranians.

In short, Eagle Claw – one of the first missions ever undertaken by Delta Force – was seen as an unmitigated disaster. And the two-stage airborne insertion for Operation No Return – as the old and the bold had started to call M Squadron's Iraq mission – was a similarly risk-laden undertaking.

In mid-March the entire Squadron flew out of their base on a fleet of C130 Hercules to a remote base deep in the deserts of Jordan. There, the first of the teams to be lifted onwards to *G2* prepared to get airborne. Each Land Rover was loaded up with all the ammo, weaponry, personal kit, NBC and other gear the three men using it – plus their quad-biker – might need, with enough fuel, rations and water for a good week or more of operations.

Each man carried twelve 30-round STANAG mags for their personal weapon, the Diemaco C7 assault rifle, making 360 rounds in all. The Diemaco is a modified, ruggedized lightweight version of the standard M16 assault rifle, and it's the weapon of choice for Special Forces. The M Squadron operators also carried a secondary weapon, a Sig Sauger 9mm pistol with a 13-round magazine, plus rakes of spare ammo.

High-explosive and smoke grenades were placed around each wagon in easy reach of the occupants, plus there were extra grenades stuffed into the men's Bergens. A one-use LAW (light anti-tank weapon) 66mm rocket-launcher was strapped across the bonnet of each Pinkie, for use against larger buildings and light armour.

Each Troop had also been issued with a highly experimental *SLAR (shoulder-launched assault rocket)* – an 85mm rocket launcher that fires an enhanced blast warhead, more commonly known as a thermobaric device. The fuel–air explosive creates a firestorm at the point of impact, followed an instant later by a vacuum that collapses just about any object it hits.

The *SLAR*'s thermobaric warhead had been developed by America's Naval Surface Warfare Center, a military technology development site based just north of Washington DC. M Squadron was very lucky to have got one *SLAR* per Troop, for it was still in the experimental phases of the weapon's development, and everyone wanted to get the chance to fire one.

Armed and outfitted as they were, the one thing the Squadron wasn't equipped to take on was the Asad Babil – the 'Lion of Babylon' battle tank. The Asad Babil boasts a 125mm main gun, a 12.7mm DShK anti-aircraft cannon, plus a GPMG-type machine-gun. Its armour is twelve inches thick, and it can maintain 50 kilometres per hour off-road. Being chased by a squadron of Asad Babils wouldn't be much fun, especially as the heavily laden Pinkies weren't capable of going a lot faster and even more so when moving across rough terrain.

No doubt about it, that kind of armoured beast was best avoided.

The first C130 flight into *G2* had four Pinkies packed into it, one of which was Grey's wagon, plus a bunch of quads perched on the tail ramp. As the C130 roared through the darkened heavens, Grey sat in the shadowed interior wondering what the days ahead might hold, and how the young lads on his team were going to cope with whatever might lie ahead of them.

Grey had a massive admiration for the C130 aircrew – guys who were basically flying into a patch of dirt deep in hostile territory, trusting absolutely that those on the ground had chosen a safe landing zone. The pilots would have to put the C130 down with total trust on a night-dark patch of desert, knowing that one rock the size of a laptop could seriously mess up their landing.

If the SAS boys had missed just the one loose boulder, it could flip up and smash into the turbines. Worse still, the tip of a rock anchored in the desert could rip the guts out of the aircraft's tyres, causing no end of mayhem.

Over the years Grey had got to know some of those RAF Special Forces pilots passably well. They were fellow mavericks who were well aware that going into a Special Forces flight would rarely win them promotion. They were the guys who didn't give a toss about rank or status, and who loved flying by the seat of their pants. They were fellow can-do rebels, which made them a natural part of the SF brotherhood.

In a standard air force set-up, an aircraft can't normally get airborne if so much as a flock of seagulls menaces the runway. By contrast, these guys would fly through all weather and just about any level of threat, to put down on just about any vaguely usable piece of terrain – as their landing at *G2* was hopefully about to prove.

The Hercules arrived above the Iraqi airstrip, and began a tactical descent towards the darkened earth so as to avoid being targeted by enemy fire. The SAS had thrown a ring of steel around *G2* to enable M Squadron's safe insertion, but that wouldn't prevent an Iraqi surface-to-air missile team from targeting the C130 from out in the open desert.

Once the vehicles had dismounted from the aircraft, the C130 surged back into the sky leaving in its wake a thick and seething dust bowl. Grey, Moth and Dude found themselves marooned in a blinding, choking cloud of fine sand. To their left and right were the half-obscured silhouettes of their fellow Pinkies, but no one had a clue in which direction the waiting Chinooks lay. The plan was for the wagons to move off the C130's ramp straight into the waiting helicopter's hold, but not a thing could be seen of them. If they set off blind they risked suffering another Eagle Claw.

'Hold stationary!' Grey yelled at Moth, above the roar of the departing C130. 'Don't make a fucking move until all this shit has settled.'

Moth gave a grunt in the affirmative.

They gazed all around, wondering what the hell to do next. Grey tried flipping up his sand goggles and strapping on his NVG, to check if the enhanced night-vision kit might somehow cut through the dust cloud. But all it served to do was to drive some grains of wind-blown dust into his eyes.

He muttered a string of curses. 'Fuck that for a game of soldiers.'

Here they were, finally in Iraq, and marooned in a brownout of a dust storm.

From off to one side a voice rang out through the dark. 'Steve Grayling! Grey! You there?'

The voice sounded familiar, and Grey figured it had to be one of his mates from his days spent working with the Regiment.

'Yeah! Over here, mate! Over here!'

Two points of eerie light emerged from the gloom. They turned out to be cyalumes – chemical light sticks – one held in either hand of the SAS guy who was here to receive them. He waved Grey's wagon forward, and at walking pace they followed him across the dirt strip. They made towards the ghostly form of a waiting Chinook, which loomed out of the murk like a darker patch of shadow amongst the dust swirling all around.

Grey indicated the helo's open rear. 'Take mega fucking care when you go up the ramp.' He jerked his thumb in the direction of their tailgate. 'Especially with the camo-netting.'

'Got it, boss,' Moth confirmed.

There were only a bare couple of inches to spare on either side when driving a Pinkie into a Chinook, plus the arse-end of their wagon had a rolled up camo-net strapped across it. If that caught on anything it could rip the innards out of the helo, or damage the hydraulic system that opened and closed the tail ramp.

With all the dust in the air, the blokes had pulled *shemaghs* over the exposed skin of their faces, and sand goggles over their eyes. It was the only way to safeguard their vision, but it made it impossible to wear NVG, for both sets of kit wouldn't strap over the eyes at the same time. It was only the dim light thrown off by the cyalumes, plus the way the SAS bloke guided the wagons forward, that got them safely into the dark hold.

There were two Chinooks waiting to ferry the Squadron onwards, but each could only take one Pinkie and a couple of quads. Part of the aircraft's hold was occupied by a bulging fuel bladder, which took up precious space but added extra range. They had before them a sixty-kilometre flight, after which they'd be dropped in the open desert to the north of the Euphrates, to form up M Squadron's vanguard.

Once they'd been delivered to their open-desert LZ, the men were to establish the Squadron's forwards mounting base for the mission. This was by far the most dangerous stage of the operation so far. A small lightly armed force was flying into the unknown, tasked with holding a patch of flat, featureless terrain for three days and nights, so the rest of the Squadron could be ferried in.

As Grey waited for the helo's rotors to spool up to speed, his mind drifted to thoughts of his wife and kids back home. He couldn't help but wonder if this was the mission that was going to get him. It was rare for him to feel as anxious as he did now: in fact, he couldn't think of another moment in a lifetime of elite soldiering that had unnerved him so much. It was ominous and unsettling.

He glanced at Mucker squatting by his quad, but the tough northerner seemed to be showing no special signs of nerves or of tension. He too had a wife and young children back in the UK, so by rights he should have been equally worried. As for the Dude and Moth, Grey figured they were the lucky ones right now. Sure, they lacked operational experience, but at least the young guns didn't have the added burden of a wife and kids on their shoulders.

The turbines screamed deafeningly above them, and the Chinook clawed into the air for the next leg of the insertion. As the pilot banked the big helo round and set a course heading north, Grey could see his men checking and rechecking their weapons. Two of his team were untried and untested in combat, and he hoped and prayed that they weren't about to fly into a patch of desert packed with a hidden enemy, one that their scrutiny of the sat-photos had somehow failed to detect.

The Chinooks were operating on black light and the aircrew were flying fast, at tree-top level. They were throwing the massive, cumbersome machine around like a sports car, and the effect in the rear was electrifying. They were going in blind to a potentially hot LZ, they had no one on the ground to guide them in, and they were unsighted and defenceless – apart from the door gun-ners hunched over their miniguns.

Following the experience of Afghan ops in 2001–2, the Chinooks had been upgraded with a fantastic NEP (night enhancement package), which enabled the pilots to fly nap-of-the-earth missions even in extremely low light. The NEP included specialist night-vision technology that showed the terrain over which they were flying in glowing near-daylight, on laptop-like computer screens mounted in the cockpit. It also included a moving mapping package that displayed a 3D contour map of the ground they were crossing.

The pair of helicopters tore ahead at near-maximum speed – approaching 250 kph – the terrain flashing past barely a few dozen feet below the porthole-like windows. There was a glint of moonlight on water below them, which had to be the Euphrates, as the pilot dropped the Chinook down to hug the surface of the river. They powered across that mighty waterway, putting the barrier it rep-resented well behind the advance force of M Squadron.

For a moment Grey was reminded of the MV *Nisha* assault.

He'd sat by the Chinook's open ramp in the howling, icy draft thrown up by the wind-whipped sea. Just as now, that Chinook pilot had brought them in at ultra-low level, the wave tops seemingly tearing at their undercarriage. The assault had been carried out in the midst of a raging gale, but still the pilot had held the Chinook rock-steady as it hovered over the deck and the men went down the ropes.

Grey had every confidence in the highly-trained Special Forces aircrew doing a similarly sterling job on their insertion into Iraq. As they thundered across the desert leaving the expanse of the river behind them, and with little sense of what they were flying into, the one comfort Grey felt was in the calibre of the men flying the helicopters: the MV *Nisha* assault had more than proved them the best in the business.

The noise in the Chinook's cavernous hold was deafening – the throbbing of the rotor blades plus the roaring of the wind from the open ramp – and it made it impossible to talk. Grey got his men to don their night-vision kit, which rendered the dark interior of the helo a ghostly fluorescent green. He gave each of his team a thumbs-up, and got a silent nod and a forced smile in return.

As they neared the LZ the nerves were really starting to show. This was the kind of mission that he had trained and coached his men for relentlessly, and he hoped they were ready. He only wished they'd had more time in Kenya to prepare for what was coming – surviving and very likely fighting from their vehicles over weeks spent behind enemy lines.

But it was too late to worry about that now: they were well past the point of no return.

# CHAPTER SEVEN

The Chinook's loadmaster – the crewman responsible for getting men and materiel on and off the helicopter – flashed the five fingers of one hand in front of the men's faces. It was the signal that they were five minutes out from the LZ; it was time to mount up the Pinkie and the quad, for the helo would be touching down only long enough for the vehicles to roar down its open ramp and be gone. Those few precious seconds on the ground were all the aircrew could afford.

Grey, Moth, Dude and Mucker flipped up their NVG, pulled down their sand goggles and wrapped their *shemaghs* ever more tightly around them. Their faces were smeared in a thick layer of camouflage cream, and their combats were covered in a layer of dust that already seemed to be making its way into everything. They were starting to assume the colour and hue of the Iraqi desert in which they would be operating.

Here and there the vehicles were plastered in dun-coloured camouflage tape, to dull down any vaguely reflective surfaces. Special attention had been paid to the light units, which were completely taped over. They'd be operating on black light, so the fuses had been removed, and the switches for turning them on and off had been taped over to ensure no headlamp or brake light could be operated accidentally. This was vital tradecraft when operating in an open, sun-blasted desert environment, and something that their US Special Forces and SAS mentors had banged into them during training back in Kenya. One flash of sunlight on a patch of metal could prove fatal this far inside Iraq.

Likewise, if as seemed likely the enemy were out there scanning the desert for British Special Forces, they'd do so at night with their headlights sweeping the open terrain. So all windscreen glass had been removed from the Pinkies, and there was nothing about the wagons – or indeed the men driving them – that would reflect any hostile light.

In short, the men of M Squadron had made themselves as invisible as it was possible to be. They were a ghost force, and to that end they'd also removed all identifying marks or documents. They carried no wallets, photos of family, or ID papers of any sort, and their combats were bereft of any sign of rank or unit. If captured, there was nothing about them that would identify what nation or force they hailed from, or who they were.

Sure, the Iraqis would have ways to break a man and force him to talk. But sanitized as they were, a captured individual might at least buy his fellow warriors a good few hours or even days of precious time, before he cracked. If anyone was taken alive then the mission would still have to be considered blown, but at least the OC would have a few hours in which to try to ensure his remaining force's survival.

But right now the main threat to Grey's team was what they might be flying into at the fast-approaching LZ. Once the Chinooks had dropped them, he felt confident they could blend into the desert environment and disappear. It was standard operating procedure to evacuate the area of the LZ as quickly as possible – but whereas two Pinkies and two quads might vanish into the rock and sand, a pair of massive, thundering Chinooks was a very different matter.

As the helos tore in and put down they couldn't help but advertise their very noisy arrival. And the trouble was, Grey and his tiny force had to remain static on the LZ for a good two hours before they could make themselves scarce. The Chinooks were going to drop them at 2400 hours, and at 0200 they were scheduled to fly in again with a further batch of men and machines. In the meantime the tiny advance force had to secure and hold the LZ, or at least give ample warning to the pilots that it had been compromised and to abort.

Grey felt the contents of his stomach lurching into his throat as the massive helo decelerated from speed, while at the same time the pilot lowered its rear end towards the earth. It was 'flaring out' so as to touch down with its ramp on the desert sands, its wheels barely making contact, and keeping the rotors turning and burning. It would hang like that for a few seconds, then the wagons would away, and the aircraft would get airborne once more and head fast and low for safety.

As the Chinook lost altitude the first whips of choking dust came whirling through the open rear, the twin rotors blowing up a veritable sandstorm. Grey gave the signal to start the engines, and within seconds the hold was filled with the blue-grey smog of diesel fumes mixed with the dust. To their left and right the Chinook's door gunners were sweeping the terrain below for hostile threat, but with the rotors kicking up a brownout of swirling sand they could barely see a thing.

A thud reverberated through the airframe as the pilot settled the giant machine arse-end onto the desert. No sooner had he done so than the loadie gave the 'Go-go-go' – signalling with his gloved hand for the vehicles to get down the open ramp. Mucker went first, the quad exiting the helo like a bat out of hell. Grey's wagon followed, with Moth inching it down the ramp and nosing it all but blind into the seething, dust-filled darkness.

As their rear wheels left the ramp and hit the desert with a thump, Grey tried to shout some kind of confirmation that they were gone, but the Chinook was already getting airborne again. The pitch of the rotors whined to a scream, the aircraft rose, dipped its nose and powered away. It roared into a banking turn, the pilot swinging the giant machine onto a southerly bearing, before being was swallowed up by the dark night.

Grey and his men hunched over their weapons, trying to shield themselves from the stinging rotor-driven sand and grit. There was no point in trying to move anywhere. Visibility was at zero and it was impossible to do anything other than ride out the storm blind. They had to sit and wait until the air cleared enough to be able to see and move.

The first thing to become visible was the night sky, the brightest stars piercing the thinning halo of dust like pinpricks of molten gold. As the fine sand settled and pooled all about them, drifting to earth on the desert air, the strong, heady smell of burning aviation fuel faded into the background, as did the characteristic thwoop-thwoop-thwoop of the Chinook's double rotors.

In its place was a deep and residing stillness such as few of the men had ever experienced, plus the empty, wild, earthy smell of the cold desert night. The terrain all around them was so utterly still and devoid of life that the gentle purr of the Pinkie's engine sounded deafeningly loud, and as if it might carry for dozens of kilometres to any listening human ear.

Grey and Dude hunched behind their machine-guns, scanning their arcs. The men on the other Pinkie, commanded by Scruff, were doing likewise. Grey felt certain there were alert enemy forces out there somewhere. He could feel it in his bones. Yet his initial rapid scan revealed nothing. They had been dropped in dead-flat and open terrain, the darker shades indicating where patches of sharp black gravel lay between stretches of bare rock and lighter sand.

As soon as the air had cleared enough, Grey signalled Moth to move out. Scruff knew to fall into line behind, as they pushed out to the eastern side of the LZ. Moth nosed the wagon ahead, the ambient light thrown off by the moon and stars being strong enough to pick out a route. It was easy enough driving, the ground under foot being hard-packed, smooth and firm, and devoid of even the slightest trace of track or pathway.

They pushed ahead observing complete radio silence, just in case the Iraqis were scanning the airwaves for Coalition radio chatter. With a force as small as theirs, it was simple enough to communicate using hand signals. Grey brought Moth to a halt, then with a knife-slice motion across the throat he got him to cut the engine.

Scruff's wagon pulled in alongside them, its bonnet pointed in the opposite direction to their own. That way, they had a pair of .50-cal heavy machine-guns plus GPMGs covering them in both directions. As the second wagon cut its engine, the tiny force of British soldiers was enveloped in the silence of the night.

Grey strained his ears, and he figured he could just make out the faint beat of the Chinook's rotor blades fading into the distance.

He wondered for how many kilometres that sound might be audible, and who exactly might have heard them. There was an empty ghostliness to this place that unnerved him, and yet was strangely peaceful and calming.

It struck him that being dropped by Chinook in the Iraqi desert was something like walking out of the world's noisiest rave club in the early hours of a Sunday morning. They'd exchanged the deafening roar of the helo's turbines and the rush of the slipstream for utter stillness and silence like the grave. He flipped his NVG down and began to do a more detailed scan of the terrain.

'Mate, best keep your natural night vision,' he whispered to Moth, 'just in case we need to move out.'

If both men used their night-vision kit, then were jumped by enemy vehicles using headlights, the NVG would be 'whited-out' by the high light levels and they'd be blinded. So one operator would always keep his natural vision, to avoid that happening.

Grey was struck by how deafeningly loud those few words that he had spoken had sounded. There was a weird, wired tension underlying the quiet here. As he scanned the terrain, in each direction that he looked the frog-eyed green fluorescent glow lit up a tunnel of desert. Grey didn't particularly rate the night-vision kit. Sure, it rendered darkness into near-daylight, but at the same time it distorted everything. It condensed distance, concentrating all into a narrow-view glow that cut out all peripheral vision.

His search revealed nothing that he hadn't seen with the naked eye: all signs of human life were absent here. He leaned across to Scruff in the wagon beside him. The two men exchanged a few whispered words, their eyes barely moving from their gun sights.

'Dog's bollocks?' Grey muttered.

'The proverbial,' Scruff whispered back.

Their two wagons and the pair of quads stuck out like a sore thumb, marooned in the sea of empty desert as they were.

'Anything?' Grey queried.

'Nothing, mate. Not a thing. Plus it's quiet enough to hear a sparrow's fart.'

They'd driven maybe three hundred metres to the east of the LZ. It was far enough to keep eyes and weapons on it, and at least they weren't parked up bang where the helos had put them down. Still, this felt all wrong. After the deafening noise of the insertion they should be making haste, putting several kilometres between them and the LZ. But the British military didn't have the airframes to move an entire Special Forces squadron into Iraq in one go, and so they'd have to stay put and wait.

Had the Yanks been running such an operation, they'd have mounted up a dozen Chinooks and swept in like a scene from *Apocalypse Now*. But this being a wholly British gig, the plan had been crafted around the available assets, and they were going to have to use waves of aircraft spread over three nights.

The risks of doing so were legion. Not only were the helos audible for several klicks away as they put down on the LZ, but coming in at low level anyone on the flight track would also detect their passing. No one but British or American forces would be using helos deep in the Iraqi desert, so it didn't take a rocket scientist to work out who it was powering overhead.

'Hope it's not going to be Al Sahara all over,' Scruff whispered, referring to the Squadron's attempt to seize the airfield not far from their present location.

'Too right,' Grey grunted. 'But we're asking for it, that's for certain.'

'Boss, it goes against all we learned in Kenya,' came a quiet voice from beside him. It was Moth. 'Remember Delta Jim's words: *Bug out of your LZ like as soon as possible. Make directly for a hidden LUP.*'

'Yeah.' Grey shrugged. 'But orders are orders. Tell you another thing, I'm bloody frozen.' He flexed his fingers around the GPMG's icy grip. 'Forget a bloody brass monkey, it's cold enough to freeze my own balls off.'

'If this was a Delta mission they'd have dedicated air, wouldn't they, boss?' Moth whispered. 'They'd have air above them the whole time.'

'They would,' Grey confirmed. 'US Spec ops types don't go in unless they've got air power on call.'

Moth glanced towards the heavens. 'Guess we can't afford the fuel to fly any—'

Grey smiled. 'Welcome to the poor man's military. It's like Dad's Army, but without the panic.'

While it was important to allow the blokes to have a good moan, it was also vital to keep everyone's spirits up. It struck Grey that Moth had just spoken the most he'd heard him say in one short burst. He'd unhooked his Diemaco assault rifle from where he had it lashed against the dash in its holster, and it was cradled in his lap. No harm in doing so, just in case they did meet an Iraqi hunter force. Grey sensed that perhaps it was now that the quiet man on his team was going to start sparking.

They'd been stationary for a good thirty minutes when Grey got down from the wagon, stamped his feet and jumped about, in an effort to bring some life back into them.

'You training for the Iraqi Olympics?' Scruff needled him.

Ignoring the comment, he ran on the spot for five minutes or so.

'Okay,' he announced, sliding behind his machine-gun again. 'Moth, you're next. Feet-stamping duty.'

Two hours spent in the bitter cold, scanning arcs and staring down the freezing barrel of a machine-gun into utter emptiness: it wasn't anyone's idea of fun. They couldn't brew up, just in case a fleet of Fedayeen did decide to pitch up on the horizon. All they could do was sit and stare and try to keep alert as the icy cold seeped into them.

As they gazed into the void, each bloke in this eight-man force couldn't help but wonder who exactly was out there. Might the enemy know already that a force of British soldiers had put down deep inside their territory? M Squadron's advance party was the furthermost Special Forces unit across the entire country. No one else was anything like this far in. They'd penetrated some 240 kilometres into Iraq, and there were still days to go before the war proper was scheduled to start.

'This is shit,' Moth complained, as he blew into his frozen hands to try to get some warmth into them.

'Yep. It's crap.' Grey confirmed. 'That's war for you. Long periods of complete boredom, interrupted by the odd moment of chaos and drama.'

'Oh, I dunno,' came a quiet drawl from the wagon's rear. 'I mean, the scenery's kind of pretty wild. Reminds me of parts of the Nevada Desert back home. And I mean, you know, the company's to die for—'

There was a chorus of 'Piss-off, Dude!' from the others, and all fell silent again.

Then they heard it. Faintly, almost inaudibly, a burst of a juddering, thumping beat on the still desert air. The men strained their ears. The noise faded into silence, then drifted back in again, stronger and more audible this time as the Chinooks bore down on them. No doubt about it, they had the second flight in-bound.

Despite the fact that they were heading in at tree-top height, the pair of helos were evident from many miles away. Their rotors were kicking up a dust storm and creating a whirl of static electricity, which resulted in a distinctive blue-green 'fairy dust' halo marking out their flight path. The eerie glowing forms were visible as a flash of light on the horizon, long before the machines themselves could be seen.

The aircrew knew to put down on the same LZ, and to expect Grey and his men to be just to the east of it. If there had been no warning radio call, they knew the LZ to be clear of hostile forces. Both the aircrew and those in the helos' rear had what they wanted now – their own men on the ground with eyes on the area of the drop, but it still wasn't the way that Grey and his blokes would have wanted to do things.

The Chinooks did a repeat performance, and fifteen minutes later there were four Pinkies and a similar number of quads gathered together to the east of the LZ. Grey took the opportunity to do a final map check. He was using a specialist torch that had a bendable straw-like tube coming out of one end, with a tiny light diode attached to it. With the map in his lap and the light diode cradled in one hand, he could map-read with barely any illumination leaking out of the vehicle.

Having double-checked the location of their intended LUP, Grey gave a whispered order to Moth to move out. The wagon swung round until they were heading due south, moving out in the direction in which the Chinooks had flown in. They were going in the wrong direction for the mission, which required them to push northwards, but it didn't really matter much, for they couldn't get on the move proper until the entire Squadron had been ferried in.

Grey and Moth had settled upon a pre-arranged modus operandi for desert driving at night. As long as the conditions remained clear and bright, Grey would map-read, navigate and scan for the enemy using his natural night vision, while Moth would rely on NVG to find a way through the terrain. From long experience Grey knew that if he used NVG, he'd have to focus them at distance to navigate, then refocus on his lap to map-check, which was pretty much undoable. It was far better to rely on the diode torch and the naked eye.

Regular forces tended to use 'red illume' at night, a dim red light that's harder for an enemy to see. At its simplest, a red filter would be taped over a torch to create a beam of softer red light. But the men of the Squadron didn't favour such kit. Only soldiers used that kind of illumination, so it stood to reason that if you did see red light at night it had to be a military force. Far better to use a source of light that could be civvie.

For thirty minutes Grey navigated the patrol across the open desert, the only noise being the soft crunch of gravel under tyres and the gentle purr of the diesel engines. Another key element of the vehicle mobility craft was being able to pack a wagon so that it could move noiselessly under a heavy load. Cargo had to be lashed vice-tight to the steel lugs on the wagon's sides. Any metal objects – jerry-cans, shovels, steel sand ladders – had to be wrapped in hessian sacking, so as to prevent them clanging against the Pinkies' alloy panels.

Grey was heading for a re-entrant, a dry channel cut into the flat terrain, one that would drain the desert of any rare rainfall.

At its southernmost end the re-entrant emptied into the Euphrates River. Grey brought the convoy to the northern end of the feature, whereupon he gave word to Moth and Dude to search for a natural entry point – ideally a shallow slope leading into the bed of the feature.

Predictably, it was Dude who spotted it. From his perch on the wagon's rear he had the best all-round vision. He pointed them towards the opening, a place where the jagged rim appeared to drop away more gently and smoothly than elsewhere. Creeping ahead at dead slow, Moth edged the heavily laden wagon over the edge, large stones cracking and popping under the weight, as the tyres fought to retain their hold.

They crested the lip and began to descend, Grey getting his first glimpse down the length of the wadi. It was set maybe six feet below the surrounding terrain, the base smooth and sandy from where floodwaters had rushed along it in seething torrents, depositing sediment as they went. Here and there large boulders dotted the riverbed – ones that had proved too heavy and cumbersome for the floodwaters. It was easy enough for Moth to weave a route around them, and they pushed a good hundred metres down the wadi. They'd lowered the tyre pressures to about half the recommended amount so they could better float across such soft, sandy terrain. Only if they hit any sand dune seas would they experience any real problems.

Moth nosed the wagon into a natural harbour in the wadi wall and cut the engine. Behind them the other Pinkies did likewise, one pulling in alongside them against the eastern wall of the feature, and two occupying the western slope. That way, they could use the vehicle-mounted machine-guns to cover the terrain to both sides of the wadi, during the hours in which they'd remain here.

With first light fast approaching, M Squadron had sixteen men on the ground, plus four Pinkies and their sister quads. The vehicles were spread out a good hundred metres along the feature. They were within speaking distance of each other, but without being too bunched together to present an easy target to any enemy. They sorted sentry duty, each wagon's weapons covering one of the four points of the compass.

Grey took first watch, a two-hour shift that would last until 0630. He mounted the wagon and slid behind the GPMG. Moth had positioned the vehicle in such a way that both machine-guns could be operated. As old habits died hard Grey preferred his seat behind the 'Gimpy', as the tried and trusted weapon was called.

He settled down to what he was certain would be two hours of complete and utter boredom. He felt certain that no one could have tailed them from the LZ to their place of hiding. They'd driven on black light the whole way, and they'd passed through the desert night as silently and unseen as ghosts. For the first time since their boots had hit the desert sand, he felt himself beginning to relax a little.

Here they were, safely through the complex two-stage air insertion, which had had all the makings of a galactic bugger-up akin to the Eagle Claw debacle. They were safely out of the LZ, and well hidden. Now all they had to do was stay unseen for the next three days and nights, gather the Squadron and head north for several hundred kilometres, then take the surrender of the Iraqi 5th Corps.

What could be easier than that? he asked himself wryly.

# CHAPTER EIGHT

A faint sound of snoring drifted up from the cold bed of the wadi. Moth, Dude and Mucker were lying prone on the hard ground, each man cocooned in a sleeping-bag. They'd brought synthetic bags, as down-filled ones were useless if they got wet. There was no need for mozzie nets: the bone-dry Iraqi desert was devoid of water, without which mosquitoes couldn't thrive.

It was good the guys were getting some kip, for come sun-up the wadi would become a roasting furnace. The Iraqi sun would quickly burn off any chill, and by mid-morning the temperature would be pushing one hundred degrees – which was about the time that Grey would be trying to get his first rest following sentry.

The men had barely slept for two nights now. Over the coming nights they'd need to be back at the LZ, securing it for the further Chinook rotations. Somehow, they'd have to grab whatever kip they could during the heat of the day. It was far from ideal, and Grey worried that by the time the Squadron was assembled and ready to move, his team and Scruff's – the advance party – would be well and truly knackered. Already he could feel his eyelids

DAMIEN LEWIS

sagging. But he forced himself to stay focused, and keep his eyes on his weapon's stark iron sights, as he scanned the empty night for the enemy.

On missions such as this one, space and weight were at an absolute premium. Those who were sleeping were lying on a length of roll-mat that they'd cut down, so that it cushioned only the length of the torso and the head. Anything else was an unnecessary luxury. But at least they were wrapped up snug and warm in their doss-bags.

After the experiences of the First Gulf War, it was well known how cold and inhospitable the Iraqi desert could get. Having been forced to go on the run, the Bravo Two Zero patrol had hit appalling weather conditions – sleet, snow and freezing winds. That lesson had been well learned across British Special Forces, and before deploying to Iraq the men of M Squadron had been issued with a full set of Arctic cold-weather gear.

It was left to the blokes to make their own choice of which items of cold-weather kit to take with them, and Grey had baulked at the idea of the neoprene ski mask. It was a kind of deformed wetsuit hood, a rubberized balaclava that left just the eyes showing. But he regretted not having it now. After a couple of hours on stag his head felt frozen stiff, and his eyes were watering. His hands had seized up, and he knew he'd have trouble operating his weapon if the enemy did put in an appearance.

He heard a few whispered words from behind him. 'All right, mate? How're your lot doing?'

He turned to find it was Gav Tinker, the Squadron Sergeant Major, doing the rounds – but right now the bloke resembled some kind of nightmare apparition. He had opted to bring his ski-mask. It squeezed up what could be seen of his face into a bulging, wrinkled blob, his eyes like little piggy slits in the middle. Still, at least the SSM was warm, whereas Grey felt as if his neck was about to snap in two with the cold.

Grey couldn't help but crack up laughing. 'What the fuck do you look like.'

'Yeah, yeah, yeah, Pumbaa the warthog. Heard it all before, mate,' the SSM grunted. 'Still alive, are you? Your feet dry? Whatever, whatever. Fuck off and see you all later then.' He turned to go. 'Oh, yeah, almost forgot. Time you switched sentry. Want me to kick the next bloke into life?'

The hidden force remained where it was all that day, without the slightest sign of any enemy presence. If they'd put down on the surface of Mars it couldn't have been more devoid of life. The terrain had been baked utterly dry and lifeless and there didn't even seem to be any scorpions, or the hated Iraqi camel spiders.

At last light the men prepared to move out and retrace their steps to the LZ. The next force to fly in would be Reggie's HQ Troop, the nerve centre of the Squadron. With sixteen men and their machines safely on the ground, it was seen as being secure enough to risk inserting the OC. Even so, Grey felt it wise to run through the JTAC procedures one last time with Moth, in case they did hit trouble and needed to call in some air support.

With no dedicated air cover, British Special Forces had to tender for air on the radio net. What warplanes did exist would be held in an orbit over central Iraq, so that whatever unit needed air could call it in. That was the theory. In practice, aircraft would be busy carrying out preplanned air strikes against strategic targets, prior to the ground forces going in. A unit requiring air cover would have to compete with whatever air missions the warplanes orbiting the area were flying.

A Special Forces request for air cover should be given top priority, but there were never any guarantees. Air power was where small elite units normally had the upper hand, when on the ground in hostile territory. Tasked to penetrate several hundred kilometres behind enemy lines, it would have been nice to have something big, punchy and lethal orbiting over M Squadron, but that clearly wasn't happening on this mission.

Apart from air power, one of the few other advantages M Squadron had over the enemy was the secret comms system that each wagon also carried – a military-issue satellite phone system used when speaking to air cover, as well as being the lost-comms fall-back option. If a troop or a team was compromised and on the run, the satcom allowed secure encrypted voice comms. With a satcom antenna built into each wagon, it could even be used while on the move.

As their team's JTAC, Moth would speak to the warplanes using the satcom, but with a 'donkey dick' aerial attached to it. In that configuration it became a line-of-sight comms system via which he could talk directly to the aircrew, and guide them onto target.

The second night's airborne infil went pretty much like clockwork, and by now a third Chinook had joined the airlift. At the end of the flights in, there were some forty men and their machines gathered on the ground. The part-formed Squadron moved off from the LZ, and Grey led it to an LUP a good distance from the one of the night before. It was a golden rule of such ops never to return to an LUP if you could possibly avoid it. No matter how careful you might be, it stood to reason that the more you used one, the more telltale signs of your presence you'd leave.

By the approach of first light Grey's team were preparing to get a good hot meal down them – the first they'd had for several days. They'd been living off British Army ration packs and mostly on 'hard routine', which meant no brewing up or hot food was allowed. But with the firepower now gathered around them, those who were first onto the ground could afford to treat themselves to a little luxury.

Grey fished out a foldable hexi stove – one that utilizes small solid-fuel blocks a lot like household firelighters – and began to cook up for his entire team. He asked the blokes what they fancied from the menu – corned beef hash, chicken casserole, beef stew, Lancashire Hotpot, or the pasta.

'I'll have anything bar the corned beef hash,' Dude volunteered. He was taking the first sentry duty, and he'd eat his meal perched atop the .50-cal heavy machine-gun. 'Dunno what it is about that corned beef, but it sure blocks me up real bad, if you'll forgive me talking about my bowel movements.'

Grey glanced up at him. The young American was always so polite, and there were times when he wondered if he was secretly taking the piss. But invariably he wasn't – it was just the good clean American kid inside him shining through.

'Dude, we'll be spending weeks shitting in cling film, wrapping it in plastic bags and carrying it on the wagons,' Grey remarked. 'I'll know all there is to know about your bowel movements by the time we're done here.' He fished out one of the boil-in-the-bag meals. 'You good with a Lancashire Hotpot?'

Dude smiled. 'Kind of a Brit version of Dunkin' Donuts? Yeah, that'll do me just fine.'

Grey smiled. Anything more unlike Dunkin' Donuts he couldn't quite imagine. As far as he was concerned, the Lancashire Hotpot was the foulest thing the British Army catering department had ever managed to concoct. It was an eye-of-newt, claw-of-bat, foul-as-fuck brew, one cooked up by a coven of witches cackling over a cauldron. But if the Dude was partial to it, who was he to argue?

He handed the steaming bag across. 'Here you go, mate. All yours. Tuck in.'

'Thank you very much,' said Dude, with a one-hundred-per-cent genuine smile of gratitude.

'You finish that lot, I'll bung you a couple of my private supply of Hobnob biscuits. How's that for a deal?'

'Fantastic, boss,' Dude remarked, through a mouthful of dumpling like congealed glue.

Grey settled down to a steaming bag of chicken pasta, his favourite.

He glanced across at the HQ Troop, positioned at the centre of the LUP and surrounded by a protective screen of vehicles. He almost choked at what he saw. There, perched in the rear of the OC's wagon, was Sebastian. He had a floppy-type jungle hat perched atop his head, presumably to keep off the burning sun, and he had a pair of nail clippers in the one hand with which he appeared to be doing his toenails.

Parked alongside their wagon was that of the SAS 2iC. Neither vehicle carried any top guns, for they were weighed down with specialist communications kit and long-range aerials. They were relying on the rest of the Squadron to provide a ring of steel around them, as they coordinated ops on the ground and liaised with UKSF Headquarters.

Grey shovelled in the pasta, his eyes glued to Sebastian's nail-clipping performance. No doubt about it – as entertainment went this was as good as it got. Sebastian glanced up from what he was doing and caught Grey's eye. His face broke into a smile, and he reached behind him and pulled something out of the wagon. It was a pair of civvie-type hiking boots.

'I've got them – my boots,' Sebastian mouthed at him.

Grey gave him a thumbs-up in return. For the laughs he offered alone it was worth having Sebastian along, not to mention the practical need to have someone able to speak to a bunch of Iraqi generals. Grey watched as Sebastian finished his clipping, slipped his socks and boots back on and wandered over.

'So what d'you think?' he whispered, pointing proudly at his footwear. 'I might go to ask the RSM if he minds – check I won't get into any trouble!'

'I reckon you'll be okay,' Grey reassured him. With the Squadron infil only two-thirds done, Gav Tinker was sure to have more on his mind than Sebastian's choice of footwear.

'Jolly good show, though, going to take the surrender of the Iraqi 5th Corps.'

Grey stared at him for a long second, thinking: *You have absolutely no idea what that means, do you?* But he kept his thoughts to himself. Instead, he gave a nod towards Sebastian's boots. 'Good you got them sorted. Crucial that, if you'll be speaking to a few Iraqi generals.'

Sebastian positively glowed.

'Best you get a warm feed down you,' Grey added, as he dug deep to scrape out the last bits of pasta. 'Might not get many more chances from now on in.'

'Jolly good idea.'

'How was the weapons training with Gunner?' Grey asked.

'A bit like the time I used my shotgun back in my London apartment,' Sebastian answered. 'Only rather more noisy, rigorous and exciting.'

'What were you shooting at in your *London apartment*?' Grey asked, incredulously.

'There was a rat running around in the cellar. In my apartment, in Pimlico. So I shot it with my shotgun. Someone must have called the police. The police couldn't work out who it was had shot what with what, though. What a wheeze.'

'What d'you mean – *you shot a rat with a shotgun in your Pimlico apartment*?'

Sebastian put his hands up in front of his face and wiggled his fingers about, whisker-like. 'You know, a rat. A rat. A ratty-rat. I shot a rat.'

Grey noticed the Squadron OC move off from his vehicle. In one hand he was clutching the unmistakable shape of a roll of bog paper.

'Don't look now, but the OC's going for a dump,' he remarked. Anything, to get Sebastian off his bizarre rat-killing story.

As the OC strolled towards them Grey raised his spoon in greeting. Reggie gave a nod in return. 'Lancashire Hotpot? Hmmmm . . . lovely.'

'Not me, boss. That's the Dude's favourite. I'm on the pasta.'

Reggie paused beside them. 'How's it been, being first in, and all that?'

'No dramas,' Grey replied. 'It'd be nice to get on the move and away from the LZ, though. Been leaving a lot of tracks in the sand around here.'

Reggie shrugged. 'We're going as fast as we can, boy.'

A secondary tasking had just been radioed through to the Squadron, the OC explained. Once the force got under way they were to check out any locations en route where it might be possible to establish a TLZ (tactical landing zone) – a stretch of flat, deserted terrain where a C130 Hercules could land.

The Squadron was to mark any potential TLZs on their GPS systems, and radio back such coordinates to Headquarters, which would help establish some degree of ground truth as they went. Any one of those TLZs could then be used to airlift in an airmobile-capable force, like the men of the Parachute Regiment, so as to accelerate the occupation of northern Iraq.

If the 5th Corps' surrender could be successfully taken, plus a series of TLZs secured as springboards for getting reinforcements flown in, the inability to launch a northern front via Turkey would become much less of a problem. M Squadron would have spearheaded the takedown of northern Iraq, in a mission of truly epic proportions.

Reggie raised the bog roll and waved it in the direction of a gully that ran off to one side of the wadi. 'Just going for a spot of the obvious up there.'

'Don't worry, boss,' Grey smiled. 'I'll warn the lads not to shoot you in the arse.'

'Thanks.' The OC paused. 'Not a lot of point keeping on hard routine, is there, buddy? We'll be sixty blokes and thirty wagons, and we'll leave a motorway of tracks as we go. A few dried turds are hardly going to be a big giveaway.'

Grey shrugged. 'Hadn't given it much thought. But yeah, boss, now you mention it, it's a fair point.'

'In any case,' the OC continued, 'imagine the wagons after three weeks if we're carrying all our crap with us.'

'Yeah, not nice,' Grey agreed.

'Three weeks!' Sebastian interjected, excitedly. 'Are we really likely to be that long?'

Reggie paused. 'A good week to do the infil overland and take the Corps's surrender. Then two weeks to oversee that, as Coalition forces move up from the south of the country. I figure it's likely to be three weeks at least before we get relieved.'

'Guess we'd best ditch the bags of crap, then,' said Grey. 'I hid most of mine in Scruff's Bergen. But don't tell him, eh?'

The OC smiled. 'Mum's the word, boy. Mum's the word.'

By the time Reggie had returned from answering nature's call, Grey was taking over watch. He mounted his wagon, and prepared for one hundred and twenty minutes of mind-numbing boredom. The trouble with such operations was that one lapse of concentration could well prove fatal. They might have seen nothing for the last forty-eight hours, but that didn't mean an Iraqi Army patrol wasn't about to stumble across their hiding place.

Forcing the mind to be totally vigilant when it craved rest only added to the exhaustion. Grey settled into his seat, and as his eyes wandered across the terrain his mind also wandered. Normally, Special Forces work was never this mind-bendingly monotonous. Invariably, there was something or someone specific to keep a watch on.

He thought back over a Northern Ireland gig that he'd been on several years back – yet another joint operation with the SAS. They'd been six blokes holed up in an OP (observation position). The OP was little more than a large grave-shaped hole scooped in the sodden earth, with the thick heather sliced through and rolled back over the top of them as cover. From there they'd had eyes on a run-down barn, originally built of dark stone and grey slate but which had been repeatedly patched with rusting galvanized iron. Typically for Northern Ireland, the rain had drizzled down from a grey sky that had all but merged into the grey of the earth. It was the kind of weather that never amounted to a downpour, but nor did it ever stop seeping damp into your bones.

The rain was miserable, but all of that had seemed somehow bearable on account of the prize. The barn housed an IRA weapons stash, and one of their more notorious ASUs (active service units) was scheduled to do a pick-up, so they could mount another murderous operation. Only this time, Grey and his fellow elite operators intended to meet them with a storm of bullets.

They'd been in the OP for a good forty-eight hours by the time the ASU had shown. They'd left it to the last moment to retrieve the arms – several shotguns and a couple of AK47 assault rifles – so as to give any watchers the least possible time in which to hit them. The rules of engagement wcrc stacked so far on the bad guys' side that they could only be engaged if they were holding a weapon, and were a 'clear and present threat'.

The bad guys had exited the barn and gone to mount up their van, when the trap was sprung. The men in the OP had made the call, and a series of airborne and vehicle-mounted forces had gone in to seal off the entire area. Meanwhile, Grey and his fellow warriors had yelled out a challenge for the gunmen to throw down their weapons or face the consequences. They'd tried to hide the guns under hay bales and the like, but this time they'd been caught red-handed, and they were rolled up without a shot having been fired.

The point about that mission was that in spite of the God-awful weather and the terrain, it had been *interesting*. It had been two days during which anything could have happened, and the comings and goings at the farm had kept the guys on edge. Here in the Iraqi desert there was nothing of the sort.

For now at least, there was only an empty and burning sun-blasted stillness.

# CHAPTER NINE

Grey cursed under his breath. *Goatherds. Why was it always bastard goatherds?*

For three days and as many nights they'd seen zero sign of life here, and the Squadron was now all but complete. A few more hours and they'd be moving out as one and heading north into the unknown. Or at least that had been the case before the eerie tinkling of the bells and the appearance of the bloody goats.

Grey gripped his weapon closer, his gloved fingers poised to flick off the safety and open fire. He held his aim rock-steady, his finger laid gently on the trigger. But first he needed to assess the threat, scan for human presence – was there anyone with the herd? – and check whether they had detected the Squadron's presence. Only then would he unleash hell.

He felt his leaden fatigue evaporating, as bursts of adrenalin surged through his veins. What with the infil into Iraq, plus sentry duties and the to-ing and fro-ing from various LUPs to the LZ, he was approaching five nights with no proper sleep. He reckoned his team had had an average of three and a half hours' kip every twenty-four hours, and a lot of that during the burning heat of the day – and sleep snatched here and there was never the same as a proper full night's rest.

Bearing in mind how utterly filled-in they were, he was amazed at how his blokes were holding up. Only Scruff's lot had been on the ground for as long as they had, and he felt as if his team had gelled well. It was good to be on the ground with them. He'd been looking forward to getting the wheels turning and the mission started for real.

And now this. A fucking goatherd.

Sure enough, he detected a stick-like figure – the herder – so there was at least one Iraqi sharing the desert terrain with his scraggy animals.

Grey reflected on how it had been a lone goat-herder that had pretty much done for the Bravo Two Zero patrol a decade or so earlier in Iraq. The B2Z boys – B2Z was how British soldiers tended to refer to that iconic mission – had seen the goat-herder approach the gully in which they were hiding. They'd clocked the fact that he was just a kid. They'd seen him catch sight of them, and they'd read the shock and recognition on his features. And the decision they'd made not to open fire and slot that goat boy had cost them the security of their patrol, not to mention good men's lives. As soon as the goat boy had seen them he'd taken to his youthful heels and raised the alarm. Barely an hour later the B2Z boys had had half of the local population coming after them with guns, not to mention the Iraqi military. The patrol had been scattered, and men had died and been captured, and all because they'd let that Iraqi kid live.

Under the rules of engagement Grey knew the terms under which he had the right to shoot the goat boy. If the kid spotted the British force, then he was a clear and present threat, and

Grey was within his rights to open fire. But like the B2Z boys, he doubted whether he had it in him to gun down a young kid in cold blood.

Grey fixed the billy-goat with his IR torch to blind it and drive it off. As it turned and stumbled away Goat Boy got spooked, and started yelling what sounded like *Feringhi* – 'Foreigner!'. For once, Grey would have given anything to have had Sebastian with him on sentry. Their terp would have known exactly what the Iraqi kid was saying – whether it was a warning that a foreign military presence was in the area, or a warning to his goats to wind their necks in.

As the herd disappeared into the distance, bells clanging softly, Grey stole a glance at the HQ Troop. There was bloody Sebastian lying comatose on his fold-up camp bed. In a way it made sense that those blokes didn't stand sentry. They needed to keep well rested and sharp so as to command and control the mission, plus they had their own duty rotations to manage, so they could keep a listening ear on comms from Headquarters.

But it grated that they'd brought with them small luxuries like camp beds, and all because they could afford to carry the extra weight on their wagons, which weren't so laden down with machine-guns or ammo. Yet right now what grated most was that Grey hadn't been able to call upon Sebastian's Arabic skills, so as to check out what that kid goat-herder had meant.

It was too late to worry about it now. The moment had well and truly passed. Grey felt a silent tap on his shoulder. Moth appeared beside him like a wraith, to take over watch.

'Anything?' he queried, as he slid himself into the driver's seat.

'Yeah, maybe,' Grey hissed. 'A herd of fucking goats. Plus a goat boy. Would you believe it? Wankers.'

Moth's watery eyes were like saucers as he stared at Grey, the blue-grey of the moonlight lending them an added ghostliness. 'He see us, boss?'

Grey shrugged. 'Maybe. Maybe not. I couldn't be sure. That's why you didn't hear the Gimpy roar as it smashed a load of goats apart.'

'If he saw us he'll raise the alarm.' All traces of sleep had gone from Moth's voice now. He was stating the obvious, but it was something that needed to be said.

Grey nodded. 'He will. If he saw us. He was a kid. Maybe eleven or twelve years old. Not my style to slot him.'

'Mine neither, boss,' Moth confirmed. 'That kind of shit would torture your head for the rest of your days.'

Grey eyed the young operator for a long second. The longer they spent in the field, the more he realized there were hidden depths to Moth.

A couple of years back a troop of SBS had been sent on Operation Barras, a Special Forces hostage rescue mission in the West African country of Sierra Leone. The rebels had taken captive a load of British troops on peacekeeping and training operations, and threatened to kill them unless a set of impossible demands were met. A combined SAS/SBS force had been sent in to rescue them, and lay waste to the rebels' jungle base.

Trouble was, the rebels had recruited child soldiers by raiding villages, chopping off limbs indiscriminately, and forcing young boys to kill their own parents. The kids were fed a cocktail of powerful drugs, and their heads were filled with evil voodoo nonsense – they bathed in potions that supposedly made them 'bullet-proof'.

When the SAS/SBS assault force had hit their jungle base the kid rebels had charged fearlessly onto their guns. Most of the blokes had done whatever it took to stop them and to rescue the British soldiers. Many had come away with dark memories, ones that would trouble them for a lifetime. One even spoke about a parade of ghostly figures – rebel kids – that would march through his sleepless nights for years to come.

Moth was right: that kind of shit would most definitely mess with your head.

Grey pointed towards the southeast. 'He came from that direction.' He moved his arm northwards. 'He left in that. Keep your eyes peeled.'

'Boss,' Moth confirmed.

Grey flicked his eyes towards the east, where a faint halo of blue was starting to lighten the flat, featureless horizon. 'We're moving out in an hour's time. Keep alert for any Iraqi presence. *Anything*. I'm going to get my head down for a few minutes.'

As he burrowed into his sleeping-bag, Grey found that his mind was churning. In spite of the exhaustion, sleep just wouldn't come. He couldn't help but wonder whether they had just got compromised. It was first light on day three, and they were all but out of there – and now this shit had to happen. It was the uncertainty – had they or had they not been seen by Goat Boy? – that was really getting to him.

It stood to reason that the herder had appeared at this time of day. No one in his right mind would be out herding in the dead of night, or in the burning heat of the day. If only the goat-herder had made it to their wadi an hour or so later, the Squadron would have been out of there. As it was, Goat Boy only had to harbour a suspicion that some unknown but deadly force lurked in that wadi for him to be able to cause them real problems. If he went and reported it to the village elders they'd likely drive out to investigate. If they did, they were bound to pick up on the tracks left by close to thirty vehicles, leading into and out of the LUP. There was just no way to hide the passage of that many Pinkies and quads.

Not only that: if the Iraqis did find the LUP, they'd very likely be able to trace the Squadron's move north, as the wagons would leave a motorway trail across the desert. No matter if they moved by day or by night, their tracks could still be followed.

Grey resolved there was nothing much he could do about it now. He'd raise it at the OC's morning briefing, and they'd take it from there. He snuggled into his doss-bag, and drifted off to sleep with that thought foremost in his mind. As his breathing slowed to a regular rhythm, the fierce Iraqi sun edged towards the distant horizon – due east of their position, and in the direction of Bayji, the city stronghold of the diehard Iraqi Fedayeen.

He awoke some twenty minutes later with a driving sense of urgency to get the Squadron on the move. In spite of his intense fatigue, he felt an unshakeable sense of foreboding – as if some dark force was out there and preparing to come after them. He made his way across to the OC's briefing, and gave a report of what he'd seen during his watch.

There were others on sentry who'd also seen the herd of goats, but it didn't much alter the Squadron's intentions. Until they had absolute confirmation that they'd been compromised, the mission would continue as planned. Yet there was definitely an added sense of urgency now to get the Squadron on the move, and to be primed to deal with any threat with instant, lethal force.

From now on every vehicle or Iraqi seen would be treated as hostile, unless proved otherwise. If the life of any Squadron member was in danger in any way, the threat would be engaged and taken out. But none of that meant that they'd start mowing down any Iraqi kids that might wander past their position. No one blamed Grey for not opening fire. In his place, the rest of the blokes would have done exactly the same.

Just after first light on day three of their mission, M Squadron prepared to depart the LUP. Apart from the added urgency of getting out of there, it was crucial to make at least the first day's move in daylight. They needed good visibility to achieve the secondary tasking of their mission – to search for and waymark any TLZs.

The Pinkies assembled in an arrowhead formation, with the quad bikes making an outrider force scouting to the front and the flanks. It was the role of the quads to be the eyes and ears of the Squadron, and to help scope out the route.

The larger Squadron arrowhead was made up of three smaller V-shapes, each of which corresponded to one Troop, with HQ Troop sandwiched in the middle of them. Within each V-shape every vehicle had its set position – so that if the Squadron came under heavy attack, each of the Troops could peel off and fight as independent units.

It was this type of complicated fire-and-manoeuvre operation that the Squadron had been rehearsing during their weeks spent training in Kenya. It was complex and difficult work when coordinating thirty-odd vehicles, and in the SAS and Delta Force it took months, if not years, to perfect. M Squadron had had barely a fraction of that time to learn their craft, and right now they were about to be tested to the limits and beyond.

As the Squadron moved out, Grey spared a fleeting thought for

Sebastian. He searched for the HQ Troop, and found it at the centre of the arrowhead. Sebastian was in the back of the OC's wagon perched on the rear gunner's seat, but with no machine-gun to man. His skin was lily-white, and his nose appeared to be smeared in a thick white slick of sunblock. His jungle hat was brand-new, and looked as if it had a seriously starched rim.

The ride in the wagon's rear was rough as hell, and without the big .50-cal or a grenade launcher to keep a hold of it would be doubly uncomfortable. The blokes manning those big weapons would be continually scanning their arcs, keeping on the balls of their feet ready to ramp the weapon to left or right whenever a threat presented itself.

Sebastian was sitting there like a sore thumb, glancing all around him and using his free hand to shade his eyes. It made him look distinctly lost. Grey figured their terp might finally have realized that things were starting to get serious. Operation No Return was under way, and they had many miles of hostile terrain to cover, plus an army of a hundred thousand to find and talk into surrendering. Who knew what might lie ahead, or what each man on the Squadron – Sebastian included – might be called upon to do?

Already, hundreds of miles of hostile territory separated the Squadron from the nearest friendly forces. Essentially, they had no back-up and no rescue force to call upon. If the shit hit the fan, they were on their own out there – and more so than any other elite unit in the entire Iraq theatre. And if and when it did all go noisy, Sebastian, their newbie terp, was just as vulnerable as the rest of them.

As the wagons gathered speed, Grey glanced further behind him: the base of M Squadron's arrowhead was some four hundred metres across, with quad outriders to either side. As the Squadron thundered forward it threw up a massive dust cloud half blocking out the sun. To his eyes it looked seriously imposing, and it gave the impression that M Squadron was a force to be reckoned with.

He turned to face the way ahead, his eyes down the barrel of his weapon. Behind him he had his body armour slung over his seat. No one in their right mind would choose to wear the stuff, unless they were forced to engage in a firefight from the wagons. Hours spent bouncing through rough terrain in body armour would likely break the wearer's back, not to mention roasting him alive under the beating sun. Hung over the seat as it was, it at least provided a modicum of protection against fire from the rear.

In any case, the terrain here was billiard-table flat, apart from where the odd wadi running into the Euphrates sliced through the earth. No one was about to leopard-crawl up to the Squadron and launch a surprise attack. If the men of M Squadron did spot trouble ahead, they could clamber into their body armour before the bullets started to fly.

As the wagons forged ahead Grey and Dude were scanning their arcs to the left, right and front. Raised up on a rear turret mount, the big .50-cal was able to put down all-round fire in 360-degree defence. Grey's GPMG could unleash rounds from the driver's side across to the wagon's right rear. Pushing ahead at Squadron strength as they were, the real threat was most likely to come from the front, where the tip of the arrowhead thrust into uncharted territory.

They headed past the landing zone where the Chinooks had repeatedly put down, and Grey was more than happy to leave that patch of churned-up terrain behind them. Gradually, the landscape changed. They moved into an area consisting of vast patches of hard-crusted sand dunes, like a frozen yellow ocean. These were best avoided. Interspersed with the sand dune seas were flat and featureless gravel plains that offered zero cover in which to hide, but perfect driving conditions.

For two hours the Squadron wove its way through such terrain. The wagons were making little more than 30 kph, which was about the maximum they could manage across such ground, heavily laden as they were.

As far as Grey could tell from his position near the apex of Six Troop's arrowhead, there were no vehicles tailing them, or watching from afar. Maybe they had succeeded in moving out without any alarm being raised. On the one hand it was a wonderful feeling to have got away and be on the move, and with no visible force after them. But still Grey felt a dark sense of foreboding lying over him like a heavy cloud.

Travelling by daylight in a V-shaped formation lent the Squadron more speed. Moving at night with dozens of vehicles strung out in linear fashion made for very slow going. Yet with each set of tyres throwing up its own dust cloud, every man was forced to wrap up in *shemagh* and dust goggles. Even so, the fine sand would still get into everything and play havoc with their kit. Moving at night might be slow and cold, but at least the moisture in the air would keep the dust down.

Every few kilometres the entire formation had to halt for a navigation check. They were moving on radio silence, and commands could only be passed verbally around the vehicles. Pretty quickly, it became clear that this system was unworkable. The SSM had to keep driving up to the wagon leading the spearhead so as to pass across another set of verbal instructions. It was all very well trying to keep below the Iraqis' radar, but it was slowing things down intolerably.

It was around mid-morning when the OC made the call that radio silence would be abandoned. The driving priority was to head north as fast as practically possible, to find the Iraqi 5th Corps. The Squadron was under serious time pressure to do so. The opening thrust by Coalition ground forces into southern Iraq was scheduled to start within five days. Ideally M Squadron would be opening negotiations for the 5th Corps surrender as the Coalition offensive began. Otherwise, the men of the 5th Corps would doubtless see reports of their fellow soldiers getting smashed by British and American forces, and their resistance to any form of surrender would likely harden.

Every effort had to be made to get to speak to the 5th Corps generals as quickly as possible, yet the Squadron could drive itself only so hard. It was the burning heat of midday by the time they had found the first usable TLZ. They'd pushed some twenty kilometres north of the Chinooks' landing zone, although they'd driven almost twice that distance to navigate a way through the rugged terrain.

Once they'd radioed through a visual description and coordinates of the TLZ, they got under way once more, with Grey's wagon in the lead. It was Grey's role to keep a check on maps and navigation, and Moth's to pick the path ahead. Both men were acutely aware that one wrong move could spell disaster for them and the wagons following their lead.

With the sun almost directly overhead they faced the most difficult of driving conditions. At any other time of day any dip or rise in the terrain would cast a shadow, which would help alert them to the dangers ahead. But the harsh light of midday rendered the landscape a flat and burning whiteness.

It was hard to spot smaller undulations when scanning ahead

for the bigger drops, and a few seconds' lapse of concentration meant that even a wadi might be missed. If Moth drove over the edge of one of those, he could bring the rest of the Squadron in on top of him, as all vehicles were following his lead. They were driving tactically, so keeping a good hundred metres apart, but even so the danger was very real. Loaded down with ammo and the vehicle-mounted machine-guns, the wagons were top-heavy. If they blundered over the edge of a wadi, any number of the Pinkies might roll, with devastating consequences for those riding in them.

They were twenty minutes out from the TLZ that they'd marked, when *wham*! – Moth drove over a patch of rock, and hit the drop on the far side. It was only a couple of feet to the hard-packed gravel below, and in the flat light the drop-off had been all but invisible. As the front wheels left the rock the wagon's nose slammed down, and its underside caught on the jagged surface. The Pinkie was only doing 20 kph, but still the noise was deafening. From the harsh tearing of steel on rock, it sounded as if the wagon's guts had been ripped out.

For an instant the vehicle stuck fast, as both sets of wheels spun and the engine whined and howled. With the acrid smell of burning rubber filling their nostrils, Moth eased off the power and slipped the gearbox smoothly into low ratio.

In high ratio, the Pinkie would drive at the standard speed of a Land Rover in four-wheel drive. Low ratio doubled the gearing, so halving the speed of the wagon but boosting the torque and power transferred to the four wheels. And in low ratio Moth found he was finally able to haul the wagon off the rocky snag, and onto the flat gravel on the far side.

The Pinkie pulled to a halt in a cloud of dust. The smell of burned rubber and diesel fumes was thick on the air. For a second Grey and Moth stared at each other. They carried few if any heavy spares. They just hadn't got the capacity to do so.

It was day one of the land move north, and already they had visions of a smashed sump pissing oil into the sands, and having to abandon their vehicle.

# CHAPTER TEN

Moth slipped out of the driver's seat and under the wagon. After a few seconds he emerged with an expression of massive relief on his features. He raised his fine blond eyebrows in amazement. 'Seems to be okay. No harm done. Bloody incredible.'

Thankfully, each of the Pinkies had a sump-guard – a sheet of solid steel that ran beneath the engine – and it was that which had taken the brunt of the impact.

Grey smiled. 'Short of rolling the thing, a Pinkie's pretty much bullet-proof.' He glanced at the Dude. 'Bet you couldn't do that in a Hummer, eh?'

'Gee, I dunno – Iraqi rock versus American Humvee. It'd sure be a clash of the Titans. My pop and me were once out in our Hummer . . .'

As the Dude launched into another of his life-on-the-ranch-back-home stories, Moth got the wagon under way.

'Bit of vital tradecraft, lads,' Grey announced, once they were pushing ahead at a decent speed. 'If you can't free the wagon in low ratio what d'you do?'

Moth and Dude shook their heads.

'You unload all the heavy gear, get twelve of your biggest blokes around her and you lift her free. Bet you couldn't do that with a Humvee, either.'

The Dude laughed, good-naturedly. 'Dude, you'd need a dozen Godzillas to lift a freakin' Humvee free!'

'And here's another for you,' Grey continued. He reached forward and pulled aside an old rag, to reveal a travel kettle that he'd bolted into the footwell of the wagon. He plugged the gizmo into the Pinkie's cigarette lighter, switched it on, and the kettle started to whine as it brought the water to the boil. He delved into his bag and pulled out some boil-in-the-bag meals.

'What d'you fancy? I got pasta, beef stew, or the Dude's favourite – Lancashire Hotpot.'

He threw the chosen meals into the kettle, then settled back to let them cook. The best time – sometimes the only time – to eat a hot meal when on a mission deep behind enemy lines was on the move. Any time parked up was best spent cleaning weapons, maintaining the wagon, doing map and navigation checks, standing sentry or catching some precious moments of sleep.

In such open terrain as this, you didn't need to be finger-on-the-trigger every second, for you could see far ahead. That left time free to spoon out the hot contents of a boil-in-the-bag meal and get it down you, but only if you had the means to heat it on the go – hence the travel kettle.

'An old trick I learned with the Regiment,' Grey continued, as he handed Dude his steaming bag of Lancashire Hotpot. For some inexplicable reason the young Yank operator still seemed partial to the stuff. 'Enjoy.'

Grey indicated the kettle, which he'd covered in dull gaffer tape to camouflage its shininess. 'A few of the other OABs have got one, but try and keep it quiet. Those that haven't will be jealous as fuck once they see us lot getting a good hot feed down us. They'll have to cook up when they reach the LUP, and more 'n' likely they won't have the energy or the time.'

Grey had his bag of hot pasta jammed between his knees, so he could feed himself with one hand and keep the other on his weapon. He kept his eyes front to scan the landscape, with the map stuffed to one side of him and folded to show the patch of territory they were moving through. It showed a series of gentle contours up ahead, which meant they were approaching more undulating terrain.

He pressed the Send switch on his radio and spoke into the mouthpiece taped to his webbing. 'Zero, this is *Zero Six Bravo*. Get the quads up front to scout the higher ground to the east of us.'

'Affirm,' came back the OC's reply – call-sign *Zero*.

A few seconds later Grey saw the quad force doing what they did best. Gunner shot past in the lead, with the unmistakable figure of Mucker on his shoulder. The quads roared up and over the rocky high ground to their right, leaving Moth clear to take the even ground that bypassed it. If there was trouble up ahead – be it enemy forces or impassable ground – the quad drivers should spot it from their vantage point, and help steer the rest of the Squadron past.

During the Iraqi winter months the sun set early, and as they crawled past the high ground Grey was conscious of the pressing need to find an LUP. To their east they'd left the well and oasis of Bu Jishah well behind them, and to their northeast lay the seasonal lake bed of Muwallah. A good seventy kilometres separated the two points, and between them was a featureless expanse of wilderness. It was marked simply on the map as 'Al Jazirah – desert'.

Somewhere within this vast empty quarter Grey had to find a place to hide an entire Special Forces squadron. As he scanned the terrain to either side of him, he felt the sweat from the fierce afternoon sun trickling down his back in rivulets. It was pooling at the base of his spine where his back met the dull plastic of the seat, and spreading out in a soaking-wet patch like he'd pissed himself.

With his skin permanently wet from the sweat, the dust thrown up by the wagons stuck to it, forming a greasy brown slick. He was drinking so heavily that he dreaded to think how much water they were all consuming. He made a mental note to check on their supplies, once he'd found an LUP for the night. He had a nasty feeling they'd under-provisioned and would need to get a resupply of water flown in or air-dropped to them.

Likewise, he reckoned they might well need more fuel. He figured they'd covered seventy-five kilometres as the crow flies, but approaching double that distance as they'd sought a path through the rugged terrain. If the conditions continued like this – and there was every reason to suspect they might worsen – it was unlikely they had the fuel to make it.

As he searched all around him for a usable LUP, Grey worried about the massive dust cloud they were throwing up. It rose behind them like a storm front, the finer particles back-lit by the sun as it sank towards the horizon. Grey figured it had to be visible from a good seven kilometres away, which made the urgency of finding a usable LUP all the more pressing.

He studied the map spread across his knees. They were using the 1:50,000 scale, which meant he had a folder with thirty individual map sheets in it, so as to cover the entire mission. Each sheet lasted for no more than 45 kilometres, after which he needed to shift to the next. He noticed a feature marked on the map, to the left front of their position. It looked as if it might be a shallow wadi – and was about all there was in terms of cover.

'Moth, head north-north-west,' Grey announced. 'After five klicks we should come upon a wadi running southwest-to -northeast.'

'Boss,' Moth confirmed, spinning the steering wheel counter-clockwise to bring them round onto the correct bearing.

Fifteen minutes' driving took them to the lip of the wadi. Moth edged along it for a good few minutes more before he found what he was looking for. At one point the steep banks of the riverbed dropped away almost to nothing, forming a natural crossing-point. Moth drove into the wadi, accompanied by Gunner and Mucker on their quads. The rest of the Squadron halted in the open, waiting for the word on the LUP.

The lone Pinkie and the quads nosed up the wadi floor for a short while, before rounding a bend that put the riverbed out of view of anyone using the crossing-point. It was as good a place as any to lie up for the night. They did an about-turn and headed back to rejoin the Squadron.

'Zero, this is *Zero Six Bravo*,' Grey spoke into his radio. 'LUP is usable. Now making for the stop short.'

'Affirm,' came the OC's reply.

Their wagon moved off heading east, the rest of the Squadron following. They pulled up some three kilometres distant from the wadi, in open terrain. Last light was all but upon them, and they'd wait here in their 'stop short' position until darkness had fallen. Only then would Grey lead the Squadron back into the LUP. That way, if anyone was watching they wouldn't see exactly where the Squadron had taken refuge for the night.

It was around 1830 hours when the Pinkies plus the quad force crawled into the wadi, and took up their positions. Once all the wagons were well spaced along the riverbed, they cut their engines. For the next fifteen minutes the men did absolutely nothing but sit there and wait, watch and listen. They scanned their arcs with the heavy weapons, alert to any threat that might be out there in the darkness. If anyone had seen them go into the LUP, it was now that they were most likely to show themselves.

At last there was a squelch of static on the radios and the OC announced: 'Stand down.'

The SSM followed on the heels of that radio message, doing a walk-about of the entire Squadron. His main task was to check on sentry duties and positions. Each Troop had set its own watch rotation, so that for the next twelve hours they had eyes scanning the desert 360 degrees all around them. The SSM also asked each Troop for fuel and water stats. The only way to get these was to remove the jerry-cans of diesel and water from the wagons, then check them by feel. Over time, it became second nature to know by the weight of a jerry-can how close it was to empty.

Due to their dwindling water supplies, the men decided to put themselves onto rations of three litres of water each per day. It was far too little for the kind of conditions they were encountering, for it was well over 100 degrees during the heat of the day.

Each time they removed the jerry-cans from a wagon, they had to unpack half its contents to do so. Lighter gear was piled on top of the jerries, for that was the only stable and secure way to pack a vehicle. On Grey's vehicle they'd taken the bulky and cumbersome camo-netting and bungeed it to the rear bumper, like a frilly skirt. Otherwise, you had to pile it on top of all the gear in the wagon's rear, which meant it was continually being unloaded and reloaded.

Grey had seen pictures of Vickers Jeeps – the open-topped wagons the SAS had used during the Second World War – with camo-nets similarly tied to the bumpers, and it was from there that he'd got the idea. As he slid the jerries back into the rear bin of his wagon he heard an envious snort from behind. He glanced round and it was Scruff. He was in the process of repacking the camo-netting into his own vehicle, having reloaded the jerry-cans.

'First a bloody travel kettle,' Scruff remarked. 'Now a bloody Pinkie with a cam-net for a skirt. Don't think we didn't clock you lot getting some hot scoff on the go. Wankers.'

Grey smiled. 'Imitation is the greatest form of flattery, mate. I got no problem if you want to copy us.'

'Yeah?' Scruff glanced around the darkened wadi. 'And where do you suggest I find a travel kettle in this God-forsaken shit-hole?'

Grey shrugged. 'Dunno, mate. I searched high and low for mine. Got it in the Bournemouth Caravanning Emporium. Cost me eighteen quid 'n' all. Tell you what – make me a sensible offer and it's yours.'

'Man, you are not selling our travel kettle,' came an unmistakable drawl from the wagon's rear. It was the Dude, who was bent over the .50-cal doing some weapons maintenance. After each day's move it was vital to clean the gun's mechanism and dust off the ammo, to prevent stoppages. 'Dude, that thing is freakin' priceless. Whatever Scruff offers you, I'll double it.'

As the men on the fighting wagons busied themselves with the evening's tasks, HQ Troop were preparing to send the second sitrep (situation report) of the day. Right after first and last light the OC was supposed to radio in a 'sched', one of two daily sitreps. If one of those scheduled sitreps was missed, then Special Forces Headquarters would know that M Squadron was facing some kind of trouble, and was possibly on the run.

After a move like today's, the sitrep would be short and sweet. It would give the Squadron's coordinates, and report that the mission was progressing as planned. Fuel, ammo and water stats would be included only if there was a pressing need for a resupply. The Iraqi goat-herder of that morning wouldn't even merit a mention, because for now at least there was zero evidence that they'd been compromised.

The OC would be hoping for some kind of update on the Iraqi 5th Corps – news of their position, and perhaps that lines of communication had been opened. It would make perfect sense for MI6, or another of Britain's intelligence agencies, to have made electronic contact with the Corps's commanders, who would be sure to possess cell phones. But so far nothing of that nature seemed to be happening, and the Squadron was heading in on the sketchy intel that it had first been given.

As he readied himself to stand his first sentry duty of the night, Grey wandered past Scruff's wagon. He could tell that the bloke was preparing for his own stint on stag. The night was still as death, the atmosphere windless and brittle with the cold. They were the kind of conditions in which the faintest noise would travel for miles on the silent air.

Grey crouched down beside Scruff. 'Mate, I got this feeling—' he whispered.

'I got it too,' Scruff cut in. 'Like we're being watched.'

'Yeah, watched or followed.'

'I can't figure out why,' Scruff added, 'but I got it.'

'Maybe the goat-herder?'

Scruff shrugged. 'Maybe.'

'You seen anything? Anything at all?'

'Nothing, mate. Not even some Iraqi bloke crouched behind a sand dune taking a dump.'

Grey eyed him for a second. 'Weird, isn't it? We're throwing up a dust cloud like an atom bomb's just gone off, yet where the hell are the Iraqis?'

'Dunno, mate. But all the same I got the feeling.'

The two men parted company without another word being said.

After two hours staring into the empty abyss Grey felt totally finished. He got relieved, crawled back to his doss-bag, wriggled inside it without removing a single item of clothing, and was instantly comatose.

A few short hours' kip later he dragged himself awake to do stand-to. Long years of soldiering had taught the British military that first and last light were the times at which you were most likely to face an attack. At first light there was enough illumination to launch an assault, but your adversary was likely to still be asleep, or at least fog-bound with recent sleep, and at last light they'd be looking forward to a good feed and bed.

Every day at these times the Squadron would do stand-to, just as it was doing now. Every man was in position with his weapon locked and loaded, scanning the terrain from which an attack might come. Stand-to was supposed to be a moment of utter alertness and silence. The only trouble was, the men of the HQ Troop weren't required to do stand-to.

The desert at dawn was so quiet that the noise of Sebastian and one or two of the others dismantling their camp beds was deafening. They were clunky as fuck, which was one of the reasons that the rest of the guys only ever used a length of roll-matting to sleep on.

Grey glanced across at Moth and Dude, and rolled his eyes. 'Where I come from one does not sleep on the floor,' he whispered, in a mock-Sebastianesque accent. 'Jolly good show, though, these camp beds.'

The two younger blokes tried to stifle their sniggers. Though Grey liked Sebastian, there were times when the man's inexperience really did grate. Plus the fact that the blokes on the HQ Troop had the sheer luxury of camp beds was starting to cause real aggravation. After a few days kipping on the hard, stony ground, such things could acquire a significance out of all proportion. Such was the intensity of living in close proximity to one another 24/7, under constant threat of attack, and with exhaustion levels rising.

The Squadron moved off just after first light. Very quickly they entered the vast wastes of the Ninawa Desert, where a series of massive dry wadis slashed through what seemed to be a never-ending plateau. The desert was utterly featureless and parched, and it stretched for a good three hundred kilometres north. It should take the Squadron to within a day's drive of the 5th Corps's position.

None of the men on Grey's wagon had ever laid eyes on such godforsaken terrain. Here and there were massive sculpted seasonal lake beds that the vehicles had to skirt round, but they seemed to be baked dry and devoid of even the barest hint of water or of life. The advantage was that there were unlikely to be any Iraqis around to notice the Squadron's passing. Not even the nomadic Iraqi Bedou people – who lived in tented camps and migrated across the desert – would find it easy to live here. But the biggest downside was the total lack of cover.

The seasonal lake beds offered perilous terrain in which to go to ground, for some consisted of a hard-baked crust beneath which lurked treacherous mud and quicksand. The occasional wadi they came across was a V-shaped slash cut deep into the earth, making entry a risky undertaking when navigating the steep, boulder-strewn sides. The only real option if they were attacked here was to stand and fight, or to try to outrun the enemy over open ground.

The name of this desert – 'Ninawa' – is an Arabized version of the original name for the area, the biblical 'Nineveh'. Grey had studied its history before deployment, and was well aware how densely populated it once had been. Nineveh is mentioned in the Old Testament as being a great commercial trade centre, and a junction between the Mediterranean and Indian Oceans, linking East and West some four millennia ago. The Old Testament says that God wanted to make of 'Proud Nineveh . . . a desolation, parched like the wilderness', to punish its people for worshipping earthly gods. As far as Grey could tell, God had pretty much succeeded in getting what he wanted, for Proud Nineveh had been rendered an empty wasteland.

With the sun creeping towards the vertical on day two of their drive north, M Squadron received an unexpected message from Headquarters via the signals wagon's skywave-type radio antennae – a length of wire cable slung across the vehicle's rear – which allowed it to receive secure data messages while on the move. The data burst from Headquarters alerted the OC to the urgent need to make voice communications.

The HQ Troop pulled up in a patch of open terrain, the wagons of Four, Five and Six Troop moving in to surround them with a ring of steel. Being static under the blinding sun was unbearable. At least when on the move the air passing through the open wagons offered a modicum of relief. Moving air dried the skin, and evaporating sweat served to cool an individual down a little. Whatever the message might be, Grey figured they wanted it over and done with quickly and to get on the move again.

The comms with Headquarters done, the Squadron 2iC and the SSM moved around the vehicles spreading the word. With sixty men in the Squadron it was often too difficult to organize a Chinese parliament, and now was neither the time nor the place to do so. Stuck in the open with zero cover, the priority had to be to get the message spread, appropriate action taken, and the Squadron moving again.

Captain Andy Smith, the SAS 2iC of the Squadron, approached Grey's wagon. 'We've just had warning from Headquarters,' he announced. 'There's a force of Iraqi Fedayeen moving out from Bayji in our general direction. They're vehicle-mounted, and they have further vehicles in support. That's about as much as Head-quarters was able to tell us.'

Grey glanced at the map in his lap. Bayji was one hundred kilometres due east of the Squadron's present position. 'Any sense of their intentions?' he asked.

'Not from Headquarters, no. But they're on a rough bearing to intercept the Squadron, so go figure.'

'How many?'

'Fifty, minimum. But likely a whole lot more with the vehicles in support.'

Grey let out a long, low whistle. 'That's serious shit. They'll not be coming just to have a butchers. If they're Fedayeen, they'll be heading out to have a good poke at us.'

The 2iC nodded. 'Yeah. Looks like it. That's if they find us.'

Grey gestured at the map. 'Rather than waiting for the Boys from Bayji to hit us, why don't we make the first move? If we can work out the routes they'll likely take, we can put a couple of forces in overwatch and ambush 'em.'

'Which way d'you think they'll come?' the 2iC asked.

Grey ran his eyes over the ground due east of their position. The trouble was, it was more or less an open book. By the time the Boys from Bayji had reached the Ninawa Desert, they could take their pick in terms of routes to come in and hit the British force.

Grey glanced at the 2iC. 'Do we know how far they've got? Are they into the Ninawa Desert yet?'

'We know as much as Headquarters told us, no more.'

'If they've hit the desert there's no way of knowing which way they'll come.'

The 2iC shrugged. 'In that case, we can't guarantee to get the jump on them.'

There was a moment's heavy silence, then the 2iC indicated he was moving on to the next wagon.

If the Fedayeen were heading out to hit the Squadron, Grey could well imagine the sequence of events that had led them onto their line of march. Two days back a young Iraqi goat-herder had fled to his village with news of a strange and unknown danger lurking in a wadi. Villagers had driven out to investigate. They'd come across the tracks of thirty vehicles, and realized they could only come from a sizeable military force. In turn they had reported it to the local Fedayeen, who had taken it from there.

Grey turned to Moth. 'Batten down the hatches, mate, the Boys from Bayji are coming.'

'Shit happens,' Moth muttered.

'Yeah, but this is far from being everyday kind of shit.'

Grey glanced around at their utterly exposed and defenceless position, the wagons gathered in a circle and lacking even the slightest suggestion of any cover.

'You know what this reminds me of?' he remarked. 'It's like the Wild West, and we're the wagon train waiting for the Indians to come and whack us.'

# CHAPTER ELEVEN

The thing that worried Grey most was a distant ridge of high ground. About five hundred yards to the east a line of low hills dominated the skyline. If the Boys from Bayji got in amongst those, they could rain down fire onto the Squadron, and keep doing so for as long as it took the British vehicles to try to effect an escape.

There was little they could do to fight back, for the enemy would have perfect cover as well as the high ground. Grey just hoped the Fedayeen were still a good distance away, and that the Squadron would be on the move again soon. In the meantime, he did what he could to prepare for war. He got out three boxes of 200-round link ammo for the GPMG and clipped the belts together. That way, he was good to rock and roll for 600 rounds without having to make a belt change.

He got Dude to do the same on the .50-cal, and Moth to check that all was good to go with his JTAC kit, in case they needed to call in any air strikes. That done, there was bugger all else they could do right there and then to ready themselves for the Fedayeen.

The Dude had six boxes of ammo for the .50-cal, some 600 rounds in all. The ammo box sat on a cradle beside the weapon's breech, and when the first was exhausted he'd have to throw the empty case off and lug up another. Grey had more ammo – seven boxes of 200 rounds each – for the GPMG, but it had a faster rate of fire. You could easily squirt off 500 rounds in five minutes, so there was only really enough for three sustained firefights.

A third of the wagons were equipped with a grenade launcher, and they'd be carrying six boxes of 100 rounds each. But the volume of those 20mm grenade rounds made for a massive bulk of kit to carry in the vehicle's rear.

The wait under the burning sun dragged on and on. Grey's head felt like it was getting roasted in a giant oven. The golden sand all around them threw back the sun's rays so that they were being blasted from all sides. Grey only wore his gloves in the cold of the desert night, and his bare hands were wet and sticky where they grasped the hot grip of the GPMG.

How the hell did Headquarters know about this Fedayeen hunter force? he wondered. Did they have humint there – a source of human intelligence on the ground in Bayji – feeding back information? And if so, who might that source be? After all, Bayji lay at the heart of the Sunni Triangle, where Saddam had his hardcore followers. If they did have a man on the ground in Bayji, why didn't MI6 – or whoever was operating the humint – have a similar source in amongst the Iraqi 5th Corps, someone who could tell them exactly where they were positioned?

There was little connection in Grey's mind between the 5th Corps and the Fedayeen. In their briefings they'd been told that the Fedayeen and Iraqi regular forces were totally separate units, and they rarely worked in conjunction with one another. If the

Boys from Bayji did put in an appearance, there would be no taking a mass surrender from that lot, that was for sure.

Finally, Reggie issued a set of orders via the radios. The Squadron was to push northwards until it found a decent LUP. They'd hole up there for the remainder of the day and the coming night, and they'd double sentry duty. Plus they'd try to make the remainder of their move northwards under cover of darkness. That way they had a far greater chance of evading the Fedayeen, and making it to their mission objective – the rendezvous with the 5th Corps – undetected.

Grey felt a massive sense of relief as they got under way. It was great to be moving again. He reflected on the orders, which made perfect sense. If only they could find a decent LUP, they could lie low in a good defensive position. If the Fedayeen did track them to it, they'd be far better placed to repulse an attack. They'd be fighting at a place – and maybe even a time – of their own choosing.

In the meantime they were buying themselves some time, which should give Headquarters a chance to gather more intel on that Fedayeen force, and to pass it to the Squadron. Maybe the Fedayeen hadn't been sent out to hunt down M Squadron, after all. Maybe it was just a coincidence that they were passing through the same patch of barren wilderness as the elite British force.

Maybe.

The one thing that troubled Grey about the OC's orders was the thought of doubling sentry. By now many of the blokes – those on Grey and Scruff's wagons included – had been on the go for six nights in a row. When they weren't doing the airborne infils via Jordan into Iraq, they'd been driving and scouring the terrain for the enemy, or digging out trapped vehicles, or standing sentry, or trying to get some kip next to the wagons. In short, they were beyond bloody knackered.

It was a couple of hours before they found a wadi that was accessible enough for them to get the wagons and quads below ground-level and out of sight. By now they'd covered several hundred kilometres by air and land deep inside Iraq, and the constant strain of always being on the alert had taken its toll. It is when men are deprived of sleep and under relentless pressure that mistakes start being made. Here in the Ninawa Desert, and with a Fedayeen hunter force more than likely on their tail, they couldn't afford even the slightest lapse.

Mercifully, that night's sentry duty proved uneventful, or so it seemed. As far as the men of M Squadron could tell, there was no sign of any Fedayeen force – or of any human presence at all. But the following morning they realized that something vital might well have been missed during the depths of the night.

Grey was woken by the sound of a tense altercation. One of the Troop sergeant majors was bawling out Scruff. Apparently, at some stage during the night Six Troop's watch had fallen over, and it was Scruff's team that was responsible. In the early hours a sentry had dropped off to sleep. He'd failed to wake the next guy until 0500 hours, fully an hour after he was supposed to.

No one knew how long for sure, but for an hour at least one segment of the terrain surrounding M Squadron's LUP had been left unwatched. Six Troop's arc of fire – which stretched from the southeast to the southwest – had been left unguarded, and it was from the southeast that the Fedayeen force was most likely to make an appearance.

As soon as Scruff grasped that it was his lot that had messed up, he took full responsibility. There were four in his team, himself included, so one of them had to be responsible – but typically Scruff took it all on his own shoulders. Grey felt total sympathy for the bloke. It was the worst of things, having to stare into the formless desert night for hours on end when you were totally chinstrapped. Grey had found himself rubber-necking – falling asleep for an instant, feeling his head drop to his chest, which woke him with a start – during the night's watch. And each time you were shaken awake for your next stag, or for stand-to, it felt as if you'd only just crawled into your doss-bag.

Even so, sentry duty was day-one lesson-one kind of stuff. The fact that Scruff's watch had fallen over only reinforced the pressing need for sleep. If the Squadron was failing to get even their sentry duties right, it *proved* how utterly knackered they were. What chance did they have of evading the enemy if they couldn't even get the stags working properly?

Worst of all, it was possible that the Fedayeen hunter force had slipped past them in the night, when the sentry had been sleeping.

The OC issued a set of orders. They were to remain in the wadi all that day, so the men could get some extra kip. They were to prepare to move off at last light, under cover of darkness and driving on NVG. By moving at night they would vastly decrease the Squadron's visibility, making them less traceable by the Fedayeen force, wherever they might be.

With sentries placed in hidden positions around the rim of the wadi, the men of the Squadron tried to find some shade in which to sleep. Anything that offered a modicum of shelter from the sun was in high demand: the steep walls of the wadi, a rocky overhang, a boulder that was narrower at its base, or the lea of a vehicle.

Before Grey could get some kip, the OC tasked him with plotting the route north that the Squadron would take that night. He got his head together with Scruff and Raggy – two of the old and the bold – and together they studied the maps and the satellite photos. For the next eighty kilometres they should be able to dodge around a series of ever deepening wadis, making reasonable progress, but the terrain would work against them the further north they went.

To the far north of the Ninawa Desert lay the massif of the Jabal Sinjar, the Eagle Mountain. When it rained up there, a dry wadi here on the plain could change within seconds into a raging, boulder-strewn torrent. Flash floods from the Jabal Sinjar had carved out deep gouges in the plateau, and the Squadron was going to have its work cut out trying to avoid those, especially if driving at night.

As they left the northern end of the desert they'd hit the worst terrain of all, for the empty wilderness would be replaced by tracks, roads and populated farmland. Grey figured they could risk driving across a B-road on the approach to the Iraqi town of Tal Afar, to get them onto a minor track heading northeast for a good hundred kilometres, and maybe all the way to the approximate location of the Iraqi 5th Corps.

That was easily two days' drive and more likely three, especially if they had to move at night. Grey plotted a route using the mapping and GPS coordinates, and referencing the stars. Wherever possible he chose a path that would avoid human habitation, but there were one or two villages at the very north of their route that they'd just have to drive right through. There was no way around them.

The route-mapping done, Grey bedded down with the rest of his team. It was late afternoon when he woke to see a flock of birds alighting upon a rock face further up the wadi. He figured here might be a chance to address the pressing issue of water. In the burning heat they needed to drink far more than they were rationing themselves to, and the cumulative effects of dehydration only exacerbated the men's crushing fatigue.

He grabbed Scruff, leaving his team to check over the vehicle and weapons before tonight's drive. They headed up the narrow riverbed on foot. At their approach the birds flew off, revealing where they had settled. The two men climbed the rock face, and in the shadow of an overhang they discovered a pool of water.

The water was brackish and full of bird droppings, but it was still potable. They dropped the end of their filter tube into it, and pumped up clear, fresh water. They extracted as much as they could carry, then returned to brief the rest of the Squadron. As word went round, those who were able sent out teams to replenish their water supplies.

There was no washing or shaving allowed for the entire duration of the mission. Both were major no-noes when on behind-enemy-lines operations, because the smell of cleanliness was a dead giveaway. There was little point going sneaky-beaky far behind enemy lines if the scent of soap or deodorant gave you away to the local stray dogs. Anywhere in Iraq with human habitation there were strays, and the Squadron would soon be heading into populated territory. The more you smelled like a freshly bathed human, the more alien your scent would be to the dogs, and the more likely they were to raise the alarm. The aim of every soldier was to blend in with his environment, and to take on the smell and look of a wild animal.

Also, the Iraqi military would have tracker dogs, ones trained to pick up the human scent, and those were perhaps the single most difficult thing for an elite force to evade.

After that evening's stand-to the OC called an O-group (orders group). Headquarters had radioed through a less than encouraging update on the Fedayeen force. Somehow, they'd lost track of them. The Fedayeen fighters, plus their support vehicles, had disappeared off the face of the earth. It was ominous and unsettling.

Despite this, the OC made the call to move out. There was still no visible sign of the enemy, and the Squadron had a mission to achieve – the much anticipated surrender of the Iraqi 5th Corps.

As M Squadron prepared to head into the darkened desert, Moth was rummaging about in the wagon trying to locate a vital piece of JTAC equipment, one that enabled him to fix an enemy position and guide a warplane in to better hit the target. Grey was leading the Squadron out of the wadi, and Moth was driving, so no one was going anywhere until they were ready. The longer they waited the darker it was going to get, and the more suited to driving on night vision goggles, so Grey was hardly fretting.

Finally Moth got his JTAC kit sorted, and their vehicle crawled out of the wadi. The long line of vehicles formed up in the open desert, with Six Troop taking the lead and Grey's wagon making the head of the snake. Their diesel motor purred softly as they waited for all the vehicles to get into position behind them. It was exceptionally still and clear, with almost too much light for covert night driving.

Grey glanced at Moth. 'You good?'

Moth nodded an affirmative. 'I'm good.'

Grey grinned. 'Nice one, 'cause tonight's drive is going to fucking kill us.'

'Like how, boss?' Moth queried. 'The Fedayeen?'

'Not that. Or at least, not chiefly that. Mate, we may have got a few good hours' kip, but we need to take it easy, 'cause we're fucked.'

Moth nodded. 'Don't I fucking know it.'

Grey paused to check the night sky above him, picking out the familiar constellation of the North Star. He traced vertically downwards from that, finding the point on the horizon that was due north. Having located that, he moved his gaze east, coming to rest on the unmistakable form of Orion, also known as 'the Hunter'. No matter where you were in the world, Orion would rise on the horizon due east, and set due west. For night drives such as this one, Orion was the key navigational marker.

'Head northeast on a bearing of 060 degrees,' he told Moth. 'For the first thirty kilometres keep two fingers to the left of Orion – there.'

Orion consists of a row of three very bright stars, known as Orion's Belt, with constellations dotted all around it that represent the hunter's body and his sword. By holding his hand in front of his face and steering at a point two fingers' width to the left of that, Moth would keep the Squadron on a rough northeast bearing. Grey's priority was to keep Moth's eyes-front and scrutinizing the terrain. If he was forever glancing down at his compass or GPS, he might miss a rocky outcrop or a ravine. With a star as his reference point, Moth would always have his gaze forward of the vehicle. The terrain here was far worse than anything they'd experienced during their Kenya training. There it had all been flat sand and savanna. Here, it was a maze of bare rock slashed through with deep ravines.

Once Grey had given Moth his navigational instructions, it was up to the younger man to feel his way ahead and seek out the best route. But this was a team effort, and it was the Dude who had the best all-round view from his position high on the rear. As they moved off he kept a stream of helpful advice coming.

'You're clear to the left, Moth, mate. Clear directly ahead for a good hundred yards or so.'

For forty minutes Moth wove the vehicle through the darkened landscape, the entire Squadron following behind and showing not the faintest pinprick of light. At one stage they ended up doing a complete circle. Grey and Moth had chosen a path that had offered them no route through, and they came back to exactly where they had started.

As Grey studied the map and tried to work out an alternative route, a stream of voices came up on the radios. 'Where the fuck are we going . . . ?' 'Looping the bloody loop . . .' 'What are we, the Red Arrows . . . ?' 'Welcome to Sergeant Grey's Ninawa Desert Tours . . .'

Grey smiled to himself. He recognized most of the voices giving it some on the radio, but he didn't rise to the bait. In a way it was good to see that the rest of the blokes in the Squadron were still sparking, in spite of the crushing burden of fatigue.

The temperature dropped rapidly, and soon it was hovering around five degrees. With the wind-chill factor on the open vehicles, Grey figured it had to be well below freezing. They'd been kipping at night wrapped in doss-sacks and Gore-Tex bivi-bags, for the extra warmth. But while on the move they needed their bodies free – to drive, to keep watch, to navigate and potentially to fight. Moth's hands gripped the steering wheel encased in leather gloves for the added warmth. But those manning the machine-guns like Grey and Dude could wear only the thin air-crewman's gloves, for they needed the added dexterity.

Between 1 and 5 degrees was the temperature bracket in which snow would fall, and it struck Grey that if it rained right now over northern Iraq it would fall here in the Ninawa Desert as snow. It was bizarre. A few hours ago he'd felt as if his head was being boiled in a cauldron. Now, it was as if he was suffering from severe brain freeze.

Grey reached forward and flicked on the wagon's heater. He had the fan set to zero, so it made almost no noise, but still the hot air should waft into the footwell and seep up around him and Moth. As for the Dude, heaven only knew how the poor bastard wasn't freezing to death, perched up there on the .50-cal turret.

Grey couldn't afford for his mind to seize up. He had a thousand and one things to think about, leading the Squadron on a night drive such as this. As well as all the obvious navigational issues, he had to try to map out in his head a series of escape routes, should they get hit from out of the darkness by the enemy. He checked his map again, and issued a fresh set of navigational instructions. A dry ravine had pushed the convoy too far eastwards, and he needed Moth to compensate. He told him to steer a route due north whenever he could, using the North Star as his celestial fix.

After two hours of leading the Squadron Grey was feeling totally bollocksed. As for Moth, he was hanging out of his hoop. They stopped to do a map change, Grey using the tiny pen-light on his torch to scrutinize the maps in his folder, and to select the right sheet for the terrain they were moving into.

A wagon pulled up beside them. 'How're you blokes doing?' a voice whispered. It was Scruff. 'We're frozen solid.'

'Still alive,' Grey whispered back. 'Mate, we've had the heater on full blast the whole time.'

'Shit. Didn't think of that one.' Scruff leaned forward and flicked the switch to activate his wagon's heater. 'We're freezing our bloody nuts off.'

They pushed onwards, Grey tensing himself for the attack he felt certain was coming. If the Fedayeen had slipped past them when the previous night's sentry had fallen over, they could have set an ambush anywhere up ahead. The jumbled, chaotic terrain certainly offered them the perfect opportunity to do so. The Squadron was making around 15 kph, and at such a slow crawl it would make the perfect target to any watching gunmen.

It's standard operating procedure if hit in an ambush to keep driving. If you attempt to turn round or to stop you only make yourself a sitting target. It's far better to keep moving and fight your way through. If that Fedayeen force did hit them, Grey would have to rely on speed and the cover of darkness, plus the firepower of the Squadron, to smash their way past.

But being at the head of the snake, Grey's wagon would be the first onto the enemy guns.

# CHAPTER TWELVE

Several hours into that night drive, Moth reduced their speed to a dead slow crawl. If the lead Pinkie actually stopped, the rest would come to a halt behind it, and it generally took an age to get the convoy moving again. It was better to keep moving than to stop completely, which was why Moth had them inching ahead at no more than walking pace.

Regardless of breaking light discipline, Grey needed to use the GPS to get an exact fix on where they were, so as to take them through a series of ravines that slashed like knife cuts across their intended path. Right now the danger of going over one of those and rolling the wagon far outweighed the risk of the light thrown off by the GPS compromising them.

Even if they survived going over the edge of an unseen wadi, most were six feet or more in height and more or less vertical-sided, so getting out would present a real problem. If there was no natural exit point, the only way would be to dig a slope by hand and drive the wagon out, and that could take all night. With the men dismounted and the wagons trapped, it would present an ideal moment for the Fedayeen force to hit them.

As the convoy crept ahead, Scruff's vehicle pulled up alongside them to provide some extra cover. Grey was punching the buttons on his GPS, and he could hear Scruff cursing under his breath.

'Still freezing our bloody nuts off,' he hissed. 'Bloody heater isn't working. The last thing we thought of bloody checking before deploying.'

Grey smiled grimly to himself. While his feet and legs were reasonably toasty, his face felt frozen to the touch, his lips cracked and sore. But at least having the heater working meant he wasn't in danger of getting his nuts frozen off.

By the approach of first light the men in the lead vehicle had horribly red and bloodshot eyes – the result of staring into the artificially boosted luminosity of night vision for hours on end. Trying to find a way through an increasingly pockmarked and ravine-strewn terrain would be nightmarish in broad daylight, yet they'd been doing just that with only the fluorescent green glow of NVG to guide them.

Grey figured the patrol had made sixty kilometres max. By now they were entering the badlands of the far north of the desert, where the plateau broke up into a confusion of all but impassable terrain. It made for horrendous going, and for long stretches Moth had been managing little more than 10 kph. As the coming dawn lit the horizon to the east of them, Moth led the Squadron into a narrow ravine. It was one of the few patches of cover he could manoeuvre the wagons into. With the vehicles snaking out along the dry riverbed, they could just about keep the whole Squadron hidden from view. They pulled up in their concealed position and cut the engines.

Grey turned to Moth. 'How you doing, mate?'

Moth fixed him with a stare from eyes rimmed with painful

red. 'Boss, I'm wiped. I need several hours' solid kip or I'll be useless for tonight.'

'Get your head down, mate,' Grey told him. 'We'll worry about vehicle checks and the rest later. Grab some kip before it's too hot to do so.'

For those like Grey's team who had been first into theatre, they were starting their seventh day in Iraq. It was one hell of a length of time to have spent behind enemy lines without being hit.

During the long night's drive Grey had kept thinking about the B2Z patrol. The fate that had befallen that SAS mission had cast a long shadow over Special Forces soldiering – and especially for a band of warriors pursing a mission like the present one. All bar one of the B2Z team had been captured or killed, and they had been an eight-man patrol moving on foot. By anyone's reckoning, M Squadron was far more visible and potentially just as vulnerable.

Grey checked his map. He figured they were 120 kilometres short of the Iraqi 5th Corps's position – wherever they might be exactly. They'd covered some six hundred kilometres of the infil, the first 250 having been made via C130 and Chinook, and the last 350 overland. He checked the Pinkie's milometer: those 350 kilometres amounted to some 600 kilometres of driving.

It was some achievement to have made it thus far and not to have seen a single enemy or been in a single contact. Maybe they were going to make their rendezvous with the Iraqi 5th Corps after all. But even if they did, it was anyone's guess as to how they were going to be received once they got there.

As the Squadron prepared for another day's rest and standing sentry, not a man amongst them had the faintest clue as to what had been happening in the wider scheme of the war. They knew that the air war would be under way by now, for that was gearing up by the time they flew into Iraq on the C130 Hercules. But they were several hundred kilometres north of where any air strikes might be going in, and they'd neither seen nor heard any sign of warplanes above them. If they hadn't known differently, the men of the Squadron could have been forgiven for forgetting there was a war on at all.

Yet hundreds of kilometres to the south of their present position the air war had actually begun in earnest. As M Squadron's vehicles had been creeping through the Ninawa Desert, US warplanes had launched a series of air assaults into southern Iraq, the most recent of which had reached as far north as the Iraqi capital, Baghdad.

The first air missions were flown by a top-secret US unit called Task Force Tiger (or TF20 for short). It was made up of state-of-the-art F15E Strike Eagle fighter jets, and each aviator was hand-picked – for TF20 was specially formulated to support those first into Iraq on Special Forces operations. In early March 2003, at the same time as M Squadron was heading for Iraq, TF Tiger had deployed to an air base in Qatar. Their first major combat missions were flown over the Western Desert of Iraq, providing air cover to US Special Forces as they took airfields and other strategically important targets.

TF Tiger's next mission had been far more challenging and high-profile. The elite aviators were tasked to hit a fleet of Iraqi warships in the Tigris and Euphrates river delta, to the far south of Iraq. The chief targets were two missile cruisers with a flotilla of smaller boats providing a defensive shield.

The F15Es headed in on a bearing that took them right up

against the Iranian border, while avoiding the SAM (surface-to-air missile) batteries at Basra. The warplanes dived down and dropped 500-pound bombs with delayed-action fuses. They hit the lead missile cruiser, the bombs penetrating the deck and blasting the sides of the warship asunder, after which it capsized and sank. The other vessel took four hits before it finally went down, leaving both warships half submerged in the shallow waters at the northern end of the Gulf.

The results of those air missions were highly visible to the Iraqis, especially as Iraqi TV was pumping out such images to ramp up their propaganda campaign. The Iraqi people were being urged to make the ultimate sacrifice, so as to defend 'the mother country and to protect the father of the nation', the great leader Saddam Hussein. Saddam was urging his armed forces and the wider Iraqi public to drive the 'infidel invaders' out of Iraq, and assuring them that victory would be theirs.

With Iraqi military personnel starting to take hits from Coalition air strikes, Saddam's message would be hitting home. Doubtless, such images and propaganda were finding their way to the Iraqi 5th Corps via their radio sets and TV screens, wherever they might be positioned. In recent days the propaganda war had reached fever pitch, as warplanes from TF Tiger had flown their first missions against Baghdad itself. Those missions were taking place well beyond M Squadron's visual range. This far north the damage they were wreaking on the Iraqi military remained unseen. The Ninawa Ddesert was an oasis of empty silence, and an eerie kind of peace reigned.

But to the Iraqi people and military alike, such sorties were highly visible, and it was plain to see how their forces were getting smashed from the air. Doubtless, those images would act as both a powerful warning and a provocation to the force charged with defending the north of the country – the Iraqi Army's 5th Corps.

The sun was peeping over the edge of the sharp ravine in which they'd made their LUP by the time Grey's team had managed to get their heads down. They fell into an exhausted sleep, oblivious to the bloody combat being waged to the south of the country by fearsome warplanes like the F15 Strike Eagles, and to the impact such air strikes might have on their own mission.

At 1300 Grey was woken to take his stand on sentry. He made his way to the top of the ravine, where he found Scruff, whose watch he was relieving. Grey settled next to him, belly down on the hard rim of the ravine.

'What's the score?'

Scruff lowered his binoculars and handed them to Grey. 'Now and then there's a vehicle way to the east of us. Take a butchers. Probably moving through the desert towards the 252.'

The 252 was a B-road that ran from the fringes of the Ninawa desert northeast towards Salah. The Squadron was approaching more populated territory, and it could well be civvie traffic making for that road. But even so this was the first human presence bar the lone goat-herder they'd seen in a week spent crossing Iraq.

Grey focused the binos. 'Anything suspicious?'

'Nope. White civvie-looking wagons. No weapons visible. They don't seem to be stopping, either.'

'Probably traffic heading for the 252.'

'Probably. But they're sticking to the very limit of our visual range. Could be dickers, mate, so keep a good eye.'

'Dickers' was a phrase first used by British soldiers in Northern Ireland. It referred to gunmen masquerading as civvies and driving civilian-looking vehicles in an effort to sneak up on a British patrol or position. The dickers would recce the potential target and help call in an attack force, while all the while hiding behind a supposed civilian identity.

Those like Grey who'd operated in Northern Ireland had learned to treat every civilian as a potential enemy. Even if they were out on the piss in Belfast, it was still an operational theatre, and one of the toughest and most challenging in the world. You could never afford to let your guard down, and you never knew for sure when and in what form the enemy might hit you. And instinctively, Grey sensed there was something very similar about operating here in Iraq.

'Any sense they're connected to that Fedayeen force?' Grey asked.

Scruff shrugged. 'Could be, mate. They could be Fedayeen scouts, searching for us. But right now there's just no way of knowing.'

Scruff wriggled backwards from his position, but as he went to leave he paused. 'You still got that feeling?' he asked Grey.

'Like we're being hunted? I have. Worse than ever, mate.'

'That makes the two of us.'

Scruff turned and disappeared down the side of the wadi, urging Grey to keep a very close eye on those mystery vehicles.

The sentry point atop the ravine had a fine view, providing an arc of fire from the north round to the southeast. It struck Grey as an ideal vantage point from which to unleash a Milan anti-armour missile on any hostile vehicle that might put in an appearance – that was, if they had brought any Milans with them.

It was a big bone of contention that their Milans had been left behind, for that was the one weapon with which they would have stood a decent chance of taking out an Iraqi main battle tank. A decision had been made well above Grey's pay grade that no Milans were needed on this mission, and they had been left behind largely to save on weight.

Normally, you'd carry one Milan per Troop, so one for each sentry position. A SACLOS (semi-automatic command to line-of-sight) missile, packing a 7.1 kg wire-guided warhead that can defeat most armour, the Milan is the most powerful and accurate piece of kit that can be operated by a light vehicle or foot patrol. But the Squadron hadn't got any, so if Grey spotted a Lion of Babylon tanks chugging over the horizon they'd have no choice but to high-tail it out of there.

After spending a couple of hours scanning the terrain to the east, Grey, like Scruff, had seen only a handful of white SUV-type wagons buzzing back and forth in the far distance. He didn't know what to make of them. They probably *were* just some civvie traffic moving east towards the 252, en route to Salah. But then again, they might not be.

His sentry done, Grey returned to his wagon. It was mid-morning, and the heat lay across the wadi like a thick and suffocating blanket. Moth and Dude had found it impossible to sleep and were doing some maintenance on the vehicle-mounted weapons. Grey briefed them on what he'd seen. The guys grabbed some binoculars so they could take a look themselves.

'So what d'you reckon?' Grey asked Moth, after he'd been staring into the distance for several seconds.

'I dunno, boss. They're Toyota Land Cruiser type vehicles, and they're a long way from us. None seem to be coming any closer, either.'

'I can't see any with any weapons,' Dude remarked, from his

elevated position. 'Could just be local Iraqi farmers' vehicles, y'know.'

'Could be,' Grey confirmed. 'But it could just as easily be scouts from that Fedayeen force. Think about it. They're keeping their distance and not showing any weapons, so we can't engage them. That way, they can keep watch and get a good sense of our strength before they hit us. They hold off, watch and wait until they've gathered a strong enough force, and then they really whack us.' Grey paused, and eyed the others. 'Trouble is, without more and better intel there's no way of knowing.'

He left them to keep watch, and went to grab a jerry-can of diesel from the rear. As he up-ended it and drained the remaining contents into the wagon's tank, he did a mental check on their diesel supplies.

As with the other wagons, they'd set out with four jerry-cans of diesel, each with a five-gallon capacity. He figured they'd been averaging no more than 20 mpg over such appalling terrain. With the fuel in the vehicle's main and reserve tanks, they'd maybe got eight hundred miles' range, no more. They were also carrying one jerry of petrol for the quad, and Grey had no idea exactly how much fuel that would need. Depending on the terrain, the quads could end up doing many more miles as they buzzed about scouting for the enemy.

Either way, by the time they reached the 5th Corps's positions they'd be at – or maybe beyond – the very edge of their range. It was never wise to push the wagons to the limit of their fuel supplies, just in case the Squadron did get hit. If they had to go on the run and evade and escape from the enemy, they'd need the fuel with which to do so.

In short, they'd need a resupply sometime very soon. Most

likely, they'd get one via air-drop from a C130 Hercules. If the Squadron could identify and secure an LZ, the Herc could roll out a couple of palettes, one packed with jerry-cans of fuel and the other with water. Dropped under massive parachutes, it should be a simple enough task to get the palettes to hit the LZ, if the wind and the release point were calculated correctly.

On one level, Grey's confidence in the Squadron had been boosted massively by the past few days' operations. Compared to how they'd performed during training in Kenya, the Squadron was starting to work as one well-oiled machine. Incredibly, they'd pushed this far north without getting a single vehicle seriously bogged in, or having any serious accidents. It was pretty impressive for a unit with zero vehicle mobility experience on operations.

The Squadron was becoming slick at day and night drives, getting into their hidden LUPs unseen, establishing arcs of fire and setting sentries. Seven days on the ground, and not a man had been wounded or hurt or a vehicle lost, and not a shot exchanged with the enemy: it was one hell of an achievement, by any soldier's reckoning.

But now there were those mystery vehicles to factor into the equation. Grey just didn't know what to make of them. He was more or less certain he'd seen the same wagon tracking back and forth at the limit of their visual range. What kind of Iraqi farmer drove back and forth across the open, scorching desert for hours on end?

It was just possible that he was searching for a lost animal, or something. But to Grey's mind it was far more likely that he was getting eyes on the Squadron. If those vehicles were carrying enemy scouts, then it meant the Squadron's long night drive had

# DAMIEN LEWIS

failed to shake off any pursuers or watchers. If they were dickers, then the enemy had to know M Squadron's present location.

And they would be feeding back information to the main force, as it prepared to hit the Squadron like a whirlwind.

# CHAPTER THIRTEEN

By the time they set out on their second night drive of Operation No Return the issue of those distant vehicles had still not been resolved. But with darkness cloaking the silent terrain there was no sign of any headlights in pursuit, or even the sound of any vehicles.

The Squadron pushed ever northwards. A few hours' drive would take them into the farmland south of an Iraqi town called Sirwal, at which point they'd find a patch of cover to lie up for the remaining night hours. The Squadron was about to switch to day moves again, and for crucial reasons.

Once they left the Ninawa Desert behind them they were well out of the area of the Sunni Triangle – diehard enemy territory. By contrast, the area of northern Iraq from around the city of Salah stretching east to the border with Iran was largely the domain of the Kurds. The Kurds were the natural-born enemies of Saddam Hussein, and that should make them friends to the Coalition forces.

Over the years of his despotic rule Saddam had launched repeated offensives to wipe out the Kurdish people and other rebellious ethnic groups. In one of the most murderous, the Iraqi 5th Corps had been tasked with the 'Anfal Campaign' – *anfal* being a word from the Koran that translates as 'the spoils of war'. In that campaign, the 5th Corps's objective was to shell and burn Kurdish villages in an effort to purge the Kurdish population from Iraq.

Some fifty to a hundred thousand Kurds were killed. Eventually a 5th Corps general, along with dozens of the Corps's top officers, was executed by Saddam for refusing to bomb villages and further prosecute genocide. Following that, a group of major-generals and a further batch of officers were executed, after they were accused of trying to overthrow his regime. So while the 5th Corps had a record of being a tool of brutal oppression of the Kurds, they'd also been a focus of resistance against Saddam's autocratic rule.

The biggest challenge facing M Squadron now was locating the 5th Corps's whereabouts. With no further intel having been provided, there was only one possible means of doing so, and that was to drive up to some local villagers and ask them where the Corps was positioned. And that meant pushing ahead in broad daylight, so that the Squadron OC, plus Sebastian the terp, could try to extract that vital information.

That night the weather changed dramatically. The open skies became overcast, a thick band of cloud scooting across the heavens and blocking out stars and moon. It acted as a welcome insulating blanket, keeping some of the daytime heat in. As they pushed ahead in the inky darkness, Grey spotted the odd flash in the far distance to the southeast.

At first it looked as if it might be the flares from 2000-pounder bombs exploding somewhere over Bayji or Tikrit, but there was no accompanying roar of distant explosions. Instead, the flashes played out in an eerie blue-white silence across the horizon. The

Squadron was hundreds of kilometres north of any Coalition ground forces, not to mention the coming thrust of the military action, so air strikes this far north seemed unlikely. Finally Grey concluded it had to be an electrical storm, especially as it had the appearance of constant lightning.

But the intense darkness to their front seemed impenetrable, and it made for horrendous driving conditions. The NVG worked by boosting ambient light – that of the moon and the stars – but with the sky overcast and angry they were barely able to function. Moth kept the wagon moving at a dead crawl, but he was only just able to make headway.

The driving was made all the more challenging by the thick tufts of vegetation that had begun to appear on all sides. Grey could feel the humidity in the air here. After the bare dryness of the desert it felt claustrophobic and suffocating. The undergrowth seemed to be growing thicker with every minute, and he could hear it brushing against the thin alloy skin of their Pinkie, as Moth eased it through the densest of thickets.

This was ideal ambush territory, and at every turn Grey tensed himself to come face to face with a rank of Fedayeen machine-guns, and to meet fire with fire.

The darkness made the terrain look flat and uniform. The lack of visibility reminded him of some Arctic training he'd done in Norway. Six Troop had been on a three-day exercise, driving skidoos at night. Grey was leading, and a couple of times he'd stopped his snow-machine just metres away from a crevasse that cut across the snowfield. In the dark everything looked flat and featureless until the very last moment. Finally, the Troop commander had lost patience with Grey's stop–start progress. 'Fucking get a move on, mate,' he'd snapped. 'We don't have all bloody night.'

David Stirling, founder of the SAS, in the North African desert. Driving open-topped Pinkies – desert-adapted Land Rovers – M Squadron's 2003 Iraq operation owed much to the tradition of Stirling's long-distance desert raiding operations. *Getty*

M Squadron was fresh from a marine counter-terrorism ship assault in the English Channel – seizing the MV *Nisha*, a vessel suspected of carrying a weapon of mass destruction to attack the UK. Here some of the lads pose with a life ring, having stopped the *Nisha* reaching London. *John Doe*

For the MV *Nisha* assault the SBS were joined by a troop from the SAS, fast-roping from Chinooks on to the ship's deck to take it by surprise. Such joint SBS–SAS missions set the tone for M Squadron's Iraq mission to come. *John Doe*

An SBS Troop formed part of the SAS-led force that went in to rescue soldiers from the Royal Irish Regiment held hostage by the rebel group the West Side Boys, in the Sierra Leone jungle, in 2000. Here they pose after the operation's successful conclusion. *John Doe*

Joint SAS and SBS selection over the notorious Pen y Fan, in the Brecon Beacons, terrain that has been known to break many a man. Selection is designed to be incredibly tough both physically and psychologically, so that those who pass can survive the incredible rigours of Special Forces operations – and few tests would prove greater than M Squadron's mission into Northern Iraq. *Andrew Chittock*

American Special Operations Forces like these trained with M Squadron in Kenya, in preparation for deployment on their Iraq missions. US Special Forces often deploy alongside their British counterparts, but in the Iraq War none would secure a mission of such scope and daring as M Squadron's into northern Iraq. *Dan O'Shea*

Tier 1 Special Forces – SAS or SBS – are distinguished by their weaponry and kit such as their lightweight C7 Diemaco assault rifles (fitted with silencers). They have a Sig Sauer 226 pistol as a secondary weapon, slung on a chest rig for ease of access, and to avoid it catching as they debus from a vehicle or helicopter. They're wearing US camos, which are harder wearing, and body armour with two ceramic plates to front and rear, for extra stopping power. They're also carrying Blue Force Tracker, plus secret satellite and image-feed technology, to facilitate fast-moving operations. *John Doe*

The M Squadron operators were flown north to leapfrog over the Euphrates River by RAF aircrew piloting Chinooks. This is typical of the terrain M Squadron ran into at the northern end of their mission, as it approached the Jabal Sinjar – the Mountain of Eagles. *Corbis*

When M Squadron deployed on its Iraq mission outriders on quad bikes scouted routes ahead and kept watch for the enemy. An entire Squadron numbering some thirty vehicles was a real force to be reckoned with, but it threw up a massive dust cloud when moving through the open desert, which was visible for miles around. It was like an invitation to the enemy: *come and get us.* *Andy Chittock*

No matter how heavily camouflaged and dirtied-up they were, in the billiard-table-flat terrain of the Ninawa Desert M Squadron's vehicles stood out like the proverbial dog's bollocks. It would take them days to cross the desert, for all of which time the enemy could be tracking and hunting them. *Andy Chittock*

With Iraqi civilians always seeming to be present it was impossible to keep tabs on the enemy. The Iraqi forces used such 'dickers' – enemy watchers disguised as civilians – to track M Squadron's progress, and plan and launch the devastating series of attacks that followed. *Andy Chittock*

M Squadron's objective was to take the surrender of the Iraqi 5th Corps, some 100,000 infantry, equipped with a fearsome array of weaponry including Lion of Babylon main battle tanks, an upgraded version of the Russian T72. British intelligence reported the 5th Corps as being ripe for surrender. Events were to prove otherwise. *Getty*

Die-hard for Saddam. Fanatical Saddam loyalists, the Iraqi Fedayeen militia were known to use Saddam's hometown, Tikrit, and neighbouring Bayji, as bases from which to mount roving operations. When M Squadron was sent into the Ninawa Desert, it was on a collision course with this fanatical and trigger-happy paramilitary unit. *Getty*

A desert-adapted landrover at full pelt. Ambushed by a far superior Iraqi force, Grey, Moth, and Dude had no option but to try to outrun and outfight the enemy, as did the rest of M Squadron's operators, who were split into smaller and smaller groups scattered across the desert. *PA*

Outrun by Iraqi battle tanks, trucks and 4x4s, the men of M Squadron went to ground in a wadi, but it turned out to be a treacherous quagmire. Bogged-in vehicles were rigged with explosives, but some were captured and paraded before the media – leading to headlines that these men were 'cowards who had run away from the Iraqis'. Nothing could have been further from the truth. *Reuters*

After the battle. Days without any proper sleep and spent on the move through the blistering heat of the Iraqi desert left the men of M Squadron exhausted . . . even before the bullets started to fly. *John Doe*

He'd taken over leading the Troop and raced ahead on his skidoo. Barely minutes later he'd gone flying over a ravine. His machine had gone airborne with the trailer behind it, the rider leaving the saddle and landing face first. Grey and the others pulled to a halt at the lip of the ravine. Below them was a cartoon-like scene of a human imprint where the Troop commander had disappeared into a thick snowdrift.

No one knew quite what to say. Everyone was trying not to laugh. As they pulled him out of the snow, someone got their camera out to take a souvenir photo. 'Anyone takes a fucking photo I'll flatten the fucker,' he'd exploded, spitting out a mouthful of snow as he did so. Luckily, the only damage to the Skidoo was a broken throttle – and he'd insisted on continuing with the exercise, using a pair of pliers to operate the throttle cable.

That experience of driving through the Arctic light had taught Grey a crucial lesson: it was dead easy to miss a massive drop in such conditions, even when it was right in front of your bloody nose. Back then the Troop commander had been fortunate enough to land in soft snow. There would be no doing that here in Iraq.

With the darkness deepening, the Squadron pulled to a halt in some thick cover. If they tried to push any further, there was bound to be a serious accident or worse. It was the early hours of the morning, and this would be their LUP for the remainder of the night. Sentries were posted, while the rest of the blokes got their heads down for some much needed kip.

Grey shook himself awake for stand-to at 0500 hours. He'd got a solid four hours' sleep in the cool of the night, which was about as good as it got on such operations. He liked to get his blokes ready a full five minutes prior to stand-to. He glanced around at the other wagons, but no one seemed to be making much of an effort. They were lazing about drinking brews.

Mucker started to complain that no other fucker was readying themselves, so why couldn't they grab five minutes' extra rest? It was well out of character for him to get a bag-on like this, and it reflected how burned out they all were feeling.

The rest of the Squadron shook off their fatigue and got locked and loaded for stand-to. They were on high alert due to all the signs they'd picked up of a vehicle-borne force shadowing them. But first light revealed nothing untoward. There was no sign of any hostile presence, though the thick palm trees and reed beds cut visibility to a few hundreds yards at most. For all they knew, an entire army could be hiding out there.

The Squadron formed up in V-shaped formation for that day's drive north. Somehow, all the men on Grey's wagon knew that today was the day: it was make-or-break time for M Squadron. Either the locals would prove friendly and lead them to the 5th Corps's position, or they'd warn them that the Corps was highly unlikely to welcome the small British force. Either way, they had to know – for without that kind of intel, the Squadron was on a hiding to nothing.

The sun was rising through a narrow break in the cloud cover as the vehicles crawled across the B-road that Grey had identified from his route-mapping. After the days spent traversing a desert devoid of any man-made structures, he felt weirdly exposed and vulnerable as they hit that patch of sun-baked highway. Each wagon used its machine-guns to cover those coming after it, as they moved in formation over the open expanse of tarmac. On the far side they hit the dirt track that would lead northeast towards Sirwal town, bypassing the marshy lowland area of Duwayliyat

Khalaf. They made good time on that track, and by mid-afternoon it had turned into a well-graded gravel road.

It was around 1350 when the first concrete signs of human habitation hove into view. Straddling the dirt road was a tiny village of mud-walled houses, the larger ones boasting galvanized tin roofs. Each of them was shaded by a grove of palm trees, and scraggy dogs seemed to be running around everywhere. This was the first human habitation that the men of the Squadron had encountered since deploying to Iraq. Although it consisted of only half a dozen shepherds' hovels, it felt like a proper urban settlement after their days in the wilderness.

As Grey's wagon neared the first building, he could see a handful of women and children squatting at the roadside. The oddest thing was that they appeared to pay the approaching vehicles almost no attention at all. At the last moment a row of heads gazed up at them in curiosity, as the vehicle trundled past. There were no visible signs of fear – no screaming kids running for the cover of the nearby palm grove, or women wailing in distress and alarm.

For an instant Grey wondered whether they had mistaken the British convoy for an Iraqi military unit. Coated from head to toe in dust and grime and done up in their *shemaghs*, he figured they might just pass for some kind of elite Iraqi unit – most likely Republican Guard. And then he remembered that these were the people who would have most to fear from Iraqi troops.

He turned to Moth. 'Weird, or what? They're not scared to see us. They're not pleased to see us. What the—?'

Before Moth could respond there was a squelch of static on the radios and the OC came up on the air.

'Zero, all call-signs. Pull up in the centre of the village. It's women and children only here by the looks of things, and we have to assume they're friendly. Hand out some food, biscuits or sweets or whatever you have, in an effort to win them over. Hearts-and-minds kind of stuff and all that.'

Moth did as instructed, pulling up in a cloud of dust. Grey began heaving out the remains of their ration packs to the gathering crowd of kids, though what they'd make of boil-in-the-bag Lancashire Hotpot he couldn't say. The kids lunged at the loot, yelling excitedly and showing off to their mates what they'd managed to grab.

The HQ Troop trundled into the village at the centre of the convoy, and pulled to a stop. The OC gestured at Sebastian, making it clear he wanted his help in talking to the locals. Sebastian made some remark to the women standing nearest, and a couple wandered over. They wore the typical black headscarves bound tight around their heads, and there was a striking fatalism about the way they carried themselves.

Grey heard a few words exchanged in Arabic. Sebastian had to be explaining that the Squadron was trying to make contact with the Iraqi 5th Corps, and asking if the villagers had any idea where they might be. For a moment it struck him how strange it was that there were no adult males in the village. But then he remembered how Saddam's campaigns to wipe out the Kurds had targeted the men of fighting age.

Women and children weren't immune to such attacks, but it had been the men who were always hit first. If the villagers had mistaken M Squadron for an Iraqi military unit, that might explain why there were no men. Either way there was nothing overtly hostile about the place, and it reinforced the impression that they were moving into territory where the locals would likely be friendly.

After a bare few moments, the patrol pushed onwards again,

leaving the village behind them and passing into rich irrigated farmland. There were stands of luscious palm trees to left and right, and fields thick with a shoulder-high crop that looked as if it could be maize. It was the kind of terrain that Grey had been dreading running into, for it was well populated and lacked anywhere obvious in which to hide an entire Special Forces squadron.

It was approaching last light by the time the patrol left that terrain behind them, and headed into a drier, more open kind of landscape – somewhere more reminiscent of the Ninawa Desert.

The OC's voice came up on the air, sounding cool and confident as usual. 'Zero, all call-signs: we'll stop here for ten minutes,' he announced. 'I want to recce this grid for a TLZ.'

After scouring the ground and reporting to Headquarters the location of the TLZ, the OC led the Squadron into a shallow wadi and signalled for the blokes to cut the engines. They were now some thirty kilometres north of the village, and in a low-lying oval-shaped depression. At around fifty yards from end to end, it was just about large enough to contain all of the wagons. Ahead and to the north lay a large, sandy plain, and the lake bed was set in an area resembling the dunes you sometimes find at the top of a beach. They'd entered via a breach in the lake wall, offering a good shallow slope leading into the belly of the depression. To the far side was a steeper exit point, and all around the lakebed the walls were some six feet high and almost sheer.

It wasn't deep enough to provide complete cover from view or from fire, but otherwise it was a fine LUP. The natural walls provided good cover, and the two exit points would enable the Squadron to leave in a hurry if needed. They sure as hell weren't going to find a better patch of ground in which to overnight, and this was bound to be their last LUP before they reached the 5th Corps's positions – that was assuming they could find them.

Over the last few miles Grey had got the travel kettle going. He reached across to Moth with a steaming hot boil-in-the-bag meal. As Moth took the proffered grub, Grey noticed one of the TSMs (Troop sergeant majors) coming over to have a word.

'You and your fucking travel kettle, . . .' he remarked, enviously. 'Anyway, the OC wants everyone to know he's really pleased with the way things are going. But best get Moth ready with his JTAC gear, just in case. We need to ensure we've got air over us tonight.'

'No problem,' Grey replied. 'One more day's drive should do it – get us to the 5th Corps's location. Any intel from the villagers on where they are?'

The TSM shrugged. 'Nah, mate. Zero. We'll just have to keep asking.'

'Nothing more from Headquarters?' Grey queried.

'Nothing. Looks like it's up to us to push ahead and find 'em.'

The light was fading fast and the men had precious little time to organize themselves. They manoeuvred the wagons into positions of all-round defence, getting ten yards between each, so as not to make an easy target. The eastern side of the lake bed had the least cover, for the wall there was lower. Six Troop took the entire western wall of the LUP, while Four and Five would cover the east.

It was 1545 hours by the time they were all done, and the sun was sinking blood-red on the horizon. With 12 o'clock being due north, Six Troop had been left to cover from the 6 o'clock position through to 10 o'clock – so from due south to the northwest of the wadi. This included their entry point into the shallow depression

– a narrow neck of a gateway just large enough to squeeze a wagon through.

Five Troop had the 10 o'clock to 2 o'clock position, covering from the northwest to the northeast of the wadi. And Four Troop was covering the 2 o'clock to 6 o'clock position – from northeast to due south. In the centre of the lake bed the OC had set up his command post, which consisted of his two vehicles complete with radio antennae, plus a couple of the quads.

As they did stand-to for last light, Grey glanced over at Sebastian. He gave an awkward thumbs-up and a grin. Now that they were so close to their objective, their resident terp was really going to have to start earning his keep, and Grey felt glad to have him with them.

'All right?' he mouthed at Sebastian. 'How's your suntan?'

Sebastian mouthed something inaudible in response. Grey figured it had to be along the lines of: *Jolly good show, getting this close to those 5th Corps chaps.* Probably followed by some fascinating snippet of information about the history of the local area.

Gunner, the quad force commander, wandered over to Grey's wagon. 'You know what?' he muttered, as he sparked up a ciggie. 'This is fucking wank.'

'It is?' Grey queried.

'We're almost at the bloody mission objective, and we've yet to have a sniff of any action.'

Grey shrugged. 'Beware of what you wish for, mate.'

Despite the fact that they were now in more friendly territory, Grey couldn't shake off the feeling that he'd had almost from the very start of the mission – that they were being stalked by an unseen enemy. He glanced at his watch. It was 1815 hours. Only a few minutes more of this half-light and then the Squadron would be hidden by the welcome cloak of darkness.

One of Gunner's quad team was a Scottish guy called Angus. He was new to the Squadron, having joined around the same time as the Dude. He came over to share a last smoke. It was standard operating procedure that there was no smoking during the hours of darkness, when even the glow of a cigarette might give the position of the patrol away.

'This is fucking shit,' Angus remarked in a broad Scottish burr, echoing Gunner's sentiments. 'By now I thought we'd be flat-packing bloody ragheads.'

He took a last drag and went to flick his fag butt into the sand of the lake bed. Bang on cue there was a sudden, deafening roar from out of the desert to the north of them.

As the butt hit the deck, the gathering night was torn apart by a savage stream of tracer fire pounding in towards them.

# CHAPTER FOURTEEN

From out of the dusk Grey saw a thick stream of fiery bullets arcing over the far edge of the lake bed and hammering into the centre of their position. For an instant he was aware of Sebastian perched atop the signals wagon, with massive flaming rounds pounding past his ears, and then the Pinkies on the far side of the wadi opened up in a barrage of answering fire.

Grey had recognized the sound of the enemy weapon instantly: it was a bloody great 12.7mm DShK, the Russian-designed anti-aircraft gun that can churn out 600 12.7mm rounds per minute. Known as the 'Dushka', meaning 'sweetie' in Russian, it can only fire on automatic, and it is a devastating weapon when targeting low-level aircraft. But it could also be used in a ground-attack role to tear vehicles apart, as it was now.

The 12.7mm bullets the Dushka fires are the equivalent of the .50-calibre round. They can chew their way through walls and trees, and would make mincemeat out of the soft-skinned Pinkies, not to mention their human occupants. If Sebastian took a direct hit from one of those big armour-piercing rounds it would rip his arms and legs from his body, or tear his head clean off.

In the first few moments of the surprise attack the wagons from Five and Six Troop held their fire. Positioned along the western and northern sides of the wadi, it was impossible for the men to get eyes on whoever it was attacking them. It was from Four Troop's arc that the Dushka gunner was hammering in the rounds, and it was Four Troop's responsibility to meet fire with fire.

There seemed to be a solid stream of fire smashing into the ground right in front of Reggie's wagon. It was ricocheting into the air over the signals vehicle like some monstrous firework display. But this was no Guy Fawkes night, and these were no fireworks. Those rounds were designed to pulverize flesh and tear apart heavy armour, let alone a squadron of unarmoured Land Rovers.

Grey figured the Iraqi gunner had to be using one-in-two tracer rounds (one normal round per tracer round), which meant there were twice as many bullets as he could actually see hammering through the air. He hoped to hell Sebastian was going to get his head down, though the Pinkie offered precious little protection against such an onslaught.

Grey had no time to worry about that now. He was scanning the terrain to the southwest of their position, convinced that this was just the opening salvo in whatever the enemy might have in store for them. Sure enough, barely seconds after the first Dushka opened up, a second stream of tracer spat out of the darkness, this one hammering in towards them from the southern end of the wadi, which put Grey's wagon directly in the line of fire.

The solid stream of rounds belched out of the dusk like a dragon's scorching breath, pounding over the top of Grey and Moth's position. M Squadron was now being smashed by Dushka fire from both sides, and Grey felt certain more was coming. As he swung his weapon around to engage, he could feel the pressure waves thrown off by the bullets hammering into his skull and shoulders, which meant the massive rounds had to be passing no more than three feet away.

For an instant he flicked his eyes around to check on the Dude, perched atop of the .50-cal. He was convinced he'd see the big Yank getting the top half of his body blown off by the heavy machine-gun's bullets, leaving just a faint pink mist on the dusk air. Sure enough, big 12.7mm tracer rounds were flaming past to either side of the Dude's head, but miraculously none seemed yet to have hit him.

'FUCKING REVERSE THREE METRES DOWN SLOPE!' Grey roared at Moth, straining to make himself heard above the noise of battle.

Their priority had to be to get the Dude out of the line of enemy fire. No point engaging them first, if that got their own rear gunner blown apart. Moth revved the wagon's engine, rammed it into reverse, and with a spinning of wheels he slammed it further into the cover of the wadi and out of the line of fire.

Grey did a visual check on the Dude, saw that the Dushka rounds were now tearing past a good few feet above him, and turned back to the target. He followed the line of fiery tracer with his eyes and spotted where the enemy gunner was firing from. He was a good thousand yards away – perfect range for using the trajectory of the big machine-gun to lob rounds into the position being targeted while at the same time keeping well hidden from view. The enemy gunner was scraping rounds over the lip of a ridge that lay between his position and the lake bed, while keeping a low profile to its rear.

He'd be watching the arc of his tracer, and using that to adjust his line of fire and bring it smack-bang into the centre of the lake bed – where it would tear apart the HQ Troop, and the ricochets would smash a good number of the vehicles to either side.

But Grey could just make out the form of the enemy gunner, and that meant he could target him. There was the distinctive flash of a muzzle, and in the glare of the weapon firing he could see the unmistakable silhouette of the Dushka. He swung the GPMG around to engage. As he did so, he heard a deafening roar from right behind his head, and a solid wave of pressure slammed into the top of his skull and shoulders. The Dude had opened up with the .50-cal, the flash of the muzzle firing right above him lighting up Grey's steel gun sights in a blinding glare.

The Dude kept his finger hard on the trigger, unleashing a long and savage burst in the direction of the enemy. So much for Grey's fears for how the Dude – the Squadron's newbie and combat virgin – would react under fire. In spite of the fact that he'd had a solid stream of Dushka rounds practically ripping his head off, he was firm and steady and sparking.

Perched that much higher on the wagon, the Dude had to have a clearer view of the enemy, and Grey was able to follow his rounds in to the target. To his right, other blokes from Six Troop were struggling into their body armour, but not Grey. An instant before opening fire, he made a grab for the one bit of kit he needed above all else right now – his tactical hearing protectors. The .50-cal unleashing in his ears had rendered him deaf as a doughnut, and as the vehicle commander he needed to be able to hear any orders radioed in from the OC.

The hearing protectors consisted of a headset designed to cut out loud noises – like explosions and gunfire – but still retaining low-level acoustics. He slapped them on over the top of his radio earpiece. They would filter out all noise bar verbal communication from those near at hand, while at the same time enabling him to hear any incoming radio calls.

The moment he had the headset on, Grey was immersed in a weird and disembodied world where he could clearly see the flash and thump of weapons firing all around him, and the streams of tracer hammering in to smash them, but could barely hear any of it happening.

He fixed the distant, muted silhouette of the enemy gunman in the glowing metal V of the Gimpy's sights, squeezed the trigger and opened fire. Moments later, rounds from both his weapon and the Dude's .50-cal were slamming into the target and ricocheting high into the desert sky.

The men of M Squadron weren't using tracer, for the fiery trails laced across the night would lead an enemy gunman to them. Even so, Grey sensed his rounds were falling a fraction short. They were sparking wildly, as they rebounded off the ridge lying between him and the enemy gunner. He raised himself on the balls of his feet, leaned his weight on the weapon and brought the barrel up a fraction, and fired again. He saw his rounds spark and flare as they tore into the metal of the enemy vehicle – and, he hoped, ripped the enemy to pieces.

To his left lay the shadowed entrance to the wadi, and Grey had to keep one eye on that in case any hostile forces came thundering through. God only knew how many of them were out there in the darkness, but already he'd detected a good half-dozen streams of tracer arcing in to hit the Squadron. And with every passing second, more Dushka gunners seemed to be joining the party.

To his right the fellow wagons of Six Troop were pounding out heavy machine-gun fire and unleashing grenade rounds. Each

Troop possessed several grenade launchers, but they weren't Grey's preferred weapon to have on his vehicle. While grenade launchers were perfect for directed fire against an identified enemy, the .50-cal was accurate up to a far greater range. Right now, the grenade launchers were being used at the very limit of their reach, and if the enemy were operating from lightly armoured vehicles only the .50-cal's armour-piercing rounds could deal with those.

As soon as Grey got a bead on a Dushka operator, the driver of that vehicle seemed to move a few yards to the rear so as to get into better cover, before the gunner recommenced firing. Several times Grey was forced to reacquire the target and readjust his aim as he pounded out the fire, fighting a deadly duel across a kilometre or more of blasted desert.

As far as he could tell at such a distance, the enemy vehicles looked like Toyota pick-ups with 12.7mm Dushkas bolted to their rears. Perthaps his eyes were playing tricks on him, but he figured he could just make out that the Dushka operators were sporting the distinctive red-and-white checkered headscarves that marked them out as being Fedayeen.

More than likely, these were the Boys from Bayji – the Fedayeen hunter force. He guessed that they had been stalking the Squadron for several days, got ahead of the British force and gone to ground. They must have been lying up in hiding, and waiting for the Squadron to stumble into their trap, and most likely using one or two civvie-looking wagons to keep eyes on the British force.

From the headlights that he could see criss-crossing the desert, Grey figured there were scores more enemy vehicles converging on their position. It didn't escape his notice how fast and nimble they seemed to be. Not only was the Squadron very likely out-numbered, it was in danger of getting itself surrounded by a force driving vehicles far more manoeuvrable than their heavily laden Pinkies.

Already they had fire coming in from three points of the compass. Only due south, where their entry point to the wadi lay, did there appear to be a gap in the enemy forces converging upon their position.

For an instant, Grey considered their options if they did have to bug out of the lake bed. The escape point lying due north was clearly a no-go: there were enemy positioned there in strength, and it would lead them into flat, open terrain, which would provide zero cover. Only the southern exit point offered them any chance of making a getaway.

But maybe it didn't. Maybe it was a trap. Maybe the enemy had left the southern exit seemingly unguarded, but had a hidden force waiting out there in the darkness to ambush them.

Grey knew better than to underestimate the capabilities of the enemy they were up against. Whether or not they were Fedayeen, they clearly knew their stuff. Somehow, they'd managed to sneak up on the Squadron during stand-to, when the men were locked and loaded and scanning the terrain all around them. They'd kept themselves hidden, and secured positions from where they could lob in pinpoint-accurate fire.

They would have had no more than three feet or so of the Pinkies at which to aim their rounds, for that was all that was visible above the rim of the wadi, and they were doing so from a good kilometre away. Despite that, they'd got the fire lancing in right on top of the Squadron. They'd got the British force nailed, and all before they'd even detected the noise of their engines.

If the enemy had managed to hit the Squadron some fifteen minutes earlier, the blokes would still have been sorting their positions, as opposed to doing stand-to. As it was, the Squadron was perfectly placed to put down return fire, but still the men hadn't had the faintest clue that the enemy was out there gathering for an attack.

From behind him Grey heard the .50-cal cease firing. The Dude ripped off an empty ammo box, kicked it into the back of the wagon's rear, heaved up another, and an instant later he was feeding the belt into the weapon's breech and opening fire again. Already he was a hundred rounds down, and they were barely a couple of minutes into the firefight. If they continued at this rate of ammo consumption they'd be all done on the heavy machine-guns in fifteen minutes flat, at which point things would start to get very bloody serious indeed.

Grey himself was rapidly chewing through his first belt of two hundred rounds on the GPMG. He hunched over his weapon and concentrated on his aim, knowing how vital it was to make every bullet count. He saw rounds tear in to the nearest of the Dushka gunners, who was just visible above the ridge line. The figure slumped forward over the big machine-gun, and for an instant it fell silent. But a split second later a second fighter had climbed onto the weapon, and the Dushka's gaping muzzle began spitting fire once more.

By now there had to be six or more 12.7mm weapons to the south and west of their position, and an equal number to the north and east where the enemy seemed to have positioned their greatest concentration of firepower. That meant a dozen heavy machine-guns were hosing down an area a quarter the size of a football pitch, and the Squadron was getting blasted from all sides.

As they had learned during their Kenya training, it was standard operating procedure when you were ambushed in a good defensive position to stay put and fight it out, and to hold known terrain. But Grey sensed they were going to have real problems if the OC planned on remaining where they were.

For an instant he risked a glance behind him, to try to check on the command vehicles and get a sense of what the OC might be planning. All around the HQ Troop wagons 12.7mm rounds were smashing into the ground. Where the big tracer bullets were hitting the soft dirt of the lake bed it was laced with furrows of spurting flame. It looked as if a series of thick wires strung with blazing fire were being pulled up through the sand by some irresistible force. Grey had never seen anything remotely like it, and the HQ Troop's wagons had to be taking murderous hits.

For an instant he caught a flash of a white-faced figure crouching in the back of one of the Pinkies. He wondered what it must be like for Sebastian right now – a bloke who'd been brought along solely for his Arabic skills and who didn't even have a machine-gun with which to return fire. It had to be an absolute fucking nightmare.

At least the OC, his SAS 2iC and the signallers would be busy as hell trying to get a contact report radioed through to Headquarters. Plus they'd be checking for any available air power, and presumably figuring out what on earth they were going to do to defeat the enemy. By contrast, Sebastian was sat there with absolutely no means of taking the fight to an enemy who were doing everything in their power to kill him – bar shouting insults at them in Arabic.

The next moment Grey saw the flare of a rocket come tearing out of the darkness to the far side of the lake bed. It roared across the wadi and smacked into the rear of the signals wagon, detonating in a blinding flash around the level of the exhaust pipe and blasting the Pinkie into the air. The stricken vehicle slammed back down again, rocking wildly on its suspension, a cloud of smoke engulfing it.

The rocket had impacted no more than thirty feet from Grey's position, and he'd seen the signals wagon take a direct hit. The flaming projectile was more than likely an RPG (rocket-propelled grenade). Upon impact, the RPG is designed to fragment into hundreds of shards of razor-sharp steel, which are blasted forward from the point of the explosion in a whirlwind of death.

The signals wagon would have been raked with shrapnel, and Sebastian would more than likely have been right in the line of its blast. It looked as if they'd just lost one of their HQ vehicles, plus God only knew how many blokes. Unless the OC got his Troop moving pronto, Grey feared that every man amongst them was going to be very fucking dead very fucking quickly.

But there was bugger all that he could do about that right now. He had 12.7mm rounds smashing into his position directly from the gunners to their front, and from ricochets to their rear. He was sure their wagon was taking murderous hits, only the ear-defenders were blanketing the noise. Unless he felt himself take a bullet, or saw a round tear through a part of the wagon he could see, he'd not know what damage they'd taken until they tried to move.

The Squadron desperately needed to start winning this firefight. He raised himself on the balls of his feet and began malleting the enemy gunners, ramping the GPMG left and right, targeting muzzle flashes as they sparked in the shadows. In an arc to his right, he saw gunners on the other wagons doing likewise. They were hammering out a solid wall of fire and Grey knew they had to be finding and killing their targets.

But the enemy was good. Very good. And there were more of them than there were of M Squadron. As soon as an enemy gunner was hit he was ripped away from his Dushka position and another fighter took his place, and that made it all but impossible to reduce the level of fire the Squadron was taking.

Still, Grey felt certain they could win this firefight. They had a dozen .50-cal machine-guns and grenade launchers plus a similar number of GPMGs blasting away, which was an awesome amount of firepower. Right now, they were well able to give as good as they got. Plus they were in positions of great cover. And while the Squadron might be new to vehicle mobility work, they were the best in the business at putting down sustained and deadly accurate fire.

Grey's main worry was the limited supply of ammo the wagons carried. With unlimited ammo, they could stay put and smash the Fedayeen force until every last one of them was dead. They'd surely take casualties, but the Squadron would win the day. Yet the Fedayeen force was supposed to have vehicles in support, which would mean heavier trucks carrying spares, fuel, weaponry and ammo. In terms of who could sustain this level of fire the longest, it was more than likely the enemy.

As if to underline his worries, the Dude kicked a second empty ammo tin out of the way, and reached for a third. The barrel of his heavy machine-gun was glowing red from the heat of constant firing, and smoking like a dragon. The Dude had slammed two hundred bullets each the size of a child's wrist into the enemy positions, but still the attackers kept coming back at them with a murderous barrage of fire.

Grey felt a dull click from his own weapon. He'd reached the end of his first 200-round belt. He flung the breech open, reached for a replacement belt, dragged it across and slammed the breech closed. An instant later he was in the aim and pumping rounds into the nearest enemy positions. He saw a lucky burst rip into a Dushka gunner, the impact flinging him backwards off his vehicle. But an instant later another had taken the dead man's place.

Grey was starting to wonder whether they could win this firefight with sheer force and accuracy of fire alone. They could keep smashing the enemy until their machine-guns ran dry, then resort to their personal weapons. But there were too many of the enemy, and he figured they were too well armed. They also appeared to be oblivious to the casualties they were taking, their fighters near-suicidal in their desire to take the fight to the British enemy.

Only a Fedayeen force would be fighting with such fanatical intensity, and with such disregard for loss of life on their own side. Grey also feared that with every passing second hidden numbers of the enemy might be advancing through the darkness towards the Squadron's LUP.

To his rear a flash of movement caught his eye. It was followed by a shattering explosion. A second projectile had smashed into the lake bed, this one right on the OC's wagon's heels. Unlike the RPG, it had left no fiery rocket's trail. It blew the entire vehicle into the air, engulfing it in a thick cloud of smoke and blasted sand.

As the air cleared, Grey saw the heavy wagon sitting where it had landed: it had been thrown almost at right-angles to its original position. Only an artillery round – or, God forbid, a tank shell – would have the power to hurl a Pinkie around like that.

Grey figured the shell must have ploughed deep into the lake bed, burying itself in a layer of soft sand, which had served to mask the blast. But it was only a matter of moments before a round like that scored a direct hit, and pulverized a Pinkie – especially if an Iraqi battle tank had joined the battle.

Grey's mind was racing, the grey matter churning out dozens of thoughts per second, as he pulled the GPMG closer into his shoulder and traded fire with fire. Heavy armour was the one thing that the Squadron was ill equipped to take on. If they'd had some Milan, they could have used those wire-guided missiles to blast a battle tank asunder. More the pity then that they didn't have any.

Of course, it was blindingly obvious that the Iraqi Fedayeen didn't operate artillery or battle tanks. Only the regular Iraq Army was equipped with those types of hardware. And the only Iraqi army unit known to be operating in this area was the Iraqi 5th Corps.

*Had M Squadron just been ambushed by the very unit whose surrender they were supposed to be taking? And if so, had the Fedayeen shadowing the Squadron somehow called in the 5th Corps to join the battle?*

Either way, their only option now was to get the hell out of the LUP. With heavy shells slamming into the limited terrain of the lake bed, they had to bug out and hope to lose the enemy in the dark. At least then they'd have the advantage of night-vision equipment. The cloak of night should serve to hide them, and if they could navigate their way south into the open desert, the Squadron might be able to evade and escape from the enemy that way.

A second massive shell went screaming across the lake bed and ploughed into the soft ground on the far side of the HQ Troop's vehicles. Whatever it was that was lobbing in those rounds, it had dropped the first slightly short and the second slightly long. That meant that the gunner had the HQ Troop bracketed, and the next shell was likely to land right on top of their position.

None of the Pinkies had the space to carry any extra passengers, least of all any wounded.

If they lost a wagon or two, things would be getting desperate.

# CHAPTER FIFTEEN

From behind him Grey could hear engines revving wildly and smell the acrid stench of tortured, burning rubber. He turned to see the OC's wagon spinning its wheels as it struggled to haul itself out of the soft sand and onto firmer ground. It looked as if the OC was trying to move his Troop away from the heart of the lake bed, the epicentre of the killing ground.

His open-topped Land Rover was peppered with bullet holes, and great rents had been torn in the aluminium bodywork by shrapnel. Grey could hardly believe that it was still drivable. Behind it, and nose to tail with the OC's wagon, the signals vehicle was also on the move. For a long second Grey figured that the lead wagon was trying to tow the other out of the kill zone, which was a fucking desperate set of straits to be in.

One crippled Land Rover dragging a second stricken vehicle: this was worse than the blind leading the blind. But then he realized that both wagons had somehow got moving under their own steam, and were making for the exit to the lake bed. How both Pinkies could still be in action Grey didn't know, but at least the

OC seemed to have woken up to the fact that either they got the hell out of there, or they were dead.

As the lead wagon headed for the exit point, Grey could see that the OC had his ear-defenders on, which meant he had his radio working. A clutch of quad bikes roared past the OC's wagon, with Gunner at the head. Like sheepdogs shepherding a flock, they would be first out, scouting the way ahead and searching for the enemy. If the Boys from Bayji were out there lying in ambush, the quads might be able to radio back a warning.

Grey had heard no orders issued via the radios, so he presumed they'd follow SOP (standard operating procedure) for pulling out of the LUP. The HQ Troop would lead, followed by Four and Five Troop, with Six taking up the rear. As Grey's was the vehicle in Six Troop nearest to the exit point, he figured they'd have to be last out of the LUP.

They'd chosen this LUP carefully and they'd chosen well. It was a great defensive position. By bugging out, they were breaking all SOPs. But Grey didn't doubt for one moment that the OC's decision was the right one. With the Squadron getting hosed down by Dushka fire, RPGs and now large-calibre shells, they had no option but to leave.

As the command wagon roared through the narrow exit point, Grey knew it was up to Six Troop, and his wagon in particular, to provide vital covering fire. The exit lay to the south of the wadi, which was within their arc of responsibility, and it was Grey's vehicle that lay closest to it. They'd need to remain where they were, putting down rounds until the rest of the Squadron had got safely out of there.

They had been first into Iraq on the Chinooks, and they were going to be last out of the ambush.

So be it.

All the Six Troop vehicles were smashing rounds towards the enemy positions, throwing out a concentrated wall of fire so as to cover those escaping from the LUP. Grey could see the empty cartridges spewing out of the Gimpy's breech, each a glowing cylinder of metal lit up golden-red in the muzzle flash of the .50-cal behind him.

As he kept his finger hard on the trigger, the spent shell cases went tumbling onto the wagon's floor in one long, hot torrent of smoking metal. Already, there was a slough of spent bullet cases down there, and it was greasy and treacherous under foot. Grey had to keep booting the used brass out of the way, so as to stop himself from losing his footing as he ramped the weapon around to hit new targets.

He could only imagine that their Pinkie was riddled with fire, but the deafening noise of battle – plus the tearing impact of enemy bullets – was silenced by his ear-protectors.

As the adrenalin surged through his veins, the sense that he was cut off and insulated from the world all around him deepened, taking on a vice-like grip. Time seemed almost to freeze. It felt as if every second lasted for an age, and every action seemed etched into his mind in impossible detail and clarity.

In his heightened state of consciousness he'd become hyper-aware of every minute detail of the battle. With dreamlike lucidity, he sensed the individual movements of the machine-gun as it sucked in the rounds, punched the detonation cap and powered each bullet down the length of the barrel, spitting out a spinning projectile of death travelling at some three thousand feet per second.

It was almost as if his eyes were following those rounds as they left the barrel and rippled through the air separating him from those he wanted to kill. His knotted shoulder muscles burned and ached from the tension of hunching over the juddering weapon, and ramping out a near-continuous and deadly accurate stream of fire. But his mind blanked any pain.

As his brain processed a tumult of thoughts at the speed of light, he zeroed in on the one overriding priority right now: how to find, target and kill the enemy, and get the Squadron out of there. It burned his mind into a pure, crystal-clear focus in which nothing else in his life seemed to matter. His family back home, the mortgage, the unpaid bills, the recent arguments with his wife – it was all an irrelevance when faced with the kill-or-be-killed reality of full-on combat.

Grey had never known anything like the level and intensity of fire they were up against. Despite the solid wall of rounds that he and Dude were pouring out, the enemy seemed undaunted, and he could sense their bullets tearing metal all around him. He just prayed that none of the damage was terminal, and that none of his blokes took a direct hit.

From behind him the Dude kicked away a third empty ammo box and slammed his fourth belt onto the .50-cal. They were eating up the ammunition at a furious rate. The Dude had already burned through half of his 600 rounds, and Grey was well through the Gimpy's second belt of 200.

Standard operating procedure when going on the run was to follow the OC's lead, and to try to keep the Squadron together for as long as possible. Things started to move very quickly now. To the east of the wadi Four Troop broke fire, and one by one their Pinkies followed the OC's lead. Moments later Five Troop ceased firing, abandoning their positions to the north of the sunken terrain so they could head for the exit point.

To the far right of Grey's position the guns on Scruff's wagon were the first of Six Troop's to fall silent. Scruff's Pinkie reversed away from the edge of the lake bed, turned in a cloud of dust and kangarooed its way across the ground, which had been churned up by the passing wagons, not to mention the enemy fire.

There now remained two .50-cals, one grenade launcher, and three GPMGs putting down rounds on to the enemy, but the amount of fire they were taking in return was devastating. A second vehicle ceased firing, and turned to leave. Now it was only Grey's wagon and one other remaining, and they were fast becoming the focus of all the incoming. It was total murder.

Sgt Dave 'Jamie' Jamieson was the commander of the other vehicle, and the Six Troop Sergeant Major. He was a wiry, fit-as-fuck Scouser, and Grey knew him to be as wily as a fox and as fierce as a lion. For an instant Jamie leaned across towards Grey, and signalled for him to get his wagon out of there.

'YOU LEAVE!' Jamie yelled. 'WE'LL COVER YOU!'

'WE'RE NEAREST THE EXIT!' Grey roared back, and without taking his trigger finger off the juddering, smoking-hot weapon. 'WE'RE LAST OUT! GET THE FUCK ON YOUR WAY!'

Grey gestured for Jamie to pull his wagon out while he still could, and with their Pinkie providing covering fire. Jamie hesitated for an instant, then signalled his thanks, and his driver finally got their vehicle under way. When the shit hit the proverbial fan, the men of the Squadron would fight to the death for each other. That was the Special Forces ethos, and the spirit that bound such elite warriors together.

Jamie's wagon reversed, powered forwards and made a mad dash for the narrow exit. Only when it was clawing its way out of the sunken lake bed did Grey finally give the order.

'FUCKING CEASE FIRE! LET'S GET MOVING!'

Moth gunned the engine on their wagon and ramped it into a screaming turn. As he did so Grey and Dude remained hunched over their weapons, but they eased their fingers off the triggers. For the first time in what felt like an age the guns of M Squadron had fallen silent.

As Moth slammed the Pinkie into first and floored the accelerator, Grey took one last look at the position they were evacuating. It was pure Armageddon in there. Streams of 12.7mm tracer rounds were slamming into it from all directions, transforming the lake bed into a raging sea of fire.

Moth raced for the exit, weaving the Pinkie through savage bursts of 12.7mm. For an instant, Grey saw a massive explosion engulf the area where the command vehicle had been positioned, throwing a fist of blasted sand high into the air. It left behind a huge smoking crater, where a few moments earlier the HQ Troop had been positioned. They'd got out of there not a moment too soon.

The nose of Grey's Pinkie was thrusting its way into the narrow neck of the exit when he sensed a massive shadowed form behind him. He turned to see the hulking great shape of an armoured beast come thundering over the far side of the lake bed. For a moment it teetered on the six-foot-high lip of the wadi, then it tilted forward and the tracks of the vehicle slammed down onto the soft sand, the wall of the lake bed half collapsing under its weight.

As the Iraqi armour hit the level ground of the lakebed, Grey's wagon powered ahead and careered around the corner at the high end of the exit point. The worry now was what awaited him and his men on the far side, when they hit the open desert.

To the east Grey spotted a thick dust trail snaking off into the darkness. That had to be the route the other wagons had taken.

'FOLLOW THAT DUST TRAIL!' he yelled into Moth's ear. 'WHATEVER IT TAKES – DON'T FUCKING LOSE IT!'

As Moth accelerated in that direction, their wagon rounded the eastern side of the wadi. Grey glanced towards the position they'd just evacuated, and in amongst the dust and the smoke rising from the lake bed he spotted three indistinct silhouettes. They were vehicles, perched on the very rim of the lake bed and occupying the high ground overlooking it.

For a moment he wondered whether they were some of M Squadron's wagons, which had somehow doubled back to the LUP. But when he took a closer look, the reality hit him like a steam train: they were far too large to be Pinkies.

Even in the gathering darkness those indistinct forms looked like Kraz 225s – a Soviet-era six-wheeled steel monster of a truck, one that was in widespread use with the Iraqi military. The Kraz 225 was a fantastic off-road vehicle, capable of 75 kph over just about any kind of terrain.

Scores of figures were leaping off the backs of the trucks, and within moments Grey had spotted the distinctive silhouettes of Iraqi Army forage caps, plus AK47 assault rifles. There was no doubt in his mind any more: the trucks were carrying a regular Iraqi infantry unit.

The Iraqi soldiers must have been trucked across the open desert to the very lip of the wadi, under cover of the Dushka fire. They were now going in to finish off the Squadron, in a ground assault – only, the British force had just bugged out of there. This had been a textbook deliberate attack, one executed by a highly mobile, extremely well-coordinated and professional force.

The men of M Squadron had been briefed that the Iraqi infantry were conscripts lacking in morale. They'd been told the Iraqi forces were ill-trained and ill-equipped, and that they were not up for the fight. From where Grey was sitting, it certainly didn't bloody look that way.

Automatically, his GPMG had swung round to face the new threat. His gun moved wherever he was looking, following his eye-line. That way, if he spotted an enemy position he could open fire on it instantly. Such vehicle-borne combat was often won or lost in the split second it took one side to recognize the other and open fire, which was why Grey had drilled and drilled to keep his weapon shadowing his line of sight.

But right now he forced himself to ease off his trigger finger and hold his fire, and with the flash of a hand signal he indicated for Dude to do likewise. If they opened up, they'd have three truck-loads of Iraqi soldiers returning fire, to say nothing of whatever else there might be lurking out there in the desert.

As the Iraqi troops surged over the rim of the wadi, Grey just had to hope that none of them spotted their fleeing vehicle. All it would take was one AK47 round into a tyre, and they'd be toast. The Pinkies had tubeless tyres fitted with some kind of run-flat self-sealing solution, which should give a shot-up tyre enough usability to get a wagon out of the immediate killing range. But with three Kraz 225s parked up no more than two hundred yards away, it didn't take a rocket scientist to work out that they'd be rapidly pursued and hunted down. The last thing they needed was for those monster Iraqi Army trucks to come steaming and snorting after them. They were big enough and nasty enough to run right over a Pinkie and squash it flat as a tin can.

A fleeting thought flashed through Grey's mind,. He'd heard

somewhere about a sister patrol to Bravo Two Zero, one that had gone into the Western Desert during the First Gulf War. They were mounted on vehicles and they'd stumbled on a mass of Iraqi infantry camped up in the desert. It was the dead of night, and somehow those SAS wagons had sneaked right through the enemy lines.

They'd been close enough to see the glow of the Iraqi sentry's cigarette, and to catch the distinctive smell of burning tobacco. But they'd held their nerve, and held their fire, and managed to slip through. Grey hoped and prayed their lone vehicle could do the same right now. In Special Force operations, knowing when not to engage the enemy was as vital as knowing when to open fire and smash seven bales of shit out of them.

'Keep after that fucking dust trail!' Grey urged Moth. 'Whatever you do, don't fucking lose it!'

Moth put his pedal to the metal, and within seconds the Pinkie was practically airborne as it bucked and cannoned its way across the rough terrain. Grey leaned forward and grabbed a smoke grenade from the dash, ripped the pin out and let the arming lever fly. He raised himself in his seat, half turned round and hurled the grenade out of the wagon's rear. If he could lay down enough smoke, it might buy them some much needed time. If nothing else it should make it difficult for the enemy to follow their trail, at least for the few minutes it took the grenades to stop gushing out their thick, choking smoke. Grey kept on hurling them until his very last was gone.

At the same time he was urging Moth to keep his speed up and to catch the rearmost vehicles. If they lost the Squadron's tail end they'd never find it again, of that he was certain. They'd be on their own – three blokes in one soft-skinned wagon that had fired off more than half of its ammo and exhausted all of its smoke grenades. It wouldn't take long for the forces gathered in and around that lake bed to realize that the Squadron had made their exit, and come roaring after them.

Night had well and truly fallen by now. Above them was another overcast sky, and it was as black as a witch's tit out there in the desert. It was great conditions in which to try to shake off an Iraqi hunter force, but it was also perfect for losing the rest of the Squadron.

For a good two minutes the men pushed onwards in a tense and nervous silence. Grey ripped off his ear-defenders, so he could better hear what was happening. He scanned the night for the noise of vehicle engines, straining to catch the distinctive note of a Pinkie's diesel motor reverberating out of the dust cloud before them. And from behind, he was dreading catching the deep throaty roar of a Kraz 225 powering its way forward.

Moth was ramping the Pinkie across the rough terrain at break-neck speed. It was on the tip of Grey's tongue to warn him to slow down a little, for if they hit a rock or a significant drop they'd be sure to smash up the wagon. And if they lost their vehicle at a moment like this, there was no way in the world they'd be able to evade the kind of forces that were coming after them on foot.

They'd gone a good three kilometres, and it looked increasingly likely that they had lost contact with the Squadron. If so, they'd have to try to use the radios and hope some of the wagons were still within range. They'd have to ask them for a grid, and for the rest of the squadron to remain stationary on that grid while their own vehicle tried to reach the others. But with the Iraqi force at their backs, the request to remain static would likely go down like the proverbial turd in a punchbowl.

To be able to use the radios they'd have to get stationary, for they were unworkable with Moth tearing across the desert like this. The wind noise alone drowned out any words spoken into the mouthpiece, and made it impossible to hear anything in return. But the last thing Grey wanted right now was to call a halt. They needed to put more distance between them and the enemy, and they needed to marry up with the Squadron so they had some real firepower again.

If they couldn't make contact with the Squadron via the radios, they'd have to go to ground in some kind of a hide, then use the satcom to call up SF Headquarters and try to locate the Squadron that way. And if that failed, they'd have no option but to call for a hot extraction – a rescue by Chinook under the threat of enemy fire. There was no way that a lone Pinkie was about to fight its way out of this one.

Finally, after what felt like an age, the vague form of a vehicle began to emerge from the dust and gloom up ahead. Grey strained his eyes, trying to work out if it was a Pinkie, or one of the Fedayeen Toyota pick-ups. From a distance, and in such conditions, it would be very easy to mistake one for the other.

The vehicle ahead was showing no lights, so it was more than likely friendly. But maybe the Fedayeen had switched to operating on black light themselves, now that the ambush had been sprung and the hunt was well and truly on.

Grey leaned across at Moth: 'Slow the fuck down, 'cause it may be the bad guys. Don't close the gap until we're sure.'

Moth nodded his assent, and eased off the gas. The wagon decelerated to something more like a more normal patrol speed. As they crept closer, the image up ahead finally resolved itself into that of an open-topped Land Rover. It was one of the most welcome sights that Grey, Moth and the Dude had ever seen.

Grey figured they'd covered a good four kilometres from the LUP. At the pace Moth had been doing, he should have won the Land Rover land speed record.

The rearmost vehicle was Raggy's. Grey could see the familar form of Rag-bag chucking smoke grenades out of the back. He was doing so in typical Raggy fashion, using a lazy lob to wing it over his shoulder. Grey could see the spare grenades lined up on their Pinkie's dash.

Throwing smoke was a fine way for the Squadron to lose any pursuers, but it had done absolutely zero to help Grey and Moth find the tail end of the convoy. As their wagon closed the distance with Raggy's, Grey caught the distinctive firework-smell of the fumes put out by the grenades. Now that their wagon had finally caught up with the Squadron, Raggy's smoke screen should aid their escape no end.

More vehicles loomed out of the darkness. The nearest one was stationary, and it had the unmistakable whippy antennae of one of the HQ Troop vehicles. As Grey neared it, he saw the OC standing up in the front seat and counting in the wagons of his Squadron. His face broke into a broad smile of relief as he spotted Grey's wagon – the last out of the LUP, and the last to emerge from out of the smoke and the dust.

As they approached Grey saw the OC give a thumbs-up. 'Okay, buddy?' he mouthed at them.

Grey returned the greeting, and got a wink from the OC in return.

But at that very instant he saw a burst of tracer fire tear through the darkness, and slam into the desert barely yards to the rear of the OC's vehicle. More rounds followed, and from the crack and thump that they made as they tore past Grey's wagon, he could tell that they were 12.7mm. Somehow, those bloody Dushka gunners were on their tail again.

The Squadron had shaken itself out into a linear formation stretching a good kilometre from end to end. Now that Grey's wagon was within range, he tuned into the radio chat. Gunner and his quad force were at the tip of the spear, and Grey could hear him banging on about the need to find a new lie-up point (LUP) so as to get out of the line of enemy fire.

The wagons thundered ahead into the darkness, the odd burst of 12.7mm fire chasing them through the night. They'd made about six kilometres when the OC called a halt, and they pulled up in a broadside position. No one dismounted. It was too hot to do so.

They were now strung out in linear fashion, but with the wagons parked side-on to the enemy. It was a perfect position from which to open up on the forces in pursuit, using every gun of the Squadron in synchrony. Grey figured the OC was preparing to brass up the enemy big time. In which case, the OC and the rest were likely oblivious to the fact that there were some seriously heavy firepower coming after them.

There was a quick head count, just to make sure that everyone was present and correct. Grey figured they had to have wounded, but as no one was making a big deal out of that right now it looked as if no one's injuries could be life-threatening.

There followed a general exchange between vehicles on the radios, so everyone got a heads-up on what the others had seen. Grey shared the news that he'd positively indentified an Iraqi infantry unit, which had presumably been led to the LUP by the Fedayeen force. He described the Iraqi soldiers that he'd seen pouring into the LUP, complete with their monster Kraz 225 trucks, and the glimpse he'd got of their heavy armour.

For a second the radio net fell silent, as the news sank in.

When a Special Force unit was deep behind enemy lines and acting on sketchy intel, the plan had to evolve as it went along. It was continually being adjusted to take account of what each of the men in the unit had witnessed. Grey's warning about the kind of forces they had coming after them completely altered the game plan. There was no limit to the kind of hardware the Iraqi Army might bring to bear – all except for air power, for the Coalition controlled the skies over Iraq.

Gunner's voice was the first up on the net: 'Fuck it, in that case we've got to find a new LUP like yesterday!'

As if to stress the point that he'd made, a savage stream of 12.7mm tracer hammered in towards the wagons, groping for a target. The Squadron was clearly a long way from being out of the shit just yet. The OC gave the order to move out. For now at least, any plans to use the broadside to smash the pursuing enemy had been abandoned.

'Go Four, Five, Six!' Gunner yelled over the net.

'Go Four, Five, Six!' voices echoed. 'Go Four, Five, Six!'

When in escape and evasion mode, the standard orbat (order of battle) for the Squadron was for Four Troop to lead, with Five following and Six Troop bringing up the rear. Once again it would be Grey's vehicle last in line, and closest to the pursuing enemy.

It seemed to take an age to get the Squadron on the move as one cohesive linear force. In the seconds they had to stay put as the tail-end Charlies, Grey and his men scanned the silence of the night searching for the enemy. Grey's mind was churning, as he tried to make sense of exactly who it was had hit them in that LUP.

The enemy had mounted a carefully planned and deliberate attack – there could be no arguing with that. It had involved a strike force of highly mobile Fedayeen, sporting Dushkas. They'd provided covering fire for truck-mounted infantry, and at least one armoured vehicle to move in. All of that had been coordinated in the gathering darkness, so that all units acted in tight partnership with one another and avoided hitting each other with friendly fire.

Grey was gobsmacked: the enemy had achieved a tight and lethal attack, which was absolutely covert in nature until the trap was sprung. If the Squadron had remained in that LUP trading fire with the Dushka gunners for a few minutes more, they wouldn't have seen the armour, or the Iraqi infantry, until they were right on top of them. It was sheer luck – combined with the OC's foresight – that had got them out of there. If the Squadron had stayed put in the LUP for only a few minutes more, they'd have been finished. All of the wagons would have been smashed, and the men would have been killed, captured, or forced to go on the run on foot.

To coordinate getting those troops and armour in so swiftly, and all the time keeping the Squadron under such a blistering barrage of fire, required an incredible level of military professionalism. It was a superbly conceived set of attack orders, and brilliantly executed.

Contrary to what the intel briefings had told them, the Fedayeen and the Iraqi Army clearly did work in close conjunction with one another. Here, they were acting as one well-oiled machine. And contrary to the intel briefings, these were far from being the actions of an enemy that was demotivated and lacking in morale. Not a man amongst that attack force seemed likely to surrender, and Grey was more suspicious than ever now that they were up against the forces of the Iraqi 5th Corps.

In which case, their entire mission had been predicated on a massive intelligence failing, and they'd been sent in here on little less than a lie.

# CHAPTER SIXTEEN

Grey had little time to dwell on such bleak thoughts. A second and a third burst of tracer fire arced out of the night, smashing into the dirt barely yards from their vehicle. Between Grey's wagon and the enemy lay the void of the night, awash with the thick and drifting smog of the smoke screen. And not a vehicle amongst the Squadron was showing any lights.

In which case, how the hell was the enemy managing to target them? They certainly wouldn't be able to see the Squadron with the naked eye, or even using night-vision binoculars. The screen of smoke blocked their sight, and even NVG kit wouldn't allow the enemy to see through that.

Only infrared thermal imaging kit would enable them to pierce the smoke and the darkness and pick up on the Squadron's heat signatures. Via thermal imaging optics the Iraqis would be able to detect any warm objects just as Predator sees them in the movies. A fire, a warm vehicle engine or a living being would form a distinctive hot white blob.

Even the tracks left by the hot tyres of the Pinkies and quads as they churned across the desert would leave a faint signature.

Using thermal imaging kit, the Iraqis would be able to follow those tracks until the Squadron's rearmost vehicles came into range and right now they'd be picking up the glowing heat of the wagons' engines and the hot barrels of the machine-guns. Only elite Iraqi units were issued with thermal imaging kit, which made Grey wonder just who the hell it was they were up against?

It took a good sixty seconds for the lead elements of the Squadron to pull out in their order of march, during all of which time Grey's wagon was taking fire. The maximum range of the Dushka was two thousand yards, so Grey could only assume the enemy were closing fast. As the wagons of Six Troop waited their turn to move, he felt a growing sense of frustration bordering on anger.

'Fucking speed up at the front,' Grey yelled over the radio, ''cause *Zero Six Bravo* are getting smashed back here!'

'Roger that,' came back Gunner's reply.

As they waited impatiently for their wagon's turn to move, the enemy fire intensified, long bursts of tracer tearing out of the smoke to their rear, and ricocheting off the hard, rocky earth. Grey heard the distinctive steel-on-steel howl as a 12.7mm round ripped into the underside of their vehicle. He felt it rock back on its spring with the impact, as further rounds smashed into the bare ground, throwing up a fountain of fire to either side.

He locked eyes with Moth. It was a golden rule of vehicle mobility ops never to break the line of march. If you did, one wagon might see another where it didn't expect there to be one, and open fire. There was double the risk of such friendly fire when the enemy were driving similar vehicles to their own – light 4WDs with heavy machine-guns mounted in the rear. But it felt like pure murder stuck here at the back taking accurate fire as the rest of the Squadron got itself under way.

All of a sudden Grey saw Moth reach for the cowboy holster that held his weapon, grab it and dive out of the vehicle. Before he could stop him, the young operator had sunk to one knee, grabbed a handful of grenade rounds from out of his webbing, and ratcheted the first 40mm round into the weapon's under-slung grenade launcher.

He planted the weapon at a 45-degree angle, butt firmly in the sand like a makeshift mortar, and opened fire. Grey stared in amazement as Moth started lobbing grenades high into the air in the direction of the enemy, so as to achieve maximum range. He realised how horrendous it must have been for Moth back at the LUP, sitting at the wagon's wheel with the engine running and unable to return fire, while he and the Dude unleashed hell.

This was the first time they'd gone static, and they'd got a good idea where the enemy vehicles were. They were just about within range of Moth's 40mm grenade launcher, when using it as he was now. They weren't going anywhere until the rest of the Squadron got moving, and so Moth had seized his chance.

But even so, what Moth was doing right now was likely to get them all killed, especially as big nasty tracer rounds kept sparking all around him. He was crouching there without even the protection of body armour, for no one on Grey's wagon had had the time or opportunity to pull any on. They'd been too busy returning fire, or running from the enemy.

Grey saw the faint flashes of detonations in the distance, as Moth's grenade rounds exploded, and the dull thud of the blasts drifted back to them through the smoke. From this distance he had next to zero chance of hitting the enemy.

'GET THE FUCK BACK IN THE FUCKING WAGON!' Grey

screamed. 'They fucking blow your legs off, we're finished! GET BACK IN HERE, NOW!'

He heard the characteristic thwup-thwup-thwup as Moth unleashed a last burst of grenade rounds. Then he turned and leapt for the wagon. He made the driver's seat, slapped his smoking grenade launcher back into its makeshift holster, and glanced at Grey.

'I thought I'd hold 'em off!' he yelled. 'Buy the rest of the lads some time—'

'*The rest of the lads!*' Grey roared. '*What about fucking us?*'

'Yeah, us 'n' all.'

'Well fucking nice one, John Wayne,' Grey snorted. 'You almost got us all—'

His last words were lost as a violent explosion lit the horizon to the west. It was just about where Moth's grenades had been landing. It looked as if one of those 40mm rounds must have hit its target, and very likely ruptured the enemy vehicle's fuel tank. It had gone up in a tower of flame, the blast punching through the blanket of smoke like a mini nuclear explosion.

Before Grey could think of a fitting remark, the vehicle to their front roared into motion, and Moth floored the accelerator and powered after it. In spite of the unorthodoxy of what he'd just done with his grenade launcher, it was great to see Moth sparking, and especially when the Squadron was getting smashed from all sides. Any worries Grey might have had about the quiet man on his team – the mysterious, wild-card operator – were fast going out the window.

Almost as soon as Moth got the wagon motoring forwards, a savage burst of 12.7mm went smashing into the ground to their front. He gunned the engine, at the same time wrenching the steering wheel round to avoid the incoming fire. M Squadron had been stationary for no more than a couple of minutes, and there was no doubt that the enemy gunners were red-hot.

As the Squadron pushed east the enemy kept bouncing fiery streams of 12.7mm tracer off the desert to either side. It was horribly close, especially for Grey, Moth and Dude in the rearmost vehicle. Rounds were slamming into the deck not ten feet away from them, and Moth had to keep weaving the wagon to left and right in an effort to avoid being hit.

Still the enemy fire kept coming. They saw 12.7mm rounds smashing into the convoy up ahead, and there was no doubt that some of those shots had to be finding their targets. Either the enemy had night-vision kit or they were using thermal imaging gear, most likely a combination of the two. There was no other way they could keep following the line of fast-moving British vehicles, and targeting them so quickly.

The Iraqis were chasing after a fast moving target heading through pitch-black terrain, and yet still they were managing to shoot effectively while doing so. That was the ultimate skill to master when it came to vehicle-based mobility combat, and it was one that it was very hard to train for and perfect.

The Squadron was going back over the same ground that it had driven in on. It was 1900 hours by now. They had been under attack and returning fire for a good ninety minutes, and there was still not the slightest sign of them shaking off the enemy.

As they pushed through the bullet-torn night, Grey marvelled that their wagon was still functioning and that none of his team had yet taken a hit. One of the great things about the Pinkie was its aluminium shell. On the downside it provided zero protection from fire, but the upside was that it offered near-zero resistance to an enemy bullet. You could take a hammer and punch a nail through the alloy shell without too much effort.

The 12.7 mm rounds would be punching holes clean through the wagon's bodywork, the bullets taking no damage at all from the impact. They'd pass straight through without fragmenting into deadly shards of shrapnel. So unless a 12.7 mm round hit a solid steel component – the engine, transmission, gearbox or the chassis – the Pinkie could keep on taking hits and only suffer cosmetic damage.

As to taking injuries, Grey figured they must have wounded men on the wagons up front. But there was bugger all they could do about that right now. They were hardly about to stop and administer first aid with the Iraqis hot on their tail. Each bloke in the Squadron carried a couple of emergency dressings in his webbing pouches, and it would be up to the injured man to patch up his own wounds as best he could, at least until they'd shaken off the enemy.

Straining his eyes to scan the dark terrain to their rear, Grey figured he'd caught the silhouette of a main battle tank. It was a frightening vision – a massive, squat black form churning ahead, the long finger of the main cannon swinging from side to side as it sought targets. All around them was open, trackless desert, so there were no Iraqi farmsteads or villages for the enemy forces to worry about hitting. It was a shooting gallery – a free fire zone – with M Squadron bang out in the midst of it.

Grey felt his shoulders tense in anticipation of the crump of a heavy gun firing at their backs, and the scream of an incoming shell, as the tank lobbed a round into the rear of their wagon turning them into a mush of shredded Pinkie mixed with pulverized flesh and gore. Instead, there was a squelch of static on the radio and the OC's voice came up on the radio.

'All call-signs, Zero. We have at least three main battle tanks to our rear. They've got to be using IR thermal imaging kit so as to hit us with their 12.7 mm. Gunner's taking us into a new LUP, so be ready for a sharp turn to the north and a new line of march.'

The OC sounded remarkably calm. Grey couldn't imagine why. The Squadron had just escaped getting trapped and smashed, and by the skin of its teeth. They now had the hunter force from hell on their tail. Worse still, there was nothing they could do against the Iraqi tanks. Unless they could hide themselves very bloody effectively and very bloody quickly, the tanks would find them and tear them to pieces.

The vehicles had made a good three kilometres from their static position when the lead element turned sharp left and started to veer northwards. Just off their southeasterly line of march Gunner had spotted a narrow wadi-like depression, and that was what he was making for.

By making this turn at right-angles to their present line of march, the Squadron was 'breaking track' – making a ninety-degree turn to get them out of the enemy's line of fire. The aim now was to achieve a major burst of speed, and to let the dark night swallow them. By the time they made it into the wadi, they'd have gone to earth below ground and out of sight.

It was a fine move by Gunner to have brought them thus far, and if they could get into that wadi unseen they might just lose their pursuers. But if they went to ground only to have a force of main battle tanks roar over the wadi's edge and swamp them, then they were pretty much done for. After all, that was exactly what the enemy had tried to do when ambushing them at their first LUP.

Within seconds of making that ninety-degree turn, Gunner

must have opened his throttle to the max. Behind him the rest of quad force did likewise, and the lead elements of the Squadron threw caution to the wind as they got their wagons flying across the landscape. The entire Squadron was hammering across the desert towards the wadi, Grey's wagon practically shaking itself to pieces as it raced along in the rear.

From his position in the Pinkie's front Grey found the noise deafening. It was the tortured sound of an overloaded and half-shot-up Land Rover being thrashed across the hard, rocky terrain. There was the smashing together of heavy ammo tins in the rear, the sharp crump of the suspension bottoming out as the wagon hit rough ground, the worrying shriek of bodywork that was about to tear itself apart, not to mention the thud-like punch to the stomach as the sump-guard hit a large rock below.

By the time they reached the entrance to the wadi, the wagons were bunched up far closer than was optimal. In classic desert mobility ops the squadron OC would have sent the quads forward to recce the wadi before the wagons entered, and they wouldn't follow right on each other's heels. But there was no time for that now. Right now, the priority was to get the entire force below ground and well hidden before the enemy spotted them.

As the first wagons rumbled down the steep and rocky slope that led into the dry lake bed, Grey felt Moth ease off the gas a little. He'd learned his vehicle mobility craft well, and he was putting a fraction more space between him and the wagon in front as they prepared to enter the depression.

Up ahead, Grey saw Six Troop's foremost wagon swing into the entranceway and slide out of view. He felt a massive sense of relief as those wagons disappeared from sight. One thing was for sure: the lake bed was deep enough to hide the Squadron's Pinkies.

Maybe their luck had turned. Maybe they were starting to win this one, after all.

But as Moth swung the wagon round and eased its nose into the steep-sided entry point, Grey spotted Gunner's quad coming haring back up the incline. The quad was caked in a thick layer of what looked like black dust, and Gunner was yelling and gesticulating wildly for the wagons of Six Troop to stop and do an about-turn.

Moth already had the Pinkie heading down the narrow V-shaped incline. There was nothing he could do to stop. There was no turning room, and the slope was too steep and friable to reverse the heavy wagon out of there. They had no option but to plough onwards and run into whatever trouble might await.

Their wagon hit the bottom of the slope, and Grey could see that it opened out into a flat, circular lake bed some three hundred metres across. At first glance it seemed to be an ideal LUP. Steep walls a good ten feet in height enclosed an expanse of flat, open terrain that was more than large enough to hold all the vehicles. As a bonus, at the far end there was what looked like a second exit point.

But as he looked again, Grey noticed that strung out across the terrain to their front were the vehicles of the Squadron. They were still pretty much in a linear formation, and bunched up close together after the speed-dash across the desert. But very few, if any, of them were moving. As he fixed on the nearest wagon, trying to make out the detail in the darkness, he knew that something was badly amiss: it was sitting far too low on the floor of the lake bed.

An instant later, figures began bailing out of the vehicle. Grey realized that he could barely even see its wheels. Somehow, the wagon had sunk up to its axles in the lake bed, and was hopelessly bogged. The line of Pinkies to the front seemed similarly mired. Only the odd one was still moving, its wheels churning desperately and its engine howling like a banshee, as it tried to haul itself and its occupants out of whatever shit they had stumbled into.

'FUCKING SLAM HER INTO LOW RATIO!' Grey screamed at Moth. 'TURN THE BITCH AROUND AND DON'T STOP UNTIL WE'RE OUT OF HERE!'

The vehicle was supposed to be stationary to change ratios, but right here and right now Moth went to crash it through from high to low without stopping.

For an instant the wagon felt as if it had hit a brick wall as the cogs ground and snarled against one another. And then the gears meshed in low, and the tyres began churning through the mud and the dust with the engine emitting a tortured, high-pitched scream.

'FUCKING GENTLY DOES IT!' Grey yelled. 'GENTLY AS SHE GOES!'

It's a basic rule of off-road driving that whenever you turn a vehicle, you lose traction. Grey could see that several of the Pinkies ahead of them had tried to turn aside from the line of march, but they were too far into the mire and had turned too sharply to make it back to solid ground.

Because they'd had that warning from Gunner, and they'd seen the plight of the wagons to their front, they'd started to reverse course that much earlier. They were barely thirty yards into the wadi by now, but if Moth turned too violently, the wagon would plough in deep, and die.

To the left and right of him Grey could see the other vehicles of Six Troop likewise doing a series of desperate about-turns. Moth was spooling the steering wheel through his fingers as the Pinkie chewed its way through the hard crust of sun-baked mud. The tyres were spinning wildly and throwing out a solid wave of gunk to their rear, which went splattering over the wagons directly behind them.

It was the weirdest of sensations, as the wagon floated through whatever gloopy crap was under the wheels. She was moving no faster than the speed of a slow-going fishing boat, and there was something of a sickening all-at-sea-like feel about the gliding, sliding progress she was making. Most worrying of all, with every second the wagon's forward momentum seemed to keep slowing.

The smell had hit Grey's nostrils almost instantly – that of an evil-smelling, stagnant, gooey swamp. As sod's law would have it, M Squadron had chosen to go to ground in one of the few dry lake beds in northern Iraq that was actually a quagmire right now. The hard, crusty surface hid below it a slough of dark, fetid mud, and if the Iraqis had wanted to set a better trap for M Squadron, Grey couldn't think of one.

How many similar features had the Squadron driven through or holed up in over the past few days? Dozens, that was for sure, and not one of them had been anything other than dry as a bone and solid-bottomed. It had been exactly the right thing to do – to break the line of march, as the OC had decided. And Gunner had led them into exactly the right kind of feature in which to hide – for who was to know it was a treacherous swamp?

The Squadron was in a whole world of shit right now. As far as Grey was concerned, this was seriously bad juju. Thirty seconds earlier he'd believed that by good luck and foresight they'd started to win this one and had shaken off the enemy. Now, in an instant, everything had changed for the sixty men of M Squadron. From what he could see, they had pretty much every wagon in front of their Troop's bogged in, and even Six Troop's foremost wagons were unlikely to make it out of there.

Deprived of their mobility and their firepower, and with a bunch of main battle tanks, plus truck-mounted infantry and highly-mobile Fedayeen after them, what the hell were they supposed to do?

Every second was precious, and it was critical that they save at least a few of the wagons. If they did that, maybe they could cram the rest of the blokes aboard the surviving vehicles. They'd be murderously overloaded, and the passengers would block the machine-gun's lines of fire, so they'd be largely defenceless. But at least they'd not be on the run on foot – for there was no way they could evade and escape from the force that was coming after them if they had to try to leg it.

Wheels spinning crazily, Moth executed a gradual arc with the Pinkie and somehow kept her moving. As the entry point drew closer and closer, Grey urged the wagon onwards: *Come on, you bastard, come on.*

But still their progress kept slowing, and he was praying that their wagon wasn't going to sink up to its guts in the swamp.

# CHAPTER SEVENTEEN

Grey risked a momentary glance to their rear. Right behind their wagon another was executing the same kind of manoeuvre as they were. It, plus the blokes riding in it, were caked in a thick layer of stinking shit thrown up by the leading wagon's tyres, making them all but unrecognizable. He figured their vehicle stood about as much chance of making it out of here as he did.

Beyond that a third wagon was still on the move. Grey reckoned it was the unmistakable figure of Scruff in the vehicle commander's seat. But the fourth of Six Troop's wagons was clearly a gonner, for already it was up to the tops of its wheels in the shit, and the rest of the Squadron's transport-cum-firepower seemed to be well and truly finished.

Then he spotted movement to the far end of the lake bed. Two wagons were trying to claw their way up the eastern side of the wadi. From the long antennae Grey could tell that they had to be the command wagons – so it looked as if both vehicles from the HQ Troop were also going to make it out of there.

The HQ Pinkies were something like half a tonne lighter than the rest, for they weren't loaded down with machine-guns and ammo. It would make sense for them to have fought their way through the quagmire, as they had a far greater chance of floating across its treacherous surface. It looked as if the OC Troop's wagons at least might survive, complete with all their communications systems.

Moth's skill with the wagon was breathtaking, as he nursed it through the impossible terrain. For an instant the front wheels ceased their wild spinning, as the tyres found a momentary grip. With solid ground beneath them again, those wheels began to commandeer the lion's share of the engine's power and transfer it into traction and forward motion.

Within seconds they had dragged the wagon ahead, and as the rear wheels also found their grip it hauled itself onto firm ground. It was then a forty-metre scramble back the way they had come, before finally they made the lip of the wadi and the high ground. The only other vehicle there was Gunner's quad, and they were all now equally covered in the thick, black stinking mud.

'Nice choice for a bloody LUP!' Grey yelled.

Gunner stared at him in stunned silence. Grey regretted having made the comment almost instantly, for the quad commander was clearly beating himself up over having led the Squadron into that fateful wadi.

Grey had little idea how Gunner had managed to turn his quad around and get himself out of there, especially as he had been first into the wadi. But he was known for being an ace quad driver, in addition to which the quads boasted a fantastic tyre-surface-to-weight ratio, one far better than the Pinkies'.

The quad was also a more instinctive off-road vehicle. Sitting astride the machine, the driver was closer to and more intimately in touch with the terrain. With a 350cc motor and permanent four-wheel drive, it had the power and the grip to haul itself through the most challenging ground. Still, it was remarkable that Gunner had extricated himself from the gluey mess of that lake bed, and especially since he'd doubled back to the entry point in an effort to warn the rest of the Squadron.

Yet right now the sum of M Squadron's vehicles that had definitely made it out of the wadi was a lone Pinkie plus a quad. With the number of wagons they were losing here, the decision to take the turn into that lakebed was doubtless going to cost them dear.

There was a screaming of diesel engines from behind, and one after the other two further wagons hauled themselves up the incline and onto the high ground. They were so caked in crap as to be almost unrecognizable as Land Rovers, and without their sand goggles Grey figured the drivers would have been blinded by the amount of shit thrown up in their faces. Yet at least they'd done the seemingly impossible and made it out of there.

One of the wagons was that of Scruff's. The other belonged to Edward 'Ed' Smith, the Captain in overall command of Six Troop. An officer pretty much fresh out of the factory, Ed was still seen as very much one of the lads. He was combat-inexperienced, but at the same time he was a down-to-earth bloke with none of the public school attitude that so often rubbed the men up the wrong way.

For a long moment those who'd made it out of the wadi stared at the exit point, willing further vehicles to appear. And then it struck them that there was no more screaming of strained diesel engines coming from that lake bed. It had fallen silent down there, and it didn't look as if any other wagons were going to make it through.

But right now there was no time to linger on the fate that had befallen those vehicles. A sudden fiery burst of 12.7mm went slamming into the wadi rim, just a few dozen yards to the west of Gunner's quad. More rounds followed, as the enemy gunners followed the tracer of that first burst, groping towards their target.

Grey searched the horizon to the west, and even with the naked eye the enemy hunter force was well-visible. There was a line of headlights, like pinpricks in the darkness, some three kilometres distant and bearing down on them. Some of those lights were closer to the ground, so he figured they would be the Fedayeen in their Toyota pick-ups. But there were a handful set twice as high, and Grey could just imagine those big Kraz 225 trucks thundering onwards.

Worst of all, here and there a cone of illumination could be seen swinging backwards and forwards across the terrain. It could only be the turret-mounted searchlight of an Asad Babil – a 'Lion of Babylon' – and seeing those beams of light groping this way and that was like an invitation to the very pits of hell.

Just to torture himself some more, Grey ran the capabilities of the Asad Babil through his mind. It weighed in at a mighty 41.5 tonnes, more than enough to crush a Pinkie under its tracks. It boasted a 125mm main gun mounted in a turret encased in twelve inches of armour, plus a 12.7mm Dushka and a GPMG-type machine-gun mounted on pivots in the armoured beast's hull.

'Whatever you do, don't return fire!' Grey yelled at the other wagons.

If they opened up on the enemy they'd signal their exact whereabouts, and they still had dozens of blokes and their vehicles trapped down below.

It was now that voices started coming up on the radios, as teams reported in that they were up to their axles in the mud and abandoning their wagons. But the remarkable thing was that no one seemed to be losing their cool down there. Somehow, the men of M Squadron appeared to be holding their nerve, and holding it together despite the fact that they were becoming ever more hopelessly trapped.

Those mired in the swamp were pretty much bumper to bumper, so they were able to speak across the vehicles. They must have got some kind of communal heads-up amongst themselves, and some very tough decisions must have been made. It was clear to the men on the lip of the wadi that the wagons would have to be blown, but it was another thing entirely to make the call.

'Right, that's it, time to blow the vehicles,' a voice came up on the radio. 'Rip out all the sensitive kit you can carry, then prep your charges.'

The speaker sounded strangely calm, as if he was giving some kind of an order during an exercise on Salisbury Plain. In truth, the situation M Squadron now found itself in was totally unprecedented. It was a total fluke, the worst kind of bad juju that could ever have befallen an elite force many hundreds of kilometres behind enemy lines.

During their Kenya exercises they'd rehearsed their 'actions-on' – the measures to be taken for each forseeable eventuality – including losing a vehicle, or having a vehicle-load of wounded. With the seats on every wagon occupied, there was zero fat in the Squadron system, and the Pinkies weren't designed to carry more than three men. The wagons of the HQ Troop had each been loaded with a stretcher, and if they did take several wounded they'd have to put the injured men on those, and lash them to the Pinkies.

But now the decision had been made to blow any number of

vehicles. That being the case, it was crucial to remove as much of the top-secret and sensitive kit as possible. Each Pinkie was fitted with specially shaped explosive charge designed to provide a larger explosive surface than a conventional saucer-shaped mine, so there was a greater chance of a tank hitting it. It was equally useful as a makeshift demolition charge when laid crossways in a Pinkie, just to the rear of the front seats.

The charges in the Pinkies were fitted with an improvised fuse system, so they could be triggered manually. But the fuse lasted for only ninety seconds, so crucially all the mines would need to be triggered at the same time. Otherwise, you'd have vehicles blowing at different moments, and blokes were bound to get caught in the blast.

In the precious few moments left before triggering the charges, the men were in a whirlwind of fevered activity trying to decide what the hell to strip from the wagons.

But on the lip of the wadi it had all gone very quiet. Apart from the odd, probing burst of incoming fire, the overriding sound was the cries of shouted instructions from below, plus the noise of a bits of kit being torn out of the vehicles.

To the west of them they could hear the faint but throaty growl of engines moving through the night. The enemy were clearly working their way through the smoke screen left by the Squadron, and tracing the tracks they had left across the desert. Even if they missed the ninety-degree turn made by the wagons, one sweep with their thermal imaging kit and they'd detect the hot engines of the three Pinkies perched on the rim of the lake bed.

Grey sensed it was only a matter of moments before they got seriously whacked. He glanced around at their position. They were perched atop a mound of rock that gave them a slight vantage point. It was the only position from which they could be seen from the lake bed, so that those abandoning their vehicles would know which way to come.

Grey was torn between trying to keep a watch for blokes emerging from the wadi, and scanning the darkness to the west for the enemy, plus he was also trying to get a glimpse of where the HQ Troop's wagons might have got to. It was hard to see how things could get any worse, but it sure as hell wouldn't help if the Squadron got split up and Grey and those with him got cut off from the OC.

One thing was clear: only the wagons on the lip of that lake bed could provide covering fire for those bugging out on foot, if and when the enemy came thundering out of the void of the night. Without some kind of force to defend them, those on foot would be mown down like so much summer hay, as they staggered out of the quagmire laden down with gear.

Grey swept the darkness with his weapon, as he prepared to defend the majority of the Squadron, who were dismounted and bereft of their heavy machine-guns. It was clear to all that their position offered zero cover and that they had negligible firepower compared to what was coming. Yet somehow, they had to hold this ground.

'We're in a totally shit position,' he grunted, 'but the lads below are in a shittier one. Prepare to fucking mallet any enemy that get near us.'

In response, he heard a sharp clack-clack as the Dude double-checked that he had a round chambered in the .50-cal. As for Moth, he reached forward and unhooked his assault rifle cum grenade launcher from its holster, and punched in a 40mm grenade round. Grey figured it was a fair one. Desperate situations called for desperate measures.

A voice drifted across to them from one of the other wagons. 'They've got onto us every bloody time.' It was Scruff. 'Sooner or later they'll do the same here. They'll see us through the smoke.'

'Yep,' Grey replied. 'I reckon we'll get opened up on, any second now—'

'You heard the fucking score on the air power?'

'Nope. Must have missed it in all the carnage.'

'There is none. At least not right now. Fucking what wouldn't you give for a pair of A10s?'

'The sky's the fucking limit, mate.'

The A10 Warthog is an American ground-attack aircraft, and a superlative tank-busting warplane. Its nose-mounted, seven-barrel Gatling-type cannon would make short work of even an Iraqi Asad Babil, so more the pity there was no air power available.

Waiting to get torn to pieces like this was the worst of all feelings. For a second, Grey considered how he would go about finishing off the Squadron, were he that force of Iraqis. They'd know by now that smashing in the 12.7mm rounds from two thousand yards hadn't quite done the job. They were also sure to know that the Squadron was equipped with nothing that could kill heavy armour.

Grey had to assume that the Iraqi military had been briefed on NATO weaponry, just as the Squadron had been briefed on available Iraqi firepower. By now they must have worked out that the Squadron had no Milan or equivalent weaponry, and that they weren't about to bring in any air power.

In the Iraqis' place, Grey would opt to sneak up on the British force. He'd get the three wagons on the rocky knoll pinned in his gun sights, and mallet them from a couple of hundred yards away.

He'd opt to blow them apart and tear the wagons to pieces, using either the tank's Dushka or its main cannon. At that kind of range, Grey and his fellows wouldn't even see the bullets coming. The only positive for the beleaguered operators was that they'd be dead before they knew it.

A voice came up on the radios: 'All call-signs, confirm with me when ready to blow charges.'

With every passing second, Grey was growing more and more anxious and edgy. He could sense the deadly threat out there in the dark, and that it was hunting for them remorselessly. He leaned across to Moth, and gestured at his GPMG.

'I'm going to check on the others – your weapon, mate.'

He slipped from the wagon and jogged down the incline leading into the lake bed. A well-worn track snaked into the depression, so at some time of the year it had to be passable. It was sod's law that the Squadron had chosen to use it just when it happened to be a treacherous swamp. He reached the bed of the wadi, and the first thing he saw was the arse-end of the rearmost wagon, with blokes clustered around it.

Ahead of it lay a column of vehicles similarly up to their doors in the mud. He kept flipping his NVG up and down, so he could check on the men's whereabouts, while maintaining his natural night vision. He counted eight wagons in all, stretching across the lake bed.

At the far end he figured he could see a lone Pinkie perched on the wadi's rim, with a couple of quads near by. It wasn't a command vehicle, so presumably one wagon from Four or Five Troop had made it through the swamp. By his reckoning that was all of their Land Rovers accounted for. They'd lost eight bogged in; three were on the lip of the wadi behind him; two from HQ

Troop had gone east; and one had got out of the northern exit point with a few quads for company.

Moving south across the wadi towards him were the first of the figures on foot – those that were abandoning their vehicles, in preparation to blow them. Grey counted a dozen figures heading his way. In the eerie light of the NVG it was a ghostly scene, as the blokes struggled their way through. In spite of the urgency of the situation, they seemed to be moving in painfully slow motion, laden down with gear as they were and wading through the thick and cloying mud.

Grey raised an arm and yelled at them to make for the wagons above, then turned and ran up the incline. As he powered up the steep slope his mind was racing. The Squadron had lost almost two-thirds of their wagons and their firepower, and maybe a similar number of quads. The situation was pretty close to terminal. In fact, he couldn't really see how it could get a great deal worse.

'We've got eight wagons bogged in, and blokes coming our way on foot!' he yelled, once he was back with the vehicles. 'Make room for a shedload of passengers.'

The eight wagons bogged in would equate to twenty-four men, and with all the will in the world there was no way they could load that many onto the waiting Pinkies. Hopefully, some would have gone north to join the small force of vehicles gathered there.

In spite of the blokes' apparent calm, what was unfolding here was their worst ever nightmare. They'd got the entire Squadron minus a handful of wagons and quads mired in an Iraqi swamp, and about to be blown to smithereens. And that meant they'd got sixty elite operators about to go on the run deep behind enemy lines, without the vehicles to carry them. They could easily lose half the Squadron or more here – injured, dead or captured.

Grey heard a yell over the radios: 'Fire in the hole! Fire in the hole!'

It was time for the last blokes to get the hell off the vehicles, for they were about to blow. To trigger the fuses you had to unwrap the gaffer tape protecting them, push the plunger, then make a run for it. The plunger worked on a ninety-second fuse which set off a length of detonation cord, and that in turn would punch into the charge with enough force to trigger it.

Grey had seen such charges in action. Designed to take out a main battle tank, they had the power to visibly lift a T-72 off the deck when detonated beneath it. They'd totally shred the soft-skinned Pinkies, thus denying the enemy the vehicles as well as any sensitive equipment that might remain on them.

Grey gave the word to Moth to move the wagon a good few feet off the rocky knoll. Up there, they'd be exposed to any blast thrown off by the charges, plus the ammo carried by the wagons would cook off in the heat of the explosions. They dropped the three Land Rovers down to where the high ground shielded them from the coming explosions but where the blokes bugging out should still find them.

The first ghostly figure appeared, stumbling up the incline. The apparition was made all the more eerie because he was caked from head to toe in the black, gooey shit. Laden down with weapons and sensitive gear from his wagon, he was moving horribly slowly. Others emerged, strung out in a ragged line behind him.

'I wish they'd get a fucking move on,' Grey remarked to Moth, as he scanned the darkness with his weapon.

He couldn't believe the enemy hadn't hit them yet, and at any second he was expecting a 125mm tank shell to come howling down his throat.

The lead figure flung himself onto the rear of Grey's vehicle. Others clambered aboard wherever they could, clinging on to the .50-cal and surrounding the Dude in his gun turret. They were exhausted from having to fight their way through the swamp, and they'd come out carrying only their personal weapons and whatever sensitive kit they could manage.

Scruff's and Ed's wagons each got loaded up with a similar number of men, who perched on the wagons' sides and clung to the heavy weapons for support. Gunner got the commander of Four Troop perched on the rack of his quad, which was designed as a one-rider vehicle. At that stage they were about as overloaded as it was possible to get.

One of the last blokes to clamber aboard a vehicle was Angus, the Scottish guy who was new into the Squadron. A short while before, back in the LUP, he'd been moaning on about how he'd hoped to be 'flat-packing ragheads'. Two hours later he'd been forced to abandon his bogged-in wagon and beg a lift on someone else's vehicle, and all so they could go on the run from the hunter force that was right on their tail.

It struck Grey as the ultimate irony: *Beware of what you wish for indeed.*

Just as the four vehicles were about to pull out, a lone individual came stumbling up the incline. It was Raggy.

'FUCKING MOVE IT!' Grey yelled.

It seemed to take for ever for the last man to make it to the wagons. He glanced around for a second, before throwing himself across Grey's bonnet, which was about the only space left available. As was typical of Raggy, he was the last to reach them, yet he seemed totally unflustered. As he wrapped his arms around the M72 LAW (light anti-tank weapon) strapped to the wagon's bonnet, to hold on, he let out this wild laugh.

'Better late than never, mate,' Grey grunted.

'Fucking hell, mate, this is shit! Ninety-second fuses on the wagons.'

'Best we get the fuck out of here. But fucked if I can use the Gimpy with you there.'

Grey didn't know for sure how many blokes were packed onto each of the Pinkies. But one thing was certain: with the number they had clinging to their vehicle, it had rendered the machine-guns totally unusable. Grey's arc of fire was blocked by Raggy, and the Dude's .50-cal was packed around with blokes on all sides.

Those who'd joined Grey's wagon were passengers in more ways than one. Grey was his vehicle's commander, and Moth and Dude were his driver and gunner. That was the basic operational unit, and they ran their own wagon. Those who'd clambered aboard were going where Grey and his team went, and they'd have little say in the matter. It would have been the same had Grey and his lot clambered aboard *their* wagon.

Grey heard a series of sharp cracks from below, as the .22 rounds went off – part of the charges' final trigger system.

There were only seconds now, and those eight wagons down in the wadi were set to blow sky high.

# CHAPTER EIGHTEEN

Grey pointed due east. 'Only one way to go,' he remarked to Moth, ' – away from the enemy's line of march.'

Moth nodded, and eased the wagon into forward motion. He edged it further into the line of enemy sight, so he could do a ponderous turn. The Land Rover was painfully overloaded, and the steering felt horribly spongy and unresponsive due to all the extra weight on the back. He got the wheels pointing east and nursed the Pinkie into gear.

But as they were moving off a terrible thought struck Grey. What if they'd left a man behind? They'd just presumed that the rest of the lads from the bogged Pinkies had headed north and linked up with the vehicles there. But what if they were still trying to fight their way out of the quagmire? What if they were coming south, to link up with their wagons?

*What if they were about to leave some of their own behind?*

He grabbed Moth's arm. 'Hold it!' He eyed Raggy, sprawled across the wagon's front: 'Mate, are you the last?'

'Yeah, I'm the last man,' Raggy confirmed. 'Let's fucking go.'

Grey spoke into his radio, so all could hear. 'Ed, Raggy says he's the last man out.'

'I reckon that's everyone,' Ed replied. 'Grey, you lead off. Let's fuck off while we still can.'

As far as Grey could tell, they had a mixed bag of blokes from Four, Five and Six Troops on the wagons. They also had one of Four Troop's commanders perched on the rear of Gunner's quad, and an officer from Five Troop in the rear of one of the Pinkies. But as the three wagons here were Six Troop vehicles, by rights that made Captain Ed Smith the officer in command of this force.

As they pulled away from the lake bed, Grey breathed the longest sigh of relief ever. It was pure ecstasy to be on the move again and getting away from the wadi of death, not to mention the threat of heavy tank fire. If the Squadron's tracks didn't lead the enemy to that lake bed, the coming explosions certainly would. They'd light up the Iraqi desert like Blackpool Illuminations on LSD.

The three wagons swung eastwards and Gunner's quad moved into the lead, so he could scout the way ahead. As they gathered speed Grey glanced at Moth. He could see the same kind of exhilaration in the young operator's eyes as he himself was feeling. It was pure madness, really. The fact they were on the move didn't change their predicament one jot. In reality, it was still the mother of all cluster-fucks.

With Raggy clinging to the bonnet, Moth could barely see to drive, and Grey couldn't use his weapon. To their rear they had half a dozen unexpected passengers, and the wagon was now overweight by an extra six hundred kilos. The springs were groaning under the load.

In truth, this was a total game-changer.

None of the wagons was able to fight effectively any more; they could barely move across the terrain, or at any pace much above a slow crawl; and right now they were cut off from the rest of the Squadron, including the OC. In short, they couldn't hope to do much more than find somewhere to hide, and with a bit of luck get airlifted out of there.

Every bloke present knew the gravity of their predicament, and nothing much needed to be said about any of this right now. The inconceivable had happened – something that they'd never rehearsed, trained for, game-planned, let alone imagined. But no one was about to drag it over the coals. They'd speak if they had something to say. Otherwise, they'd shut the fuck up and try to keep a constant watch for the enemy.

As the unwieldy convoy nosed eastwards, Raggy kept trying to shift around so as to give Moth a better line of sight out front.

'Can you see all right, mate?' he asked.

'Yeah, just about,' Moth replied.

Raggy shifted again. 'Is it better if I lie this way? Can you see better like that?'

'Stop fucking wriggling, or you'll roll off,' Grey told him. 'Just keep fucking still.'

If the situation hadn't been so utterly desperate, they'd all have seen the funny side of things right now. But as it was, no one was so much as cracking a smile as Raggy squirmed around on the Pinkie's bonnet.

Bang on cue there was a huge blast from their rear, a blinding white flash lighting up the entire length of the lake bed. It made the distinctive sharp crack of a steel-on-steel explosion – the shrapnel of the charge tearing into the wagon's chassis. If it had been a tank shell landing in the wadi, it would have made the duller thump of shrapnel exploding in amongst soft sand and mud.

An instant later the night sky dissolved into a raging sea of fire, as series of further explosions punched a huge fist of smoke and flame high into the air. The blasts were followed by a massive firework display that seemed to light up the entire night sky, as the ammo on the vehicles started to kick off a fiery orange.

As the first of the bogged-in Pinkies went up, the three wagons on the move were no more than a hundred yards away. A crazed barrage of rounds went tearing past overhead, as boxes of .50-cal and 7.62mm ammo fired off in the blistering heat. Instinctively the blokes on the wagons ducked their heads, as the angry buzz of bullets cut through the air all around them.

Grey jerked a thumb in the direction of the blown-up vehicles. 'That's it,' he yelled at Moth and Raggy. 'They sure as hell fucking know where we are now.'

For several long seconds the exploding ammo cooked off a blinding firestorm. With the enemy moving in from the west, east was the only way to run now. If they'd headed in any other direction, their wagons would have been silhouetted by the conflagration in the lake bed and clearly visible. It was a stroke of luck that that fiery hellhole lay between them and the advancing threat.

It struck Grey that by blowing the wagons, they might also have brought themselves a little time. With all the ammo cooking off, it would look as if a massive firefight had erupted in the wadi. The enemy had to be wondering what the hell the force they were hunting was up to now. They'd be drawn to that violent conflagration, but presumably they'd approach it with some degree of caution, especially as further wagons proceeded to explode.

Grey forced his mind and his senses back to the terrain to their front and the route they needed to go. Automatically, he went to grip his GPMG and swing it onto his eye-line. It was second nature to be on his weapon whenever the wagons were on the move, and scanning his arcs. But overloaded as they were, the Gimpy was unusable. He felt as if he'd had both his hands cut off at the elbows, he was that useless right now.

But if he could spot the enemy early, at least he could get Moth to try to steer a path to evade them. Ahead was an open and gently undulating expanse of terrain. It was shitty ground on which to try to lose a highly mobile enemy force, but at least there was one blessing: the night sky above them remained sullen, overcast and dark. There was little if any ambient light, and if the enemy were equipped with night-vision goggles they'd have precious little chance of using them.

He was acutely aware that they were balanced on a knife-edge now. If they lost one more vehicle, there simply wasn't the room to load any more on board. If another went down, some of the blokes at least would be forced to go on the run on foot. At which point, what would the others do? After all, they were hardly likely to abandon their fellow operators.

If they did go down to two wagons, he guessed they'd have no option but to bin every last piece of kit they carried. Ammo, weaponry, food, water and fuel – all would have to be dumped, in an effort to somehow cram the extra blokes aboard. It didn't bear thinking about. He tried to blank such thoughts from his mind and concentrate on the one overriding priority right now: survival.

They were no more than a couple of hundred yards away from the wadi of death when there was a series of further massive explosions in quick succession, as more of the abandoned Pinkies blew. The entire night sky behind them was transformed into a curtain of raging fire, as the ammo went off and a barrage of rounds hammered high into the heavens.

Grey counted four detonations, which meant that there were two vehicles still to blow. It was a good minute or more after those last explosions when he began to feel seriously worried. All the charges would have been fitted with ninety-second fuses, and he'd started to suspect that one or two of the detonators might be duds. If they were, the charge would fail to blow, and unless the wagon was caught in a neighbouring vehicle's blast it would be left undamaged.

Grey stole a quick glance behind him. Their vehicle was cresting a small ridge, which provided a vantage point from which he could see along the whole of the wadi. The fierce white light of the explosions had lit up its entire length. It was a raging inferno, with twisted, blown-up hulks burning fiercely.

He searched for anyone they might have inadvertently left behind. He couldn't see anyone moving down there. He was pretty certain there was no one they'd forgotten, which meant that no one had been caught in the shrapnel as the wagons blew, or worse still, abandoned to the mercy of the enemy. But with the Squadron scattered, he couldn't know for sure.

Yet the far end of the wadi of death he figured he could just make out the forms of one or two wagons that seemed untouched by the flames. And if that was the case, some hugely sensitive kit might be about to fall into enemy hands, not to mention the Pinkies themselves.

More worrying still, what had happened to the blokes who'd been operating those vehicles? Had they failed to trigger the charges because the enemy had somehow overrun them? The nightmare scenario right now was a couple of teams being taken alive.

The Iraqis would torture them to secure intelligence on the

nature of the mission, parade them before the world's media to prove how the Coalition was far from invincible, and by doing so they'd torture the blokes' families in turn.

It would be a massive propaganda victory for the enemy, not to mention a disaster for British and allied forces operating here. And all before the ground war proper had really even started.

Unbeknown to the scattered forces of M Squadron, that very night British and American troops would begin their push across the border from Kuwait into southern Iraq. At any moment now the ground offensive would begin, the opening sortie of which would be an air-mobile assault by British Royal Marines to take the Al Faw peninsula, the southernmost territory of Iraq.

But right now, the course of the wider war was an irrelevancy to the men of M Squadron. Right now, their every fibre was focused on the desperate struggle to escape from and evade an enemy who were faster, more mobile, better equipped, better armed and far more numerous than the scattered forces of M Squadron.

The three wagons were crawling away from the wadi, making no more than fifteen kilometres an hour, when Grey sensed a pop in the sky high above them. Suddenly, the landscape all around was lit up by a brilliant white light. He glanced skywards, and high above him he could see a blinding globule of fire floating gently to earth, like a giant candle flame.

He recognized it instantly as an illume round – a flare suspended beneath a parachute. His first thought was: *Fucking hell, they're managing to get illume rounds above us while moving through the desert and hunting us down.* His second thought was: *What the hell kind of weapon is managing to put up those illumes?*

Judging by the height at which they were bursting and the size of the flares, Grey reckoned that these were monster illume rounds

– 81mm minimum, perhaps larger. They'd light an area two to three kilometres across, so the wagons would be just within the enemy's visual range. He had to hope and pray the bastards didn't spot them.

It couldn't be the Fedayeen SUVs or the Iraqi Army trucks firing those flare rounds, because neither carried a weapon that could handle that calibre of ordnance. He looked west, and in the intense white light he could see scores of vehicles moving in line abreast, combing the desert terrain.

There were dozens of white Fedayeen SUVs, and in the centre of that force were the hulking forms of half a dozen Kraz 225s. The Iraqi Army was clearly working hand in hand with the Fedayeen, using their light and mobile SUVs like a pack of dogs to hunt their prey.

He caught the flare of a muzzle firing further to the west, and a stab of flame belched skywards. In the light of the muzzle flash he thought he'd seen the silhouette of enemy armour. An instant later a second flare round burst high above. In its harsh glare Grey was suddenly very certain: to the rear of the Fedayeen those cursed T-72s were churning their way forward, and it was the tanks that were putting up the illume rounds.

Pinned under that burning white light, Grey felt horribly exposed. He was also starting to feel punch-drunk. How the hell had the enemy been so quick off the mark?

They'd legged it from their first LUP just in the nick of time, but the Iraqis had scanned the surrounding terrain with their thermal imaging kit and found them. Then the Squadron had broken track by executing a ninety-degree turn, and ended up in the wadi of death and been forced to blow the vehicles.

They'd managed to salvage a handful of wagons and bug out of there, but the enemy had clearly checked out the wadi of death pretty quickly. They'd have debussed a bunch of their infantry, and just as soon as they'd realized there were a bunch of wagons bogged in and blown, they'd scanned the surroundings with their thermal imaging kit. By sheer luck, Grey and his fellow vehicles were a good distance beyond the range of such kit, but at that stage the enemy had decided to put up flares, to light up the wider terrain and nail them.

It was now that Gunner started to really earn his pay on the quad. He kept beetling backwards and forwards, recce-ing a route that would hide them from the enemy, then returning to check on the wagons. It was great to have the quad still with them. It was their only remaining means of fast and agile mobility, and it was perfect for checking out the ground ahead and to the flanks for the enemy.

A kilometre further on Gunner pulled his quad to a halt, the rest of the vehicles following suit. They'd taken no incoming fire, so for now at least they had to assume the enemy hadn't seen them. They'd left behind the cone of light thrown off by the illume rounds, and edged into the night's welcome embrace, which meant they could afford a few seconds to deal with the overriding priority right now – which was doing an accurate head count.

The wagons drew in close so they could speak to each other without dismounting. Normally, doing a head count would be a simple task of asking the Troop leaders to check that all their men were present. But right now that didn't cut it, because the Troops had been split left, right and centre.

Ed, Scruff and Grey got the names and call-signs of all the blokes on their vehicles, Ed scribbling a list of them in his note-book. The results confirmed how the Squadron had been scattered.

There were a total of twenty-six blokes with the three Pinkies, plus the two on the quad. With the Squadron numbering some sixty blokes, that meant there was an equal number out there somewhere unaccounted for.

They'd got most of those from Five Troop and half from Four Troop clinging onto their wagons. They'd lost one of the Six Troop Land Rovers plus every one of their quads. Grey had no idea where the fourth man of his team, Mucker, had got to, or even if his quad had made it out of the wadi. Instead, they had Gunner from Four Troop with them, driving their only quad.

No one had much of an idea where the OC might have got to, or even whether his Troop was mobile. There had been no comms from the HQ Troop, and the OC hadn't responded to Ed's repeated radio calls, which had to mean that wherever the HQ Troop might be right now they were out of range of the radios.

But their overriding concerns were for the third group, which had been perched on the northern rim of the wadi. They were pretty certain the wagons of HQ Troop had made it out of there. Sure, they'd be deprived of the protection of the Squadron's heavy weapons, but so what? The three wagons right here could hardly use their machine-guns, and at least the HQ Troop should be reasonably mobile in their lighter vehicles.

By contrast, the lone Pinkie and the handful of quads on the northern rim of the wadi could be in a seriously shit state. If most of the missing blokes had headed for their position, they'd be hopelessly overloaded with the extra bodies. But the alternative scenario was even more desperate: if the missing men hadn't made it to those vehicles, they would be scattered across the Iraqi desert on the run on foot.

Ed had one of the Six Troop signallers with him in his wagon.

He got him to try to raise UK Special Forces Headquarters via the vehicle-mounted satcom. They didn't have a second to fuck around here, but it was just possible that the other elements of the Squadron had reported in to SFHQ, in which case they could get confirmation that all the blokes were accounted for. They might even get a workable RV – a rendezvous point where the Squadron could gather together.

Ed spoke into the handset. 'Zero, this is OC Six Troop. Zero, this is OC Six Troop. Contact status report. Come on – come on – answer!'

The air was thick with tension as he waited for a response. Then: 'OC Six Troop, this is Zero. Go ahead.'

'Zero, OC Six Troop – sitrep: Squadron bogged down in wadi, blown six to eight wagons, split up and forced to go on the run. We are now a mixed unit of blokes, with three LRs and one quad, facing a superior enemy force.'

'Give casualties and head count,' came the tense reply.

'Twenty-eight present with my force. No serious casualties.'

'Give call-signs.'

Ed passed across the call-signs of all present in his group. 'We need air support,' he continued. 'Repeat: we need air. Plus we need a grid for a hot extraction.'

Ed began to add something else, but there was a hollow thud and a hiss and a dazzling flash in the sky to the west, as the enemy put up another illume. It was too distant to light them up completely, but with each flare they were creeping closer. The noise of its bursting drowned out much of what Ed was saying.

'We've had six vehicles disappear from Blue Force Tracker,' came the call from Headquarters. 'What's happened to them?'

'Understand the situation: we got bogged down,' Ed repeated.

232

'We blew the bogged-in vehicles. Those guys cross-decked to other wagons. That's why we're three LRs and one quad with twenty-eight blokes.'

'Will get helos on standby for a forty-min flight time to your position. Stand by for a grid. Repeat: stand by for a grid.'

Ed came off the air, wiping an exhausted hand across his mud-stained features. 'Zero's finding us a grid. Plus they're getting together some close air support for us. For now, keep heading south. Grey, you got the next map?'

'I got it,' Grey confirmed. He'd done a map change just as soon as they'd left the wadi of death, for they'd hit the edge of one 45-kilometre-square sheet.

For a few moments Grey and Ed studied the map together, searching for some open, flat terrain where they might call in a couple of Chinooks to carry out a hot extraction. A patch of possible ground sorted, they prepared to move out.

'Any news on the others?' Grey asked.

'Nope,' Ed replied, his voice thick with worry. 'There's been nothing from HQ Troop, and the third group hasn't come up on comms.'

'What about Blue Force Tracker? Surely, they can track their position on those?'

'Zero says they've been trying to, but it's total bloody confusion right now.'

Each of the wagons was fitted with a BFT (Blue Force Tracker) system – a small gizmo housed in a black box that worked via a satellite antenna. BFT was designed to send data to Head-quarters on the location of each of the vehicles. In the operations room, each wagon would show up as an individual icon displayed on a giant computer screen. Each BFT unit sent a signal unique to the wagon's call-sign, so each vehicle could be tracked individually.

The BFT system also had an emergency button, which sent a message akin to a Mayday call. Apparently, some of M Squadron's Mayday buttons had been pressed. In fact, Headquarters had received Mayday calls from wagons scattered dozens of kilometres apart – which was how they'd first realized that M Squadron was in serious trouble.

But without a sitrep from anyone in the Squadron, those Mayday calls had caused total confusion at Headquarters. How could they be coming from vehicles scattered so far apart? Had some of the wagons been captured by the Iraqis, who were now tearing about in them and messing with the BFT systems? Or – as unlikely as it might seem – had an entire Squadron somehow been scattered across the Iraqi desert?

To make matters worse, half -a-dozen of the BFT systems had suddenly gone off air, as the wagons in the wadi of death had been blown. Understandably, that had caused chaos at Headquarters, for it seemed to show that six wagons had just been taken out by the enemy, and pretty much in one go.

As they had begun to wake up to what was happening to M Squadron, the SF Ops Room had been transformed into a whirl-wind of activity. Ed's sitrep had shed some welcome light on the situation, but the word from Headquarters hadn't made things look a great deal more positive, for neither the HQ Troop nor the third force had come up on comms.

As impossible as it might seem, right now they might have lost half of the entire Squadron.

# CHAPTER NINETEEN

From the wagon to his left, Grey heard a voice start banging on about the need to split up. He didn't recognize who it was, so it was probably a bloke from Four or Five Troop. With sixty men to the Squadron there were some you'd barely know by name, let alone be able to recognize from a few words uttered across the tense darkness.

Due west eighty kilometres or so lay the border with Syria. For most of their journey the Squadron had been paralleling it. Their final option, if all else failed, would be to try to make a run for that border, as the lads from the Bravo Two Zero patrol had done, back in 1991. But lying between the M Squadron operators and their escape route was the Iraqi hunter force – so it had to be a total non-starter right now.

Just as soon as they'd been compromised by the Iraqi goat-herder, the B2Z boys had headed for Syria, but only one of them had made it. En route, the rest of the patrol had been shot up, killed or captured. Plus the one patrol member who had made it into Syria on foot had hardly been welcomed. He was arrested, beaten and interrogated before the British government pressurized the Syrians into handing him over.

Even if the remnants of M Squadron could reach Syria, it would offer only very dubious sanctuary. The Syrian regime was no friend to the West, and it would hardly welcome half a British Special Forces squadron piling across into its territory. In spite of this, that same voice kept going on about the need to split up: 'We've got to split up, like they did in Bravo Two Zero. It's the only way. We've got to split up.'

Finally, Grey lost it. 'That's the last fucking thing we need to do. We need to stick together. We need to stick together and find the rest of the Squadron. There are blokes missing out there, including the OC, and who knows what kind of shit they're in. We need to stick together and find them, so let's get fucking sparking.'

'But if we split into smaller groups we're less visible,' the bloke continued. 'We split up and head for the Syrian border—'

'If we split up we can't coordinate the hot extraction, 'cause some wagons don't have satcom,' Grey cut him off. 'Plus if we go in three directions, who's heading back the way we've come? 'Cause that's the suicide option. And who's going east, further into Iraq? And even fucking west towards Syria we know there's a shedload of enemy. Think about it. It just doesn't fucking add up. We keep together and head south on a bearing for a hot extraction.'

'Grey's right: no one's splitting up,' Ed cut in. 'We keep together as one unit, and make for a hot-extraction grid.'

That seemed to shut the bloke up.

Ed turned to Grey. 'I need you to plot a course that gets us out of here and into the open desert – somewhere we can hide, in case we can't make an extraction grid. Double-check your map-reading, 'cause we need to know exactly where we are at all times. Your wagon will take the lead. And budge up, 'cause I'll get someone riding shotgun with you to help with the mapping.'

Ed got the rupert from Five Troop to squeeze himself into the seat beside Grey – which meant that the front of their wagon was like the proverbial sardines in a tin, especially as they still had Raggy sprawled across the bonnet. Luckily, the Five Troop officer was a skinny shrimp of a bloke, which left Moth just about enough free space still to use the gearstick.

'Two heads are better than one,' Ed explained. 'If we're going to get the helos in for a hot extraction, we need to make fucking sure we don't mess up on the mapping.'

Grey figured it was a fair one. But as the Pinkie pulled away he was struggling with the map sheets – and with the rupert practically perched on his lap. It wasn't going to make the task of navigating any the bloody easier.

'Head south,' he told Moth. 'For now, make for the Southern Cross. I'll check the maps as we go.'

The Southern Cross is a bright bluish star lying in the heart of the Milky Way, and it's a rough pointer for south. Grey figured if they headed due south, then sooner or later they'd hit the Ninawa Desert, which should give them the space and the terrain in which to lose the enemy. If they lost their pursuers they could contact Headquarters, radio in their position and act as an RV for the remainder of the Squadron. Hell, they might even be able to head out in a couple of the Pinkies and bring the missing blokes in.

As they pushed ahead at little more than a crawl, a thought struck Grey from out of the night. An image had come unbidden into his head: it was of Reggie, the Squadron OC. He was his super-cool self, mug of coffee clasped in the one hand: *Okay, boy, okay, thanks for that, buddy . . . I'll have a think on that one.* Would he still be keeping his famous cool, Grey wondered, with his Squadron scattered to the four corners, and stuck in a hole as he now had to be?

Grey bloody hoped he would. The last thing they needed right now was the OC getting captured. For a British Special Forces Major and SAS veteran to fall into the hands of the enemy would be a propaganda victory par excellence for the Iraqis. Not only that, the OC would be privy to all the bigger-picture intelligence about the wider war effort. He might well be a quiet, dagger-between-the-teeth kind of a bloke, but the Iraqis had ways of making even the toughest talk.

It was then that he remembered Sebastian. *A spot of foreign adventure, indeed.* Their poor bloody terp must have realized by now that he'd bitten off a massive hunk of *foreign adventure*, far more than he had ever bargained for. Sebastian would be with the HQ Troop sharing whatever fate had befallen them, and if the Iraqis got hold of him Grey dreaded to think what they might do to him.

Moth was struggling to pick a route through the rough landscape. The night was black as hell and it made for impossible driving, especially with a wagon as overburdened as theirs. But on one level, that was the least of their worries right now. Suddenly, there was the howl of an incoming round. Right in the path of the vehicle out front – Gunner's lone quad – was an almighty great explosion.

For an instant, Grey saw Gunner and the officer riding pillion silhouetted against the white-hot blast. He figured with the next shell the both of them would be pulverized. But an instant later Gunner had spun the quad into a crazed turn to the right, to get them out of the line of fire. Moth followed his lead, the blokes hanging onto the rear of the wagon practically being thrown off as he ramped it into a screaming turn.

The second he did so, a shell aimed with pinpoint accuracy slammed into the patch of desert that they'd just vacated. Blasted rock and sand hammered into the rear of their Pinkie, the shock-wave rocking it savagely from side to side. They were under fire from what had to be those enemy tanks, the T-72 Lions of Babylon unleashing their massive, fearsome 125mm shells.

This time, Grey didn't need to tell Gunner to pull his throttle to the max. Ahead of him the quad shot ahead like a bullet out of a gun, and – bugger the blokes hanging onto their vehicle – Moth floored the Pinkie's accelerator. All three wagons started to buck and kangaroo their way across the terrain, the extra blokes hanging on for dear life.

None of the Pinkies could return fire, for their extra passengers were blocking their arcs of fire. Even if they could have done, there was jack shit they could do against those T-72s. Their only hope was to try to outrun them and disappear into the dark desert, and to evade and escape from the enemy that way.

Those in the back of Grey's wagon were on their feet now, using their knees to cushion the blows as the vehicle cannoned into dips and off ridges, their hands gripped tight to whatever they could find close by. Yet no matter how hard Moth pushed the Pinkie, the hunter force kept coming.

Grey could sense the 12.7mm Dushka rounds tearing past overhead now, as blast waves from further salvos of 125mm tank shells pounded them from either side. He figured the T-72s had opened up from no more than a kilometre away. Most likely, the enemy armour had sneaked closer while they were doing their head count, hoping to tear them apart from point-blank range.

As the wagons had got on the move again, the tank commander must have decided to hammer in the rounds anyway. The only thing that was preventing the wagons from getting hit was the way Gunner was weaving the convoy through any patches of cover he could find, plus the thick blanket of darkness.

But they were at the total mercy of the elements right now. If the cloud cover cleared and the moon came out, they'd be finished. They had an enemy force closing on them, and they were ploughing ahead as fast as their vehicles could go. If the clouds blew over and the sky brightened they'd be silhouetted in the moonlight, and they'd be toast.

As they careered across the terrain Grey's wagon went flying over a ridge with a sharp drop on the far side. For a good few seconds the Pinkie was airborne, and then the wheels hit the deck with a tortured groan as the weight of the human and other cargo slammed down. There was a horrible crack as the springs bottomed out. Moth fought to control the speeding vehicle, as the heavier rear end tried to slide forwards and overtake the front, sending them into a wild spin.

Moth won the battle and wrestled the Pinkie under control again. Grey was tempted to tell him to slow it a little. A couple more incidents like that, and the wagon was surely going to shake itself apart. But to their rear the Iraqi tanks were coming on fast, and the only option they had was to run and run. There was only so much battle damage a Land Rover could take, and he feared theirs was fast approaching the limits of its endurance.

Another worrying thought struck Grey: *Where the hell were the Fedayeen?* They had armour to their rear hammering in the 125mm shells, but the militia were nowhere to be seen. Their Toyotas were way faster than the Pinkies, and they were very likely familiar with the terrain here. Grey couldn't help but think they were going to run into those bastard Fedayeen sometime soon.

A voice came up over the radios, from the rearmost of the vehicles. 'What you guys got to the front? We've got fucking armour to the back of us. And on the right there – can you see those vehicles? They're moving to head us off. We've got to split up!'

'Fucking bullshit,' Grey snapped. 'Keep the force together.'

He glanced to their right, and sure enough a line of headlamps low to the ground had appeared from behind the cover of a slight rise. They were speeding along, and seemed to be making good use of the tracks that criss-crossed the sands, while the British vehicles were churning across the rough of the open desert. It had to be the Fedayeen.

More alarming still, they looked as if they were making towards the south of the British patrol's line of march, to cut off their escape. This had become a desperate race to get far enough south to lose the enemy armour and before the Fedayeen could intercept the British force and trap them. Grey had few doubts as to who was going to win this particular struggle.

The Fedayeen vehicles thundered ahead with their lights on full beam, making no attempt to conceal themselves. When you were a force as fast and as potent as they were, Grey figured, you didn't really have to hide. The nearest of their Toyotas were closing fast, and shortly they were barely three hundred yards away. As they drew level with the British vehicles, Gunner slowed the convoy to a crawl.

Moments later, he pulled to a halt, and the wagons behind him did likewise. Every bloke held his breath as the enemy force approached. The lead Toyotas tore past going at breakneck speed, and no more than 150 yards away. The blokes on the Pinkies kept as quiet and as still as they could. They barely dared to breathe, as one after another the Toyotas powered onwards.

At this range, they could make out the enemy force in detail. The open rear of each of the vehicles was crammed full of fighters, clustered around a tripod-mounted Dushka. Each was dressed from head to toe in white – a long robe topped off by a *shemagh* wrapped around the head that left just the eyes showing. Their vehicles looked brand spanking new, and the fighters riding in them were armed with smart-looking AK47 assault rifles.

There were some half-dozen in the rear of each wagon, so eight or more per vehicle. With a good dozen Fedayeen wagons out there, that made a force of pushing one hundred fighters. They looked hardcore, well disciplined and up for the fight, plus they packed some serious firepower. They had the air of fanaticism about them that the briefings back at the forward mounting base had suggested.

These, then, were Saddam's diehard militia.

They had one disadvantage right now, compared to the tiny British force. With their headlights on full beam those behind were lighting up the vehicles in front, and they would have acquired little if any natural night vision. In effect they would be blinded by their own lights, which meant that the desert outside the cone of illumination thrown off by their convoy would be an impenetrable wall of darkness. By contrast, the British wagons were totally unlit. More than likely, the Fedayeen would spot the hidden force only if one of their Toyotas got lucky and swung its headlamps across a Pinkie's flank.

Sure enough, the convoy of enemy vehicles swung eastwards, and as their headlamps swept round it looked for a moment as if they were going to spotlight the lead Pinkie in their glare. Blokes were poised to dive off the rear of the British wagons so that the heavy machine-gun operators could use their weapons to defend the small force. Even so, the Fedayeen seemed set on getting the drop on them.

Yet as luck would have it none of the Toyotas seemed so much as to slow, and within seconds the last of the hunter force had surged onwards into the night. The Fedayeen had failed to spot the British vehicles, and were racing on ahead to block the route south.

For now the threat was past. Grey breathed out a long sigh of relief, and glanced at the open map in his lap. His heart was hammering against his rib cage, and he fought to get his pulse rate under control again. That had been bloody close. He was trying to read the map without using any light at all. If the barest pinprick was visible, it would draw all the demons from hell onto their position.

From the map their situation looked pretty close to hopeless. To their north they had the Iraqi armour. To the south were now the Fedayeen. Going east would only take them further into Iraq, and they'd quickly be into built-up areas and major roads, which would be perfect terrain for the Iraqi forces to run them to ground.

He figured there was only one option left open to them. If they swung west, it might enable them to sneak between the Fedayeen force to their south and the armour to their north. But somewhere out there was likely to be the Iraqi infantry in their trucks, and heading west risked running onto their guns. In short, Grey didn't have much of a clue where next to steer the patrol.

As he scrutinized his map, desperately trying to find a safe route through, he was tempted to hit the Mayday button on his Blue

Force Tracker system. If he did, an emergency burst of data would be emitted, which would be picked up first in the American military's operations room – for theirs was the central coordinating point for all BFT traffic. From there it would go to British SFHQ, alerting them that more M Squadron wagons were in serious trouble.

He glanced across to the BFT unit. Hidden deep in the dash the tiny light diode was flickering away, indicating it was switched on and operational. There were only three buttons on the unit: 'on', 'off' and 'Mayday'. For a second, his finger hovered over the third. Then he told himself not to be so fucking defeatist: *I'm not going to bloody do it. Whatever it takes, we'll get ourselves out of this shit.*

After all, what would it achieve? Headquarters had already received several Mayday calls, but all it had served to do was add to the confusion. Without having a fully coordinated sitrep from the Squadron as a whole, there was no way of knowing the fate of all sixty men. Right now, each scattered unit knew only its own, very confused circumstances, and another Mayday call was hardly going to help.

What they needed was to re-form the Squadron and get this shit sorted.

They still had options, Grey told himself. Sure, they could do sod all against an Iraqi main battle tank. But they still had a LAW 66mm anti-armour weapon strapped across the bonnet of each of the Pinkies. The LAW was the NATO version of the RPG. It was a bit dated, with a remarkably crude sight, but it was actually very effective. The LAW was more than good enough for taking out one of those Kraz 225 infantry trucks, or you could smash it into the ground next to a group of infantry and cause some real carnage.

Plus they still had Six Troop's one *SLAR* – the shoulder-launched multipurpose assault weapon – the state-of-the-art 85mm rocket launcher. The *SLAR* was still in the experimental stages of development, so who knew the limits of its thermobaric warhead? It came complete with six thermobaric rockets, and right now that represented the patrol's greatest firepower. If they could just get into a decent position from which to fight, they could still do some serious damage.

Grey glanced up from the map. 'Take a right turn onto a southwesterly bearing,' he told Moth. 'Keep on that bearing until—'

'Hold on a minute, are you sure you're on the right map sheet?' the rupert sitting next to Grey cut in. Grey had pretty much forgotten about the bloke up until now. 'I think you've made a mistake—'

Grey fixed him with a look like murder. 'You want to take over? Be my fucking guest, mate.'

That killed the issue. Moth eased the wagon into motion, swung right and got them onto a southwesterly bearing. To his rear the rest of the wagons came after them, while Gunner accelerated the quad until it was scouting the terrain to their front.

'We're heading southwest for reasons that should be obvious,' Grey announced on the radios. 'Keep your eyes peeled for those fucking Iraqi infantry trucks.'

Gunner responded to Grey's warning by speeding ahead still further, so he could probe the territory they were moving into. He crested a shallow rise. No sooner had he done so than he pulled the quad to a sudden halt. A line of powerful headlights had emerged from the gloom. They lay a good two kilometres west of the British force, and it was obvious at once that this had to be the fleet of Iraqi infantry trucks. They blocked any escape route west.

He did a quick about-turn and raced back towards the wagons. As he did so, he radioed through a hurried warning, and in response a chorus of voices came up on the radios:

'That's it – we've got fucking enemy infantry to the west' . . . 'Plus Fedayeen to the south, as a blocking force' . . . 'Plus we've got armour to the rear' . . . 'And east it's fucking bedlam' . . . 'We've got to fucking split up' . . . 'Yeah, we've got to split up' . . .

'No way! That's fucking bullshit!' Grey countered. 'Keep the wagons together.'

'Keep the unit together,' Ed's voice cut in. 'Keep the unit together. I repeat, we keep the unit together.'

But others kept crashing in on the radio net.

'We've got to split up.'

'We've got to split up.'

It was then that Gunner's voice came up on the air. He was screaming to make himself heard above the revving of his quad bike's engine and the roar of the speeding vehicle's slipstream. It made comms with him extremely difficult, which added to the confusion.

'If we're splitting up, I'm off to Syria! See you blokes in Syria!'

'KEEP THE UNIT TOGETHER!' Ed roared, but his command was drowned out by the chaos on the net, as voices shouted and yelled across each other.

'We're splitting up!'

'Let's head for Syria!'

'Split up and head for the border!'

The Six Troop signaller came up on the net, desperately trying to cut through the radio traffic. 'Negative! Negative! Stick with the unit! Stick with the unit! All call-signs, stick with the unit!'

'See you blokes in Syria! See you blokes in Syria!' came back

Gunner's response. It was drowned out by the screaming of the quad's engine, and it was obvious he wouldn't be able to hear much of what was being said on the net and probably hadn't heard the order.

By now the sound of Gunner's quad was fading to a ghostly whisper. Even though he was two-up on the machine, it was far more nimble than the Pinkies. He was soon lost in the night, the silhouette of his fast-moving machine being swallowed by the desert horizon, and with the rupert clinging desperately to the rear.

Grey turned to Moth. 'What the fuck?'

Moth shrugged. 'Sounded like he couldn't hear us.'

Grey jerked a thumb towards the rearmost vehicle. 'Yeah. With those twats crapping on about splitting up, it's hardly bloody surprising.'

'He sounded pretty pissed off too.'

Grey smiled grimly. 'It's probably sharing his quad with a rupert that's got him so twitched. That alone is enough to get him pissed off.'

In spite of their predicament, Moth gave a short bark of a laugh. With the days spent driving through the heat and dust, Gunner's radio might have packed up completely. Who knows?

For a few long moments there was chaos on the radio net, as voices ranted on about the need to follow Gunner's lead and to split up. A far greater number were adamant that the force needed to stick together. Finally, Ed cut it short. They needed to stick to their standard operating procedures, he announced, which meant going through the ERV (emergency rendezvous) procedures.

Grey couldn't have agreed more. It was the only logical thing to do right now.

As the Squadron had pushed northwards through Iraq it had established a series of ERV points. First was the 'Coastal RV' – the name being a hangover from M Squadron's maritime operations that referred to their point of entry into theatre. In this case, the Squadron's Coastal RV was the original landing zone where the Chinooks had dropped them, north of the Euphrates River. After that, a series of additional ERVs had been established, each fifty kilometres or so further north and distinguished by some special feature – one that would be memorable enough not to have to be marked on the maps.

A marked-up map was a big no-no for Special Forces operations. If a marked-up map fell into the hands of the enemy, it would give away all the ERVs – hence the need to commit them to memory.

Whichever RV you made for, when you reached it you'd mark it with a distinctive sign – maybe a cross made of stones – to signal that you'd arrived, before moving off a good distance to find an LUP. That way, there was less risk of compromising the RV point, but others in the Squadron would know that you were there.

The last-ditch rendezvous was the 'Combat RV' – the escape route if all other options failed – which in this case was to make for the Syrian border. Right now, Gunner had thrown steps one to nine out of the window, and was heading direct for the Combat RV. But in a sense it was hardly his fault. With all the calls to split up, he must have thought the entire force was heading for the Combat RV, in which case he'd made a break for Syria along with what he believed was the rest of them.

Things were getting shittier by the second now. M Squadron was split into at least four separate units. Gunner had been doing a fantastic job of shepherding the three wagons, but now they had well and truly lost him. Their force was deprived of its last quad, which had constituted their only remaining fast-mobility and recce capability.

They were down to three Pinkies careering across the desert sands, with twenty-six blokes clinging on for their lives.

# CHAPTER TWENTY

If only Grey could navigate the wagons to their last ERV point, there was just a chance that they might find the rest of the Squadron there (minus Gunner and his passenger, of course). If the OC and the third group had followed standard operating procedure, that was where they would have headed – assuming they were able to get on the move at all, what with the numbers of men they'd be carrying and the presence of the enemy.

If they didn't find anyone at the ERV, at least they'd know that the rest of the blokes hadn't been able to make it – which would mean they'd been captured or killed, or that they'd lost their mobility and gone into a hide. Either way, it would give them some concrete, usable intel to go on. Plus the ERV was a known point at which they could try to call in a Chinook, to lift them out of there.

The Squadron's last ERV was a four-way junction of dirt tracks, set at the extreme northern end of the Ninawa Desert. It had been chosen because it was visually distinctive and memorable, with the ruin of an ancient stone-walled fortress lying to the north side of the crossroads. It was to there that Grey decided to try to charter a route, using his compass and his mapping.

He turned to Moth. 'Ignore all those twats crapping on about splitting up. Head three fingers to the left of the Southern Cross. Forty kilometres south is the first ERV. Get up as much speed as you can, 'cause that's where we're bloody going.'

Moth swung the wagon round to the new bearing, the other vehicles moving into line behind him. For now at least, they were holding together as a unit. As they probed ahead into the hostile night Grey had an image in his mind of a lone quad haring across the desert. Gunner would have to box around the Iraqi forces, which meant it would probably be a good two-hundred-kilometre round trip across rough terrain before he hit the Syrian border.

Luckily, he'd have his silk escape map threaded into the waistband of his trousers, so he'd have the means to navigate his way towards the Combat RV. The map was 1:200,000 scale and covered the whole of Iraq, so it was like a massive parachute when unrolled, but it was more than good enough to plan a route to hit an unmissable feature like the Syrian border. He'd also have the half-dozen gold sovereigns provided to all SF operators sewn into his clothing somewhere crafty. If it came to it, he could use those to bribe whatever Syrian forces he came across to allow him and his passenger through.

Most of Gunner's spare fuel would be on one of the Pinkies, so he'd only have whatever was in the bike's tank, plus maybe a small can of extra fuel strapped to his quad. But presumably he had enough to make it to the border, or he wouldn't have made a break for it alone – he'd have stuck with one of the wagons. Gunner was a slick operator and a smart navigator, and he'd not have set off for the Combat RV without the juice to get there.

It was the officer clinging onto the rear of the quad that Grey really felt for. Perched back there on the metal rack, he'd hardly have been privy to Gunner's decision to split. After a ride like the one that lay ahead of them, his backside was going to be so sore he wouldn't be able to sit down for a week. As Grey played the image through his mind, he couldn't help but crack up laughing.

He didn't keep smiling for long, though. The alternative scenario was that the two of them wouldn't make it. There were any number of reasons why they might fail. They might run out of fuel. They might shoot over a ravine in the dark, and roll the quad. They might go into a hide during the day, and the enemy might find them.

Worst of all, if Gunner tried to box around south they might blunder into the Fedayeen and get taken captive. Grey shuddered to think what would happen to them if they did. If there was one thing that Grey was determined to avoid above all else, it was falling into their bastard hands alive.

Grey took a quick glance behind him. The three wagons were well spaced apart and showing no lights, and the sky above them remained blissfully dark. They no longer had Gunner probing the way ahead, but even so he figured they had a half-decent chance of making it through the screen of enemy forces unseen. If they did, they'd loop around southeast and make direct for their ERV.

But all of that was predicated upon the Fedayeen remaining stationary in their positions, and unfortunately that was something they just couldn't count on. The Fedayeen had been constituted as a fast guerrilla-type force able to rove around in their highly manoeuvrable vehicles doing hit-and-run style operations. They had an organic, flexible command structure, and staying put really wasn't their style.

The three wagons pushed onwards for twenty minutes or so in

a tense and brittle silence. Instinctively, all the blokes knew this was their last-gasp effort. It seemed to Grey like the silent desert was holding its breath, as it waited to see if they'd make it through the wall of steel all around them.

It was then that a crescent of headlights emerged from the desert to their front, stretching across their path. As Grey stared into that swathe of illumination, he was forced to accept that the enemy had comprehensively outmanoeuvred and outsmarted the British force. They had double-guessed their intended line of escape and cut them off in every direction so as to cover all points southeast through to southwest.

Grey took one last look at the map nestled in his lap, but he knew they were out of options. If they kept running in any direction southeast to southwest they'd blunder into that screen of waiting Fedayeen, which outnumbered them four to one and outgunned them even more comprehensively.

It was twelve o'clock midnight by now, and they'd been running and fighting for six hours. The Squadron had been brassed up, smashed up, bogged in and forced to blow its vehicles, plus they'd lost half the guys and were split into at least four separate units. Now their force of three Pinkies and twenty-six blokes had been boxed in by a vastly superior enemy force, and with no way to use their heavy machine-guns, due to all the bodies clinging to the wagons.

There wasn't a man amongst them who gave a shit any more as to who exactly the Iraqi forces they were up against might be. The Fedayeen were a known quantity – these had to be the Boys from Bayji. But very likely the regular infantry and armour were units hailing from their mission objective, the Iraqi 5th Corps. Not for the first time the intel they'd been given had proved a total crock of shit. It would be hard to imagine a force less likely to surrender than the men who were coming after them now.

Every which way Grey looked at it, from the get-go theirs had been a true mission impossible. They had driven into what amounted to an ambush, one very likely planned and conceived over several days. Just as he had feared from the start, they were sixty blokes up against a force of a hundred thousand – that's if the entire 5th Corps had decided to join in the hunt for the Squadron.

Right now he couldn't see any way out of the trap that had been set for them. In fact, the force whose surrender the Squadron had been sent in to take looked poised to annihilate them, for there was no way that Grey and his ilk were likely to surrender. It was the ultimate irony, in a mission defined by such travesties.

Grey figured it was time to face the music. He turned to Moth. 'Mate, there's no way through. There's nowhere left to run. Best you slow the wagon.'

Without making a comment or giving any visible reaction, Moth eased off on the gas. As he did so, there was no denying the young operator's icy cool.

Grey scanned the terrain all around them. 'Let's try to find some decent cover, eh?'

Moth indicated a patch of darker shadow lying just to their left front. He drove the wagon into it, and it proved to be a miniature lake bed set just below the level of the surrounding terrain. The bed of the depression was solid as a rock, so this was no wadi of death – or at least, not in the way the last had been. It would provide some cover from being seen, plus minimal cover from fire, which was far better than none at all.

Moth got them into position, and cut the engine. The other

wagons pulled in close. Grey leaned across to Ed so he could have words.

'We're boxed in,' he whispered, as the quiet closed all around them. 'The enemy's to the west and the north of us, and we'll hit Fedayeen if we continue south. If we cut east we'll hit the N252, and a load of other roads and built-up shit. So, the question is – where's left to fucking run?'

Ed didn't answer. It was hardly surprising. In truth, there was zero room for manoeuvre.

'Okay, this is my suggestion,' Grey continued. 'We stop running. We go firm. We get the extra lads off the wagons and into all-round defence. At least that way we can use the heavy machine-guns. The night's dark and they'll take a while to find us. In the mean-time, Moth can dial up some fast air.'

Ed nodded. The relief was clear on his features. 'Let's do it. There's no way out of this shit without some air cover. Get the lads into position, and I'll dial up Headquarters.'

Now that every man had a role to play and was no longer just a useless passenger, they started sparking. Any ideas about split-ting up were instantly forgotten. The blokes piled off the wagons and unlashed the M72 LAWs from the Land Rovers' bonnets, plus Scruff grabbed the *SLAR* 85mm rocket launcher together with its thermobaric warheads. They moved into defensive posi-tions all around the wadi rim, concentrating on the areas of greatest threat.

The M72 LAW is a single-use weapon, so once those three rocket-launchers had been fired they were done. By contrast, the *SLAR* offered the blokes some repeat-use firepower, of untested potency. Back at their forward mounting base they'd dry-rehearsed using the *SLAR*, but with no warheads to spare no one had yet managed to fire the thing, to assess the potency of one of those thermobaric rockets.

For the first time in what felt like an age, the gunners on the three wagons were able to take possession of their two .50-cal machine-guns, the one grenade launcher, plus the three GPMGs. As they swung the weapons round to cover the oncoming Fedayeen and bunched their shoulders in preparation for the coming firefight, they felt strangely calm and empowered.

While they had bullets left and could use the heavy weapons, they were still a force of elite operators to be reckoned with. Every man amongst them knew to hold his fire until the very last moment, and then to unleash hell – for once they opened up, the enemy was sure get an illume round bang over their position, which would make them sitting targets.

With the defences set, Grey, Moth and Ed got sparking. Ed cranked up the radio, to check in to SF Headquarters. Grey began working out the exact grid of the patrol's position to pass to Headquarters. Meanwhile, Moth got on the satcom, dialling up any warplanes he could beg, borrow or steal from the racetrack system they'd be flying over central Iraq.

'This is *Zero Six Bravo* making an any-stations call,' Moth intoned into the satcom. 'This is our situation: we're a British Special Forces patrol eighty kilometres to the southeast of Salah. This is our grid: 15839501. Repeat: 15839501. We're surrounded by the enemy and in need of fast air. Do any call-signs copy?'

All he got in reply was an echoing void of static.

'Repeat: *Zero Six Bravo* requesting fast air, at grid 15839501. This is the codeword: *battleaxe*. Repeat *battleaxe*.'

'Battleaxe' was the codeword for a Special Forces patrol in need of air support. The codeword was changed every twenty-four hours, and passed down from SFHQ to the various patrols. Fortunately, Moth had had the foresight to get the present codeword from the HQ Troop, just before stand-to at the LUP where the enemy had first hit them.

There was silence for a long second. Then: 'Roger that, *Zero Six Bravo*, this is *Viper Five Three*. I'm hearing you loud and clear. We're a pair of F16s, three hundred klicks south of your position. We've got full payloads and four-zero, repeat four-zero minutes' play time. What can I do for ya?'

The pilot's voice was badly distorted by the range of the call and the interference, plus it was filtered through the alien suck-and-blow of his oxygen mask. But he had an unmistakably broad American drawl, and that voice was one of the most welcome sounds that the men had ever heard.

'*Viper Five Three*, *Zero Six Bravo*. We're under attack from Iraqi main battle tanks and infantry trucks to the north and west of our grid, plus Fedayeen in SUVs to the south. I need you overhead to smash them. Our grid is 15839501. Repeat: 15839501. Read back.'

'Roger that, *Zero Six Bravo*, your grid is 15839501. Repeat: 15839501. We'll be in your overhead in approximately ten, repeat one-zero minutes. Out.'

The radio traffic had been short and sweet, not to mention decisive. Moth replaced the satcom handset and his ice-blue eyes met those of Grey. 'We'll have a pair of F16s overhead in ten minutes. They've got full loads of ordnance and forty minutes' play time. Fucking result.'

Grey broke into a smile. 'You hear that, Dude, Uncle Sam's coming to the fucking rescue? That's why we love you Yanks, Dude. Let's get the fucking bombs in and smash them.'

The General Dynamics F16 Fighting Falcon flies at almost twice the speed of sound, or 2,410 kph. It comes equipped with a 21mm seven-barrelled M61 Vulcan Gatling gun, plus 7,300 kilograms of ordnance. The pair of jets in-bound had full payloads, which meant they'd be fully bombed up. The F16 could carry four massive 2,000-pound JDAMs – joint direct attack munition guided smart bombs – or as many as eight smaller CBU87s (combined-effects munition bombs), or similar.

The M61 Gatling gun would be armed with 511 cannon rounds. A couple of strafes with that, and the warplanes' armoured-piercing bullets would rip the guts out of the Iraqi T-72s, not to mention the infantry trucks and Fedayeen wagons. In theory, all the blokes had to do was stay hidden for ten minutes, and they'd have a pair of F16s overhead tearing up the bad guys.

Grey passed the word around the patrol. It was the first piece of positive news that the men had had since battle had been joined, and it lifted their spirits immensely. It felt good not to be running any more. It felt good to have made the decision to stand and fight, and especially with those fast jets in-bound.

A few short moments later Ed succeeded in raising Headquarters. He came off the air and glanced across at Grey. 'They're going to try to pull us out by Chinook. They've got helos on standby on thirty minutes' notice. They'll need to give us coordinates for an LZ to do the hot extraction, and they'll need time to de-conflict and clear an air corridor with the Yanks.'

'What's wrong with doing the hot extraction from right here?' Grey queried. 'We've drawn the bulk of the enemy onto us, so why delay? Let's get the fuck out of here.'

Like every man in the Squadron, Grey had total confidence in the Chinook pilots. This was like calling for the fire brigade with the house burning down around you, and you and your kids trapped on the top floor. It might seem impossible, but somehow they'd chop their way in with axes, or put ladders against the burning walls and pluck you out of there. Likewise, the Chinook aircrew would know they were flying into a shit-fight pretty much blind, but that's what those Special Forces pilots did best.

Once they'd split from the main force and gone on the run, Gunner and his rupert passenger had become a CSAR (combat search-and-rescue) case, which was one step more serious than a hot extraction. They were on the run, position unknown, and with no way of making comms with Headquarters. The only way to find them and pull them out was to launch a CSAR flight, and scour the Iraqi terrain for a lone quad heading for the Syrian border.

But right now the remnants of Six Troop were in a known static location, and they'd passed their grid to Headquarters. The enemy forces were close, but when had that ever stopped the Chinooks flying a hot-extraction mission? If the blokes had to choose between getting plucked out by a pair of helos, or staying to fight the kind of forces that had them surrounded, they'd choose the hot extraction every time – and even with a couple of F16s in-bound.

'Headquarters has just managed to make contact with the OC,' Ed explained. 'He's come up on comms, which is fucking great news. There's a load of blokes with the OC, and only enough Chinooks to pull one lot out at a time, so they're going to try to get that lot out first. They're trying to establish exact casualties, but they've prioritized getting the OC out first. We've got to buy ourselves some time, get a grid sorted with Headquarters, so they can pull us out when they can.'

According to the word from Headquarters, the OC of M Squadron had gone into a hide somewhere to the northeast of the wadi of death. His small force was totally unsighted, but they could still hear tank fire rumbling across the darkness and see the light of flare rounds being fired, plus the occasional burst of tracer arcing across the heavens.

This pretty much confirmed what Grey already suspected, that it was their force – the remnants of Six Troop – that had drawn the bulk of the enemy fire. The enemy had opted to follow their line of march from the wadi of death – that much was pretty obvious from their present place of hiding. Seemingly from all around them they could hear the grunt of powerful diesel engines, as the enemy continued to scour the desert terrain.

'What about the third force?' Grey asked. 'The wagon and the quads that went north from the wadi?'

Ed shrugged. 'Nothing's been heard of them at all. They're a CSAR job, unless they come up on air. HQ's suggested a grid for us to head for, where they'll try to get the helos in for a hot extraction: 64732857. Take a look at the maps, mate.'

Grey plotted the grid. Headquarters would be choosing an extraction point from what they could see on the maps and sat-photos, plus what they could tell from Blue Force Tracker. They weren't able to take account of enemy forces on the ground, especially without any air cover to give them eyes on the battlefield.

'It's no good,' Grey told Ed. 'It's smack bang on the far side of that Fedayeen hunter force. There are masses of enemy that way. Get another.'

Ed radioed Headquarters, and came back with a second grid. It was further to the southwest and Grey figured it was just about doable. But Moth took one look at the map and he wasn't happy. From a JTAC's perspective the grid was bad news.

'It's no good. It puts us twenty klicks short of the Syrian border. That's a no-no for any fast air. Those F16s won't operate that close to the Syrian border.'

Moth's words were drowned out by a long burst of 12.7mm that went flaring past overhead. It didn't mean that they'd been spotted, necessarily, but it was a sharp reminder of what was out there just beyond the rim of the wadi.

'Like how's it no good?' Ed demanded.

'Fast air's all we can get over us quickly this far north of Baghdad,' Moth explained. 'Fast air won't operate that close to the Syrian border 'cause at the speed they fly they'll risk straying into Syrian airspace. We'd have to wait on that grid for extraction with no air cover over us, which is a fucking nightmare.'

'So where are those F16s, anyway?' Ed asked.

Moth grabbed his satcom. '*Viper Five Three, Zero Six Bravo*: what's your locstat?'

'We'll be in your overhead in five, repeat five minutes,' came the pilot's instant reply.

A second and a third burst of 12.7mm went thundering over their position. It felt as if the fire was getting closer. Leaving Ed and Moth to sort another grid for the helo pick-up, Grey went to check on the enemy. He scuttled over to the wadi rim, coming up on Scruff's shoulder.

Scruff stretched an arm towards the north. 'Tanks.' He swung the arm south. 'Iraqi infantry.' He swung it further south, then west. 'Fedayeen. Take your pick, mate, but sooner or later we're going to have to start smashing 'em.'

Having moved to block the route south, the Fedayeen had swung east and west to almost encircle them. Grey couldn't believe how quickly the Iraqis had got them surrounded. Plus it looked as if they'd worked out that the British force had gone to ground. They were moving methodically across the desert, lights on full beam, searching as they went, and bit by bit they were converging on their hidden position.

To the north the squat forms of the T-72s were crawling forwards, their blazing searchlights sweeping the desert to either side of them. And Grey didn't doubt that to the west the truck-mounted infantry were closing in, lights on full beam. The Fedayeen wagons were the nearest threat – no more than five hundred yards away – the tanks maybe double that distance, but creeping ever nearer.

Grey glanced at Scruff. 'Hold your fire until the last possible moment. Let's get the jets in.'

He ducked down and scuttled back towards the vehicles. As he did so, he fancied he could hear the faint rumble of jet engines at high altitude and far to the south of their position.

*Fucking great,* he told himself. *Let's get the bombs in.*

# CHAPTER TWENTY-ONE

'Same old same old – we've got enemy on all sides,' Grey reported, once he was back at the wagons. 'Moth, get the jets in to mallet the Fedayeen, 'cause they're right on top of us.'

Moth gave a thumbs-up. He got on the air and began to talk the F16 pilots around the battlefield. As the jets bore down on them, he gave the pilots a detailed sketch of their own and the enemy positions. That done, he asked the lead pilot to smash the Fedayeen vehicles that were nearest to their place of hiding, and just as soon as they were ready to engage.

'Am in your overhead carrying out my air recces,' came back the lead pilot's reply. 'Stand by.'

'They're preparing to smash the Fedayeen,' Moth reported to Grey and Ed. 'Any moment now.'

'*Zero Six Bravo, Viper Five Three*,' the pilot came up on the air again. 'No can do. There are vehicles everywhere that I'm looking. They are too numerous to ID friend from foe, and I can't de-conflict with your position. *Zero Six Bravo*, I can't do the drop.'

Moth spat out a string of curses. He turned to Ed and Grey. 'He can't do the drop! The Fedayeen are too close to us.'

'Fuck that!' snarled Grey. 'Get him to smash the tanks. We'll get the guns working on the Fedayeen.'

'*Viper Five Three, Zero Six Bravo*: can you see those Iraqi main battle tanks, a thousand yards due north of us? If you can, get in and smash them.'

'Affirmative, we see them. Trouble is, you've got remnants of your Squadron in unidentified locations all around the battlefield. We understand you've been split into four units, and command has asked us not to execute drops until all units are accounted for. There's too much risk of a blue-on-blue.'

'But what about those battle tanks? Surely it's obvious they're not bloody friendlies?'

'Negative. From where we're sitting I can see vehicles to every cardinal all around your position, many danger-close. There's so many we can't differentiate friend from foe, so as to ID enemy targets. There's too much risk of friendly fire to make any drops.'

Moth paused over the satcom. He was racking his brains to think of a way to direct the pilots onto the enemy, and to give them the confidence to make the drops. Maybe he could use his laser to paint the vehicles he wanted hit. But the one thing he couldn't do was find and identify all friendly forces, and especially not when some of them were scattered across the field of battle, in unknown locations and with no way of coming up on comms.

He fixed Grey and Ed with a look of utter desolation. 'Pilot says there's so many vehicles in the vicinity they can't differentiate targets. There's too great a risk of friendly fire.'

There was a moment of crushing silence as the three men stared at each other in disbelief. The word from the pilots just didn't make any sense. They were surrounded and about to get torn to pieces, and they had a pair of warplanes smack bang above them – but they couldn't do any drops. How the hell did that compute?

The whole point of going into a hide had been so they could call in some air power. That they had done, only to be told that the pilots were unable to hit the enemy. They were boiling up with frustration. What the fuck were they supposed to do now? Bug out of the lake bed and get the wagons on the move again? And if so, where to? As the F16 pilots had so eloquently told them, they had enemy forces surrounding them to every point of the compass.

'*Zero Six Bravo, Viper Five Three*,' came the lead F16 pilot's voice again. 'There *is* one thing we can do for ya. We can come in lower than a snake's belly doing low level passes with sonic boom. That'll scare the crap out of those Iraqi sons-of-bitches.'

'Stand by.' Moth turned to the others. 'Pilot's offering to fly low-level shows of force.'

'We're about to get overrun, and that's all he can do,' Grey snorted. 'Still, it's better than fucking nothing.'

'Get the jets in,' Ed confirmed. 'Maybe it'll buy us some time.'

Moth radioed the pilots. 'Bring your jets in right over our position, on a north–south bearing, and as low as you can get them.'

'Affirmative. Preparing to fly show of force, coming in from a northerly bearing bang on top of you guys. We're three minutes out and closing.'

Grey felt his head sink into his hands, exhaustedly. How long could they hope to hold the enemy off like this? The Iraqi infantry might opt to stay hidden, for the F16s could easily tear their trucks to pieces. Likewise the armour, for they'd be reluctant to lose a squadron of main battle tanks to air strikes. But Grey felt certain there was only one way to stop a force as brainwashed and fanatical as the Fedayeen – and that was to kill them.

With the jets unable to mount any attacking runs, he figured they'd have to try to break out, which would likely mean a stand-up fight in the open desert. And all things considered, he'd prefer to take on the Iraqi infantry rather than the diehard lunatic Boys from Bayji, or a fleet of Iraqi T-72s.

He'd once been on a mission to a certain African country where the rebels had been fighting a war for decades. They'd learned to defeat main battle tanks by digging a hole in the likely path of attack, and hiding in it. As soon as the tank had driven over them they'd climb aboard its rear, and kill the crew with small-arms fire. They'd captured scores of enemy tanks that way, and had even learned to operate them, before turning them against the government forces.

But to do that took days of careful planning, and a serious fighting force to back you up. The tanks had to be channelled along specific routes, where the tank-trappers were hiding. And with the best will in the world – not to mention a good dose of suicidal bravery – no one from the remnant force of Six Troop was going to pull off a trick like that. If nothing else the desert was far too open, offering the tanks any number of avenues of attack.

He didn't rate their chances very highly against the Iraqi infantry, either, but if they could catch them in their trucks, the Kraz 225s made for big, bulky targets. They could slam the LAWs – plus some *SLAR* warheads – into those, and maybe incinerate the lot of them in their vehicles. Then they could head west for the raging inferno that marked their position, and try and pass right through them. They'd have the Iraqi tanks to their north and the Fedayeen to their south, but assuming the infantry had been incinerated, they might just make it through. And with the F16s flying shows of force, maybe they could sneak away and lose them all.

There was a rushed heads-up amongst the blokes, and they agreed on Grey's idea as a plan of attack. Assuming the F16s' low-level passes had the desired effect, they'd bug out under the cover of their fly-pasts, then head west, stopping only when they had to fight. They'd mallet the Iraqi infantry, and force a path through. It was a plan born out of sheer desperation, but what other options did they have right now?

Ed got back on the radio, trying to get another set of coordinates agreed with Headquarters, and a hot-extraction grid set to the west of their position. As he did so, Grey issued a set of combat orders: the blokes were only to engage the Fedayeen if they opened fire or started advancing on the British position. Once the route west was declared on, they were to move out pronto.

A few seconds later there was a faint rumble from the skies to their north. It grew rapidly to a throaty roar, like an avalanche was sweeping across the open desert. For an instant this dark, shadowed arrow loomed out of the pitch black like some monster alien spacecraft, a thunderous snarl tearing apart the night with ear-shattering violence.

The warplane flashed overhead so close that you could have thrown a rock at it. The howl of its jet engines was powerful enough to rattle the Pinkies, as if a giant hand had grabbed hold and was shaking them about. The blokes atop the heavy machine-guns ducked involuntarily, as if the jet was about to rip their heads off. They'd known it was coming, but still the sheer force and ferocity of the thing was awe-inspiring and fearsome.

It was dead-hard to achieve a sonic boom on demand, and only the best of the best could manage it. The F16 pilot would have to pull up violently right over the Fedayeen's heads, the jet engines' thrust colliding with the air to create a massive boom.

The lead F16 bottomed out into a screaming turn above the enemy, the air in its tortured wake glowing like a ghostly steam cloud. Moments later the jet's afterburners cut in, trailing a comet of fire as the F16s climbed almost vertically.

Then: KABOOOOOM!

The ear-splitting sound rolled across the open terrain, thundering over the British position like a tidal wave. As the jet climbed, the pilot fired off a blinding burst of flares in his wake, like a salvo of missiles pummelling the earth all around the Fedayeen's positions. Barely thirty seconds later the second F16 came screaming in and did a repeat performance, the sonic boom of its afterburners echoing like an atomic explosion across the battlefield.

All around the desert to the south and west of their position, vehicle lights had gone out. The Fedayeen had doused their headlamps in an effort to hide themselves from the warplanes.

'*Zero Six Bravo*, *Viper Five Three*,' came the voice of the lead pilot, 'they've gone static and dark, so that's shut 'em down for a while. We've got twenty minutes' play time, but doing those low-level passes sure burns up the fuel real fast.'

'Roger, keep watching 'em,' Moth replied. 'They start moving or showing any lights, smash in another low pass. We're going to bug out west, and when we do I'll give you a warning. Do not engage three wagons moving due west on black light. Repeat: do not engage us.'

'Well copied.'

It was 0045 hours by now. The men had been in constant combat or on the run for approaching seven hours. After a week spent operating deep behind enemy lines, they had been on their chinstraps even before they'd got hit. It was only the adrenaline, plus the fear of being overrun, that was keeping them going.

The force prepared to move out, pulling blokes back from the rim of the wadi and loading up the vehicles. Using the cover of the F16s screaming in for a second low-level pass, the wagons crawled towards the lip of the lake bed, in preparation for turning west. But as the pair of warplanes roared overhead at tree-top level, the Fedayeen opened up on them, spurts of 12.7mm tracer chasing the jets through the dark skies.

The militia fighters must have woken up to the fact that the F16s weren't dropping ordnance, which wasn't good news. The Dushka was designed first and foremost as an anti-aircraft weapon, although it stood little chance of bringing down an F16. But it just went to show how quickly the Fedayeen learned from the realities of the battlefield, and adapted their actions accordingly.

The lead Pinkie was creeping up over the western edge of the wadi when the nearest of the Fedayeen vehicles swung their guns round. Within seconds, 12.7mm Duskha rounds went tearing past the blokes in the wagon, as the enemy hosed down the wadi.

With all the passengers blocking their arcs, the gunners on the Pinkies still couldn't return fire. Figures dived off to either side, sprinting for their defensive positions and to find some cover. At the same moment the .50-cals and GPMGs sparked up, smashing rounds back into the enemy, targeting the long tongues of yellow flame spitting out of the darkness.

For a few instants they traded fire with bloody fire, then the wagons reversed course back into the cover of the lake bed. It was impossible to exit from their position in the face of such a murderous assault, for there was no way they could fight when the crowded wagons were on the move.

Whether or not those low-level passes by the F16s had led the enemy onto their position Grey didn't know. But he was burning up with frustration, and the enemy sure as hell seemed to know where they were now.

The F16 pilot was on to Moth almost immediately. The warplanes were approaching zero fuel, and they'd clocked that they were under fire. It was clear that with each pass the Fedayeen were getting wise to the fact that the jets weren't killing them, which made each less effective than the last. The lead pilot warned Moth they could manage two more shows of force, by which time they'd be sipping on fumes. The British force had to break out west in the limited time that the warplanes could buy them, or they'd be overrun.

It was then that Grey had a flash of pure inspiration. He dived out of the wagon and sprinted over to Scruff, who was lying prone on the rim of the lake bed. He dropped down beside him, so both men were gazing out into the open desert due west.

'When the jets come in, unleash with the *SLAR* on whatever targets you can hit,' Grey told him. 'We've never seen a thermo-baric warhead in action and neither will the fucking enemy. Fire off as many as you can as the jets do their stuff, and hopefully the bastard Fedayeen will think the F16s have switched to drop-ping bombs.'

'Fucking nice one,' Scruff growled.

'Get one of the blokes to be your loader,' Grey added, 'and smash the warheads into them fast as you can.'

'Got it.'

Spurts of 12.7mm fire went burning across the skies above him, as Grey scuttled back to the wagons. He gave Ed the sketch and they put it out on the radios, so all would know what was happening.

'Right, here's the plan: we'll smash the Fedayeen with the *SLAR*, and maybe the Iraqi infantry too. Presumably, the enemy'll think it's the F16s in action, and they'll run for the fucking hills. They do that, we break contact and head due west. We'll break through their lines, and either we'll hit the Syrian border or get a helo in to a grid to lift us out.'

That done, Grey slid into the seat of his Pinkie and grabbed the GPMG. He swung it round, centring the metal sights on a pair of Fedayeen headlights. He paused for an instant to draw breath, and waited for the roar of the warplanes as they headed in for their third low-level pass.

As the rumble of the incoming warplanes grew in volume, a monster round from one of the T-72s came tearing across the British position and slammed into the open desert a hundred yards beyond. There was a momentary delay, and a second tank shell ploughed into the ground just short of their position. Now the gunners had them bracketed.

Grey tensed for a third shell to smash right into them, the scream of the jet engines drowning out the roar of battle. As the lead F16 streaked earthwards in a shallow dive, Scruff unleashed the first thermobaric rocket from the *SLAR*. There was a violent flash of flame from the weapon's gaping muzzle, and the rocket went tearing towards the nearest Iraqi vehicle.

The compact warhead slammed into the target, impacting with a dull thud. A small scatter charge threw out a fine mist of fuel-air explosive, which enveloped and saturated the vehicle. A split second later the secondary, igniter charge detonated, instantly transforming the fuel-air mixture into a white-hot seething fireball.

As the flame front accelerated from the epicentre of the blast, the burning vehicle careered onwards, the firestorm flaring and seething as it sucked in oxygen like a dragon devouring its prey. The blast wave flashed outwards from the heart of the conflagration, tearing into the vehicles to either side, before collapsing in on itself to form a crushing vacuum.

Moments later the incinerated vehicle shuddered to a halt, a gutted ruin. A black mushroom cloud of smoke belched skywards, right in the wake of the F16. Scruff reloaded, aimed and fired again. The entire horizon under attack from the *SLAR* seemed to dissolve into a sea of raging fire, as a second vehicle was engulfed in a white-hot blast.

With the F16s ramping up the afterburners Scruff hammered in the thermobaric rockets, and the headlights all around them went out. Even the searchlights atop the T-72s had been doused, as the enemy forces killed their movement and their lights, and went static.

For several tense moments the men of the tiny British force gazed out into a dark and apparently empty desert. The seconds ticked by. Seconds became a full minute, and still there was no sign of movement or light from the enemy. It looked as if the plan was working. Now was as good a time as any to make a run for it.

For a second time, they pulled the blokes back from the rim of the lake bed and loaded up the wagons. Then Moth got the lead vehicle nosing out of cover and into the open desert. As he did so, the F16s came in for their fourth and final pass. They screamed across the British vehicles, and then they were powering south away from the battlefield.

The lead pilot came up on the air. '*Zero Six Bravo, Viper Five Three*. We're bingo fuel and we're out of here. Stay safe down there.'

Moth offered a heartfelt thanks you for everything that the American pilots had done for them. They'd not been able to unleash their bombs or their cannon, yet to a man the blokes knew that without those warplanes they'd have been trapped in the lake bed and overrun.

The three Pinkies pushed due west, the noise of the F16s fading to a faint rumble on the still desert air. Hardly had the skies above them fallen silent than the first lights blinked on to their rear. The enemy was on the move again, but whether they'd seen the British force bugging out no one knew for sure right now. As the three wagons careered onwards, trying to put as much distance between themselves and the lake bed, a chilling thought hit Grey: even if they could break out west, they mightn't have the fuel to make it to the extraction grid.

The last time Grey had checked on the diesel was at last light, shortly before the enemy had hit them, and it had been clear then that they'd need a resupply within the next twenty-four hours. He'd figured they had a hundred kilometres max of diesel on their wagon. That was seven hours ago, and without factoring in all the desperate driving since then, plus the extra weight of the blokes they were now carrying. And he had little idea of the fuel states of the other vehicles.

He was dreading the moment when the first wagon shuddered to a halt, as its tank ran dry.

# CHAPTER TWENTY-TWO

The three Pinkies had made no more than five hundred yards from their last position when the enemy closed the noose. To their rear the lake bed they'd just vacated was transformed into a sea of fire, as the Fedayeen hosed it down with 12.7mm Dushka rounds.

At the lip of the depression the enemy pulled to a halt, and their fighters piled off the Toyotas. They swarmed into the low ground, AK47s spitting fire – at which point they must have discovered that the British force had somehow evaporated into thin air. But a set of tracks led out of the wadi, and those could be traced and followed.

As they pressed onwards, Grey did a quick check on ammo stats. He'd got two boxes of rounds left for the GPMG, so he was 800 down. Dude was in an even worse state. He'd just slung the last belt of .50-cal ammo onto the heavy machine-gun, which put him 500 rounds down. They'd each got their Diemacos, with 360 rounds apiece, but they were piss-all use against 12.7mm heavy machine-guns.

A couple more up-close firefights with the Fedayeen, and they were going to get slaughtered. Grey was in no doubt that the Iraqis would be bringing up reinforcements, and they presumably had a hundred thousand troops plus their war machines to choose from. The British force had survived thus far only thanks to the terrain, the distance and the darkness, not to mention the battle-winning air cover.

It was some five minutes later, around 0130 hours, that Grey's vehicle drew level with the scorched and twisted wreckage, which was all that remained after the *SLAR* strikes. As their wagon pushed in amongst the inferno, they passed the gutted shell of a vehicle spewing out great gouts of oily black smoke. Its tyres were still burning fiercely, thick acrid fumes barrelling into the sky.

The way ahead was all but obscured by the drifting, oily darkness. Visibility was down to near-zero, and Grey couldn't tell if there were any enemy left alive in there. They were moving through the Iraqi lines more or less blind. There was one upside: now that they were in amongst the worst of the carnage, the dense smoke should hide their position from those to their rear.

As the lead vehicle pushed ahead Grey, Moth and Dude pulled their *shemaghs* closer around their faces, to filter out the fumes. They were hyper-alert to any hostile presence, as was Raggy, who was still sprawled across the wagon's bonnet. They crawled past the wreckage – the paint blackened and blistered from the scorching heat, the steel warped and twisted.

The flames were red-hot on the exposed parts of Grey's face, and the intensity of the conflagration had rendered the vehicles all but unrecognizable. He heaved up his *shemagh* still further, to better shield his skin. As he did so he said a quick prayer for the poor bastards who'd been caught in all of this. They may have been the enemy, but it was still a horrible way to die.

They were in amongst the gutted skeletons of the vehicles, scanning the smoke to their front, when Grey chanced a quick look to their rear. His heart skipped a beat, and his pulse began to hammer away in his head ever more powerfully. He figured he could just make out a set of headlights probing the thick smoke.

It had to be those bastard Fedayeen.

He eyed Raggy on the bonnet, and took a sideways glance at Moth. 'Fedayeen to our rear, guys. They hit us again, we're fucked.'

Moth grunted an acknowledgement and kept focused on his driving.

Raggy forced an exhausted grin. 'Yeah, don't I know it, mate.'

They were maybe forty kilometres short of the border with Syria, and that way lay their only hope of sanctuary. It would be a massive embarrassment should twenty-six elite British operators get hauled into custody in Syria. But it could hardly get a great deal worse: they'd lost scores of vehicles blown up, with more than likely a couple captured intact, and God only knew what specialist kit had fallen into enemy hands.

The Squadron OC plus his Headquarters troop had been forced to go to ground, and they'd lost contact with one element of the Squadron completely – the lone Land Rover plus the clutch of quads, with however many blokes crammed onto those vehicles. Plus they'd got one quad on the run two-up, which would be crashing across the border into Syria if Gunner had his way, or falling into enemy hands if he didn't.

Either way, the Squadron had been well and truly scattered, so now probably *was* the time to head for the Combat RV. But before they could try for Syrian territory, they'd have to cross the N253, a main road that runs along the Iraqi side of the border. And if Grey had been the commander in overall charge of the Iraqi forces, it was there that he'd have the main body of his armour and infantry positioned. That way, he could use the Fedayeen to drive the British patrol onto their guns.

The lead wagon was rocketing ahead as fast as it could go, when Grey caught the ominous growl of a powerful engine just to the north of their line of march. He locked eyes with Raggy. They'd both recognized the sound. There was a tank on the prowl out there not far ahead of them, and it sounded like a monster.

Moth gunned the Land Rover, pushing it ever harder. But the terrain here was far harsher than the Ninawa Desert in terms of navigating at night and at speed. It was a flat, rocky plain, criss-crossed in every direction by dry, shallow gullies. Mostly they were oriented in a southeasterly direction, and when it rained here they'd channel the floodwaters towards the seasonal lake of the Kabrat Sunaysilah, lying on the northern border of the desert. The easiest thing would be to head for the cover of one of those gullies, yet that would channel the patrol in the opposite direction to the way they needed to go.

Syria lay west: the gullies would funnel them south and east. Instead, Moth found himself having to search for a route across the narrow, steep-sided obstructions, while the blokes clung on to the wagons for all they were worth.

As the lead Pinkie crawled down the friable slope of the next gully, Moth made the snap decision to pull up in the cover of its walls. The throaty growl of the approaching tank was growing ever louder, as it churned through the smoke and the fumes.

The two wagons behind pulled up alongside them, and the blokes piled off in all-around defence. With LAWs held at the ready and the heavy machine-guns freed for action, they were now in a snap ambush. Almost as an afterthought, Moth reached forward and unleashed his grenade launcher from its cowboy holster. If that Lion of Babylon came charging over the wadi's edge, they'd mallet it with everything they had.

The more modern Asad Babils had laminated armour to the front and rear, to provide extra protection against HEAT (high explosive anti-tank) armour-piercing projectiles, so there was little the men were likely to achieve against one of those. But it would be better to go down fighting.

The clatter of the tank tracks could be heard clearly now, as it hunted through the smoke and the wreckage. From behind them they caught the odd snarl of a speeding Toyota, but it was the howl of that T-72's massive 12-cylinder diesel engine that had them transfixed. No point going anywhere until that had been shaken off, or dealt with.

The most advanced Lions of Babylon had been fitted with Belgian-made thermal imaging sights for the 125mm smooth-bore main gun. That would explain how the enemy had been able to track the Squadron through the dark and the thick smoke as they escaped from the first LUP. If the battle tank now bearing down on them was fitted with such a system, it should be able to see through the drifting smoke.

The clanking of the approaching behemoth became ever more deafening, as the men present prepared to open fire. For an instant its squat, desert-grey form came looming out of the shadows, its nearside track tearing along the western lip of the ravine, and throwing down rocks and sand into the bed of the wadi.

There was a horrible moment when it seemed as if the lip of the wadi above them would collapse, bringing the 41.5-tonne armoured monster down on top of them. And then it had roared past, the long neck of its main cannon swinging this way and that as it scanned through the drifting smog. Getting the three wagons below ground and out of sight had more than likely saved them. But how many more times were they going to get this lucky?

The noise of the battle tank faded, and finally Moth fired up the Pinkie and nosed out of the ravine, setting a course westwards for Syria. As they pressed onwards through the relative quiet of the night a thought struck Grey: for the first time in many hours they were no longer under direct attack.

He glanced at the faintly luminous dial of his watch. It was 0200. No more than three hours left until first light. He didn't doubt that come sun-up they'd be pretty much out of options. Most likely they'd find some kind of an LUP, but Grey wasn't kidding himself that they'd be able to lie low all day long without being discovered. There were scores of enemy vehicles out there combing the terrain, and he was not even sure that they could manage to evade them during the hours of darkness, and more seemed to be joining the hunt with every passing hour.

Either they had to make it across the Syrian border, or they got the Chinooks in sometime within the next couple of hours – and all before the wagons ran out of fuel. He glanced at the gauge. The needle was hovering at just above the reserve-tank level. As overloaded as they were, they'd get maybe thirty klicks out of that – possibly less, depending on the terrain. Plus he knew they had a few glugs of diesel left in the one remaining jerry-can that hadn't been exhausted. They needed to get to a hot-extraction grid or cross into Syria bloody quickly, and before the tanks ran dry.

The lead wagon emerged from the final ghostly whips of smoke remaining from the *SLAR* attack, and pushed into the open. Grey put a call through to Ed on the radio.

'We're running low on fuel and there's precious few hours left of darkness. Let's stop for a Chinese.'

'Got it.' Ed confirmed. 'Pull over when you can find some cover.'

The lead Pinkie rolled to a halt in a shallow depression and Moth cut the engine. The two other wagons pulled up, one to either side. The top gunners covered their arcs as the extra blokes tumbled off the vehicles and gathered round. The wagons were close enough so all twenty-six could hear what was to be said.

'This is how I see it,' Grey began, speaking into the tense silence. He was one of the most battle-experienced of the lot, and he'd largely been navigating the patrol ever since they left the wadi of death. He had the skills and the experience to speak and to be heard. He outlined the patrol's predicament, then asked for any suggestions from those present. No one had much to say, so he ploughed on. He was stating the obvious, but it needed to be said so they could make the toughest of decisions.

'There's no way we can lie up around here, come daylight. We've seen enough of the enemy to know they can scour just about every inch of the terrain, and if nothing else the tracks we leave will lead them right to us.'

Raggy grunted in agreement. 'Time's fucking tight now. There's only three hours left until first light. One way or the other we've got to get ourselves gone.'

'Right, so let's go firm on a grid and get the Chinooks in,' Grey continued. 'Or let's get a grid passed from Headquarters, one we can make this side of the N253, and let's rendezvous with the helos there. That's Plan A. But if there's no helo pick-up possible by 0330, we need to face the fact that we're not getting pulled out of here. We'll need to run west and make a break for the Syrian border, 'cause there's no way we can hide around here, come sunrise.'

'Agreed,' said Ed. 'We go for the helo pick-up, and if not for Plan B – which is to make for the Combat RV before—'

His last words were cut off by a sharp burst of small-arms fire. About a kilometre to the east, tracer rounds went arcing into the sky. There was no way the fire had been aimed at the patrol, for it was well wide of the mark. It looked more like some kind of a signal, and there were no guesses as to who the signal was intended for. Everywhere to their east and south there were headlights stabbing the darkness.

Half a dozen sets of lights turned towards that burst of fire, and began to converge on it. For a moment it crossed Grey's mind that it might have signalled that the Fedayeen had found one of the scattered elements of the Squadron. It was possible they'd cornered Gunner and his rupert passenger, as they tried to evade and escape on the quad. There was just no way of knowing.

'What about the rest of the guys?' he asked Ed. 'Any news on Gunner? Or the third force – the lone Pinkie and the quads?'

'No word on Gunner,' Ed replied. 'But I was onto Headquarters as we moved out of the last LUP, and the third force has just come up on comms.'

'Nice one!'

'Fucking result!'

'So what's the score with that lot?'

'There are twenty-four blokes with them,' Ed said. 'They've got one Pinkie and half a dozen quads, so they're hopelessly overloaded, worse than us. They're into some difficult terrain – rocks, boulders and ravines. But they've gone to ground as best they can and they're playing hide-and-seek with the enemy—'

Grey whistled. 'Fucking hell, and we thought we had it bad. The quads must be double-bagged, maybe more, and they'll be burning up the juice. Plus they've got fuck-all heavy weapons.'

'Yeah, but it's the quads that saved the Squadron,' Scruff cut in. 'Far more of them got through the swamp than the Pinkies. If the lead Troop had all been riding Pinkies, they'd have been finished.'

'They taken casualties?' Grey asked. Clearly, that third group was the most vulnerable.

'Headquarters is seeking casualty stats right now,' said Ed, 'but it's a hellishly confused picture. They'll try to marry us up with that lot, so they can extract us as one force from the same grid. But Head Shed says don't worry about them right now. Our job it to get ourselves out of the shit. That's our priority.'

'Presumably, Headquarters are still looking to pull the OC out first?' Grey queried.

'Yeah. We may get a bit of a run-around as they try to pull the boss out, but that's just how it is. He's the last person we want getting captured or killed.'

'One thing,' remarked Moth. 'Let's try to get some air. We need something that can sit above us, looking nasty and ugly and ready to mallet the enemy if they get too close. That's the only way to get the Chinooks in.'

'Try for some air,' Ed confirmed. A pause. 'So, we're decided?'

There were terse nods all round.

Grey glanced at the blokes. Their faces were caked in mud and dust mixed with cordite burn marks and streaks of smoke. In their ripped and bloodied combats and with self-administered bandages slapped on here and there, they looked like a band of total desperadoes. Which right now was exactly what Grey figured they were, especially when considering their chances of getting out of this one alive.

Moth got on the satcom and put out an all-stations call to any available warplanes, while Ed dialled up Headquarters to get a usable extraction point. It was a few moments before he was able to pass the grid of the new helo pick-up to Grey.

He also had news for Moth. Headquarters had promised an AC130 Spectre gunship to be orbiting in their overhead within the next hour. The Spectre had been scrambled from the nearest friendly airbase, and was flying in specifically to give top cover to the scattered remnants of M Squadron. Having a Spectre above them would sure make all the difference right now.

The Hercules AC130 Spectre is the cream of air cover, being an armoured behemoth that can loiter in the air for several hours flying orbits above the battlefield. It boasts a 25mm GAU-12 Equalizer cannon, a 40mm Bofors auto-cannon and a 105mm M102 howitzer. It has unrivalled night-vision optics, pinpoint targeting systems and a crew of thirteen to fly and fight her – including pilots, a navigator, fire-control officers, sensor operators, loadmasters and the all-important gunners.

In short, it was the perfect air asset to de-conflict a complex and confused battle space – identifying friend from foe – and to target and hit hostile forces. The likelihood of it being unable to do any attack runs – as with the F16s – was pretty much zero. Its call-sign was *Ghost One Six*, and it would be above them in sixty minutes' time.

Grey punched the coordinates of the new helo pick-up point into his GPS, and worked it through the mapping.

'RV point with the Chinooks is five kilometres due west of our present position,' he announced, 'plus five klicks short of the N253. It's doable.'

'Right, let's get moving,' Ed confirmed.

The men mounted up the vehicles. Moth fired up their wagon and prepared to move off. But as he did so, there was a furious cry from one of the wagons to their rear.

'The wagon's fucking dying! Bastard fucking wagon's fucking died on us!'

It was Scruff. Grey could only imagine his Pinkie – like the rest of the wagons – had been torn up by the 12.7mm fire and shrapnel, and that was what had made it finally give up the ghost. It was a miracle that the three Land Rovers had kept going thus far, but now they were going to have to get the blokes from the last wagon to cross-deck onto the two that remained.

Grey ran back to Scruff's position, to find out what the hell had happened. It turned out that the rear-most of the vehicles had in fact run out of diesel. For a moment Grey was frozen with indecision and then he made the call.

'Fuck it, keep everyone on your wagon. We'll refuel it from our jerry. We've got to keep the wagons going, or we're fucked. They'll catch us.'

Bodies piled off the lead Pinkie, as Dude hauled out the last remaining jerry-can from the rear. He handed it to Grey. It had a five-gallon capacity, and it felt as if it was around one-quarter full.

Under normal circumstances the Pinkies could manage twenty mpg across rough terrain. Overloaded as they were, that was probably down to fifteen. If Grey drained the entire can into Scruff's wagon, he was giving it no more than thirty miles of fuel max. Either they got the Chinooks in pronto, or they'd be down to twenty-six blokes sharing two crippled vehicles.

Grey lugged the jerry back to Scruff's Pinkie, up-ended it and sloshed the diesel into the wagon's tank. To their rear he could see scores of headlights probing through the gloom, as the Fedayeen fanned out across the desert. Maybe they too were running short of ammo, and they were holding their fire until they were close enough to see the whites of the eyes of their prey, and could be certain of their targets.

He cursed as he tried to get the can to empty faster. As he finished draining the last of the diesel he noticed that his hands were shaking. Whether it was from the exhaustion, the adrenalin rush or the fear, he didn't know. And in a sense he was past caring.

He raced back to his wagon and set to working out a bearing to take them to the extraction grid. The wagons moved out. But after some nine hours of navigating through the darkness he was tortured with exhaustion, his eyes red-raw from staring at his map and into the hungry maw of the night. He was desperate for a break.

They got Scruff's wagon to take the lead. It made double sense, for their vehicle was arguably the most vulnerable now. It was better to have it up ahead where a problem could be instantly spotted. It hadn't escaped any of them that a round might have gone through the Pinkie's fuel lines, in which case it would piss out any diesel into the desert sands.

Fifteen minutes' hard driving later they reached the grid for the helo pick-up, with Scruff's wagon still going strong. The blokes debussed and went into all-round defence. They were flat out on their belt buckles, but it was clear right away that this was a totally shit patch of terrain from which to mount a battle. Headquarters had chosen a featureless stretch of open desert: it was perfect ground for a pair of Chinooks to put down on, but useless for repelling an attack by scores of Fedayeen wielding 12.7mm Dushkas, let alone a marauding Iraqi T-72.

They'd need a minimum of two Chinooks to lift them and their wagons out of theatre, but there was precious little cover the blokes could give the helos if they landed here. That would be the ultimate nightmare – seeing a couple of those giant twin-rotor helicopters blasted out of the sky. It would be a disaster for the RAF aircrew, who'd likely die – or get captured – if by some freak of chance they survived. And it would be a disaster for the twenty-six blokes waiting on the grid, for no one was kidding themselves that the British military would get a replacement pair of helos up and running in the few short hours before sunrise.

Ed radioed Headquarters that the patrol was in position, and gave a warning about the lack of available cover, plus that enemy forces were all around them.

He was told to stand by.

# CHAPTER TWENTY-THREE

They'd been on the ground for ten horribly tense minutes when Ed got the word. The Chinooks were en route to their grid, but they were being diverted. Reggie, the Squadron OC, had just come up on the air with his own extraction coordinates.

It made every sense to pull out the HQ Troop and all the extra blokes with them – and especially if they had seriously wounded. But it was still massively frustrating to have this happen right now, especially as it was their unit that had been drawing the bulk of the enemy fire.

Their force was to remain static on the present grid for as long as they could possibly manage. Headquarters would try to get the helos in to pick them up, once they'd lifted out the HQ Troop. If the patrol needed to bug out, they'd set another RV point further west, and try to marry up the helos and the patrol that way.

They held firm for a further five minutes, but time was dragging painfully slowly. Each second felt like a bloody lifetime, as the thought of the hunter force that would be drawing ever closer gnawed into each of the operators' minds. Eyes stared out anxiously into the dark night, keeping watch on the scores of headlights tracking back and forth across the desert.

The Fedayeen were out there not that far away, driving what looked like a series of search grids. It stood to reason that sooner or later, they'd stumble upon the force that was static at the hot-extraction grid. Grey knew it was suicide to stick around for much longer. If they did, they were going to be caught in the open with their pants down.

He had this ghostly, creepy feeling, like ice running down his spine: it was his sixth sense screaming *Danger!* From long years of elite soldiering, he knew when his instinct was telling him that the enemy was close, and it was doing so right now. He'd learned to trust that instinct, for it had saved his life on more than one occasion.

He caught the snarl of a revving motor to the east, and a Toyota SUV crawled out of a deep river gully not three hundred yards away. Grey knew that steep-sided ravine well, for it was one Moth had had real problems getting their heavy wagon out of as he'd headed for the extraction grid. The powerful, lightly loaded Toyota suffered no such difficulties as it hauled itself onto level ground.

The Fedayeen must have used the gully to push northwest, the terrain masking their engine noise until the very last moment. There was no way that the fighters riding in it could fail to spot the British vehicles. Grey saw the lead Dushka gunner swing his weapon round, scanning his arcs. It was simply a question of who got the drop on the others first and opened fire.

Grey swivelled the GPMG round, found his target, pulled the trigger and let rip. An instant later the heavy .50-cal snarled and roared from behind him, as Dude spotted the threat and opened up. Big, chunky rounds went pumping over Grey's head and slamming into the enemy vehicle.

Bursts of fire punched a neat line of holes through the windscreen of the Toyota and tore through the bodywork, chunks of metal spinning off in all directions. Within seconds the vehicle had exploded, as heavy rounds sliced through the fuel tank, igniting the diesel in a ball of boiling flame. Figures stumbled from the burning wagon, the clothes of one of them a sheet of raging fire.

The surviving Fedayeen piled off the vehicle's rear, and dived for cover. AK47s were raised and muzzles sparked as they started unleashing on automatic. To his right Grey saw Moth raise his Diemaco-mounted M203 grenade launcher and open up, pumping 40mm grenades into the enemy position. Within seconds, they'd blanketed the surviving Fedayeen in murderous fire.

Moth had proved himself ten times over as a driver, and he more than shown his mettle on the M203. He might have been the wild card on their team, but with Moth, Grey reckoned he had hit solid gold.

As the Toyota popped and burned, Grey detected the grunts of powerful engines from further down the wadi. Further Fedayeen were moving through. Where there had been one enemy vehicle there were soon going to be a whole lot more, for it sounded as if the first Toyota must have been leading a sizeable convoy.

That first vehicle continued to burn fiercely, throwing off clouds of thick, black smoke. The extraction grid had been compromised big time, the firefight ensuring that it was visible for miles around. It was like a magnet now, drawing in the bad guys. No way were they about to bring any Chinooks in here.

Voices broke out over the radios. 'Fucking mount up and move out!'

'Move it! Move it!'

'We're out of here!'

Figures sprinted across the terrain and hurled themselves into the rear of the Pinkies. Moth slipped his weapon back into its holster and fired up the wagon's engine, as Raggy dived onto his place on the bonnet, wrapping his arms around their M72 LAW in an effort to hold on.

'Head west!' Grey yelled. 'And let's fucking move it!'

They were seriously on the run now, and within seconds Moth had their Pinkie thumping its way across the rough ground, as he accelerated away from their extraction. But they'd made no more than five hundred yards when the first savage burst of 12.7mm fire tore out of the darkness, hammering overhead.

More SUVs were powering up from the riverbed, and they were onto the British vehicles almost instantly. Less than eight hundred yards separated the two forces as the Fedayeen gave chase, their convoy charging across the desert terrain. Short bursts of probing Dushka fire sparked over the blokes' heads, as the enemy gunners tried to gauge the range and fire accurately from their fast-moving Toyotas.

Blokes hanging off the rearmost Pinkie began trying to return fire with their assault rifles and grenade launchers, as others held them fast in an effort to keep them aboard. But it was all but impossible to put down accurate fire from a speeding wagon weaving through horrendous terrain. The only way to do so would have been by means of the tripod-mounted heavy weapons, and they were unusable with so many blokes clustered around them.

Yet for some reason the Fedayeen seemed to be hanging back, instead of closing for the kill.

As their wagon fought its way across the uneven ground Grey

was desperately trying to check his maps. He figured the Syrian border had to be no more than eight kilometres away. It seemed impossible that they'd make it – but hell, they had at least to try.

He glanced at Moth. 'We got to make that break for Syria, like now! Keep going due west as fast as you can go, mate.'

Moth floored the accelerator and the wagon ripped ahead, practically going airborne as it smashed through a patch of broken ground. Grey flicked his eyes down to their fuel gauge. Their reserve tank was half gone: they should have enough diesel to make it across the border – that's if they could head straight through. Too much of a run-around, and in no time they'd be sipping on fumes.

He glanced up and into the far distance, scanning the route that would take them to the border. As he did so, he almost had a heart attack on the spot. Due west of their position he'd spotted lights in a long, linear formation – ones that had just become visible on the near horizon. Up ahead they had a convoy of vehicles spread out at regular intervals on what had to be a road.

It was at the limit of his sight, so maybe three kilometres away. But via his natural night vision he figured he could just make out army trucks, and the squat forms of armour. It had to be an Iraqi military convoy on the N253. It was static, and this was where Grey figured the commander of the entire Iraqi battle effort had to be positioned. Doubtless, it was from here that he'd been over-seeing the hunt for M Squadron.

It struck Grey that they were being herded into the final trap. This had to be what the Fedayeen were trying to drive them onto – this solid front of Iraqi armour and guns. He felt the wagon slow, as Moth woke up to the new threat. It was clear as day that there was no way through to the Syrian border any more. Even that doubtful promise of sanctuary was now suddenly closed to them.

Grey flicked his eyes down at his map. 'The border kinks east, and the 255 with it!' he yelled at Moth. He grabbed the receiver, 'They're trying to herd us onto the 255. Steer north-northeast to take us away from the fuckers!'

With the Fedayeen on their heels it was the only route left open to them – though somewhere to their north lurked the hunter force of Iraqi battle tanks. Moth spun the steering wheel through his hands, and the nose of the wagon swung ninety degrees northeast.

As they came around to the new bearing, Grey could just make out the faintest trace of a fine, duck-egg blue painting the horizon due east – the first hints of the coming dawn. They'd just run out of escape options, and they were fast running out of time.

They had an Iraqi military convoy bang west of them; Fedayeen to the south and east; T-72 tanks to the north; plus a shedload of Iraqi infantry somewhere in the middle. They were totally boxed in, and they'd been left with nowhere to run or to hide. They needed some air cover – like now – or they were totally fucked.

'Where the fuck's that Spectre gunship?' Grey yelled.

Moth pointed to the comms handset bolted to the Pinkie's dash. 'Fire that up, and dial up the air. How many satellites is it showing?'

'Two.'

'Not enough. Needs three.'

The wagon careered ahead at breakneck speed, with the odd burst of tracer fire tearing through the night. Grey got their grid sorted, and then there was an audible bleep as a third satellite icon flashed up on the screen.

'Three!' he yelled. He grabbed the satcom's receiver. '*Zero Six Bravo*, calling *Ghost One Six*, d'you copy?''

A beat. Then: '*Zero Six Bravo*, this is *Ghost One Six*. I got you good and clear. How you doing down there?'

'Not fucking great! We're three jeeps with a shedload of Iraqi SUVs on our tail. We need you to smash them. Our grid is 98463782, and we've heading northeast at roughly thirty kph. The enemy is six hundred metres to the south of us and closing.'

'No can do, *Zero Six Bravo*. We're a good thirty minutes out from your location. It's that kind of time before we'll be within range and we can light those fuckers up for ya.'

'Stand by.' Grey cut the line. He let out a string of curses. The adrenalin was pumping in bucketloads, and despite the icy cold of the desert night his combats were soaked in sweat. 'They're thirty minutes out. There's no air cover. What the fuck?'

Moth shrugged. 'We need an extraction grid, like yesterday.'

As if to reinforce what he was saying, from just beneath where Raggy was lying across the bonnet the Pinkie began to emit this tortured whine. The engine sounded as if it was about to shake itself to pieces. It was hardly surprising. There were more bullet and shrapnel holes than bodywork on their wagon, and the damage to the internal components had to be terminal. The fact that it was still moving at all was little short of a miracle.

Ed's voice came up on the radios, thick with tension and urgency. 'We've got a new extraction grid! 14657389. Repeat: 14657389.'

Grey plotted it. 'Just to the north of here, and well away from the 255. It's doable. But make sure the fuckers get the Chinooks in this time, 'cause we ain't going to get a second chance.'

'It's a one-ship,' came Ed's reply. 'They've split the Chinooks so the other can lift out the OC. It'll be standing-room only, and we're gonna have to blow the vehicles.' A 'one-ship' was military-speak for a lone aircraft. They were still trying to pull the HQ Troop out, so they'd been forced to separate the two Chinooks.

Grey glanced at the cloud of steam that was boiling up from their engine, and presumably scalding Raggy's balls off. 'No fucking loss there. Ours is about to fucking pile in on us.'

'The helos are coming in with top cover from fast air,' added Ed. 'That should keep the fucking Fedayeen's heads down.'

The Chinooks would be fitted with internal fuel bladders, to give them extra range. And for sure they'd need it, given the run-around from grid to grid they'd been getting as the scattered forces of M Squadron tried to outrun and evade the enemy. The bladders sat in the hold, cutting down the space for men and cargo. With a lone helo in-bound, there would be precious little room for the twenty-six blokes, let alone all their kit and the wagons.

As Ed's voice went off the air, Grey double-checked the grid on his map. They had five klicks to go, and if the fast jets could drive off the Fedayeen they might just make it. If not, there was no way they could hold that grid, fight off the Fedayeen, and get the lone Chinook in safely.

If Grey were the Iraqi commander sitting in that convoy on the N253, just as soon as the British force went static he'd start dropping shells onto their grid. He'd get the Fedayeen to talk the rounds in, walking the 125mm tank shells and their artillery right onto the British position. Basically, any helo crew putting down amidst all of that would be committing suicide.

Grey glanced towards the heavens, and he fancied he could just about make out the faint roar of a couple of jets in-bound. That, he hoped, was the fast air escorting the lone Chinook in.

Moments later the lead pilot came up on the air. Moth gave him the talk-on, as he continued to coax their ailing wagon through the horrendous terrain. He was having to yell to make his voice heard above the screaming whine from just beneath the bonnet, to which had now been added a deafening steel-on-steel clanking sound.

'This is the sketch: we're making for an extraction grid two kilometres north of here, but we've got enemy wagons in hot pursuit. We need to go firm on that grid, and wait for a Chinook to extract us. Can you keep the enemy off our backs and away from that RV point, until we're pulled out of there?'

'Roger that,' came back the crisp tones of the lead RAF pilot. 'It's a very confused battle space down there, so we'll come in first in a low-level pass. If that doesn't do it, we'll start hitting enemy targets. Either way, we'll keep a good watch over you.'

Moments later a pair of Tornadoes came screaming out of the darkness to the southwest, tearing over the N253 and practically kissing the desert as they thundered across the Fedayeen positions. More or less the instant the jets roared past overhead, the enemy vehicles in pursuit slowed to a halt and their lights went dark.

The pair of British warplanes banked around in a burning turn, then tore back across the enemy positions like streaks of lightning blazing through the night. They dipped low over the Fedayeen positions, their pounding slipstream ripping the branches from the scattered palm trees as they practically set the desert ablaze with their afterburners.

For the first time in what felt like a lifetime, the terrain behind the three battle-weary wagons had gone dark. It was totally devoid of enemy headlights, muzzle flashes or any sign of movement.

Presumably, the enemy commander figured the jets would soon be gone, in which case he could finish off the British force at his leisure.

The one thing he couldn't know was that in the wake of those warplanes a heavy-lift Chinook was in-bound, and the twenty-six blokes on the three crippled vehicles were just a few thousand yards away from getting plucked out of the cauldron of death. If they could make it out of there, rarely would a force have snatched such a victory – or at least survival – from the jaws of defeat.

That's if the blokes could make it to that grid, get the Chinook in safely, and get pulled out alive.

# CHAPTER TWENTY-FOUR

The vehicles hammered onwards, although Moth felt able to ease off the gas just a little, with those warplanes doing their stuff above them. It was just as well, for the wagon was spitting and popping as the engine gasped its last.

Barely minutes later they pulled to a halt on a featureless patch of ground. Moth killed the motor, and just moments before it seemed destined to burst into flames. Raggy dived off the hot, smoking bonnet, as blokes piled off the rear into all-around defence.

Grey's first priority now was to blow the wagon. He started to throw out kit from the rear, so he could get to the charge and prepare to set the fuse system. He dug down to it, and his frozen fingers began feverishly to rip off the black gaffer tape that protected the trigger mechanism. In the back of his mind he knew he had to check it over first – for one or more of the wagons' fuses in the wadi of death had failed to blow.

Ed was on the radio calling for an update on the helo extraction. He came off the air following a terse exchange, balling his fists into his temples with tension.

'Change of fucking plan!' he yelled over the radios. 'We're not going to blow the wagons. If the Chinook's delayed it'll come down as the wagons blow and get caught in the blast. Rip everything out that you can salvage, and we'll leave 'em to the fast air. Chinook in-bound in five minutes.'

In spite of their utter exhaustion the blokes started sparking now. So began a fevered rush of activity, as they tried to tear all the sensitive kit out of the wagons in the short time they had remaining. In theory they were leaving them to get hit by the warplanes and denied to the enemy that way, but there were never any guarantees.

Working fast and trying not to show any lights, they started stripping sensitive kit from the Pinkies, as the Tornadoes flew close and very noisy orbits above them. Grey set about ripping the radio from its mounting, while Moth did the same with the other comms systems and their Blue Force Tracker unit.

That done, Grey grabbed the GPMG, unbolted it from its pivot mount and slung it over his shoulder. He clicked together the four hundred rounds of link, and wrapped the entire lot around his neck and torso. He hauled his Bergen and the Diemaco assault rifle out of the back of the wagon, and dumped them on the ground beside him.

To his rear the Dude moved off from the wagon staggering under the weight of the .50-cal plus a tin of ammo.

Grey stepped away from their Pinkie with the GPMG on his shoulder, Bergen on his back, ammo wrapped around him and his Diemaco in hand. In spite of his total and utter exhaustion, he was now carrying some eighty-plus kilos of weight slung around his person and somehow managing to stay on his feet.

He glanced at Moth and Raggy, plus some of the others from their wagon. Every man was plastered with mud and dust, mixed with a slick of cold, icy sweat; plus they were weighed down with all the kit that they could carry.

'You blokes ready?' Grey grunted.

He got a series of terse nods all around.

For an instant he paused, eyeing the trusted Pinkie that they were abadoning. He leaned in, checked the milometer, and did a quick mental calculation. From the reading, he figured they'd covered 1,019 kilometres since setting out from the LZ north of the Euphrates, and for a good part of that they'd been taking murderous fire. But he'd never have the chance to count the unbelievable number of hits their wagon had taken, for this was the last goodbye.

Grey turned to walk the short distance to the LZ. Not a moment too soon he detected a distant, eerie blue glow moving across the desert towards them. It was the unmistakable signature of a Chinook coming in low and fast at night. At that height, and with the way the twin rotors whipped up the air, the static electricity formed a flickering dust halo, like some kind of an alien light show.

Right now, it was the most welcome sight that any of the men had ever seen.

The lone Chinook circled in from the southeast, its twin rotors silhouetted against the glow of first light. It flared above the LZ, which Ed had marked with a distinctive symbol formed from IR cyalumes – chemical light-sticks. The helo came down in a thick, choking dust cloud, the door gunners sweeping the terrain with their miniguns as it descended, but there seemed to be nothing moving out there that was remotely close to the LZ.

The helo's ramp was down before the wheels touched the desert, and the blokes staggered aboard. Grey took one last look around him before the Chinook spooled up to speed. He tried to check that Moth, Dude, Raggy and the others were all on board, but with the choking cloud of dust kicked up by the rotors he could barely see his hand in front of his face.

The indistinct forms crouched all around him were pretty much unrecognizable, and the last thing they ever wanted to do here was to leave a man behind.

From the open ramp there came a yell: 'Twenty-six aboard!'

The helo's loadmaster had done a body count, so presumably that should be everyone. Though they were a fragmented group culled from across M Squadron, presumably all the blokes from their makeshift force were present and correct.

*Let's go.*

The turbines reached a screaming fever pitch, and the helo hauled itself into the air. With the twin-rotors powering the Chinook skywards, half the men of M Squadron were now pulling away from the desert that had so nearly been the death of them.

Through the porthole-like window Grey could see scores of burning vehicles scattered over the terrain to the north, south and the east, indicating the magnitude of the terrain over which they had done battle, plus the true the extent of the forces they had been up against.

*Sixty against a hundred thousand indeed.*

It was an overwhelming sight, and it reinforced in his mind just what a miracle it was that they were getting the hell out of there. They'd penetrated a thousand kilometres behind enemy lines, yet somehow they'd escaped from the trap that had been set for them in the cauldron that was northern Iraq. They'd done so by the very skin of their teeth, and with the gods on their side. Somehow, they were returning home from Operation No Return – as long as no one put a surface-to-air missile, or a long burst of 12.7mm fire, up their arses.

The helo banked hard, turned southwards and accelerated to its 250 kph cruising speed. As it sped low and fast across the formless desert, Grey slumped down on the cold steel floor, letting the GPMG fall from his hands. He felt his head drop to his knees. He was suddenly aware of how totally and utterly burned out he was.

He had one thought at the forefront of his mind now: there were a load of blokes from the Squadron who were still on the ground out there somewhere, desperately trying to evade and escape from the enemy. Presumably, the OC and his HQ Troop must have been plucked out of their hide by now and be on a flight out of there. Presumably Sebastian was with them, and wondering how on earth he'd survived it all.

But what about the third force, plus Gunner and his passenger? Grey wondered how many they'd lost already, and how many more they might lose in the coming hours, as the fierce Iraqi sun cast its harsh, burning light across the battlefield. Come sun-up, there would be nowhere left to hide. The only option would be to fight and die, or surrender.

This was a long way from over yet.

Where the hell was Mucker, he wondered, the fourth member of his team? He'd got two of his team out and, some might argue, the entire twenty-six-man unit, but still he'd left a man behind. He glanced at Moth and Dude. He could see a mixture of shock and relief written across their features, plus a growing sense of what almost looked like failure.

He leaned across to them. 'Lads, don't fucking worry about it!' he yelled. 'As a team we did more than okay out there.'

Moth forced a smile: 'Yeah, maybe we did all right.'

'Moth, you were mega with the wagon, not to mention the air. You drove like a fucking maniac and you smashed out the rounds from the M203. And Dude, you did a great job on the gun, mate. Plus you didn't get your head blown off, which is a bloody miracle!'

The Dude grinned, exhaustedly. Shrugged. 'Yeah. Tell you what though, we'll have some stories for our grandkids, eh? Did I ever tell you guys the one about . . .'

It was an hour's flight to the base that M Squadron had forward-mounted from, just south of the Euphrates River, at the *G2* airfield. Grey didn't get to hear the rest of the Dude's story, for he'd long since fallen into a deep sleep. Waking him from that would have been like trying to waken the dead.

The first he knew of their arrival was the helo's ramp whining open and the cold inrush of air. He levered himself to his feet, grabbed his GPMG and the rest of his kit, and turned to leave the Chinook's echoing hold. As he did so he felt a hand on his shoulder.

It was Raggy. 'Cheers for the lift, mate.'

Grey couldn't help but laugh. 'You're the only one who's bloody said thank you.'

Together with Moth, Dude and Scruff, they headed down the helo's open ramp and into the blinding light of the Iraqi dawn.

# EPILOGUE

On arrival at the *G2* airfield, the remnant force of Six Troop was reunited with M Squadron's HQ Troop. The Squadron OC and the rest of his Troop – Sebastian the interpreter included – had been pulled out of theatre by a Chinook flying a hot-extraction mission, and only shortly before their force of twenty-six had been rescued.

The HQ Troop was extracted complete with its two Pinkies, and so by then some two-thirds of the Squadron had been pulled out of Iraq, which left only the third group, plus Gunner and his quad, at large.

But that day – 24 March 2003 – news broke on Al Jazeera TV that 'ten British SAS and Special Forces had been killed in northern Iraq'. Al Jazeera cited Iraqi military sources as the basis for the story. More worrying still, footage was shown of victorious Iraqi forces riding a captured Pinkie and a quad bike – both of which were M Squadron vehicles – in order to substantiate the story.

Those men who had already been pulled out of Iraq had been placed in isolation, pending debriefs on the mission. But in spite of that, news filtered through to them regarding what the Iraqis were claiming had happened to those forces left on the ground – namely, that ten had been killed. Without doubt, this was the darkest moment of the entire mission. British forces had secured satellite images of the battlefield, which proved conclusively that the three Pinkies abandoned at the Six Troop extraction grid had been destroyed by air strikes. This meant that the captured vehicles shown on the Arab media could only come from three possible sources: from the wadi of death, from the third force still unaccounted for, or from Gunner and his passenger.

The Iraqis had also displayed a plethora of captured British kit, including various weaponry, maps and radio systems. Because the two captured Pinkies were only lightly damaged and still drivable, it seemed likely that these had been taken – along with the radio sets – at the wadi of death, and that the demolition charges had failed to blow (as many of the men had suspected). Detonators failing to go off constituted an equipment failure as opposed to human error, but still this loss weighed heavily on the Squadron.

By now day one of the Coalition war effort in Iraq was drawing to an end, and American and British forces were pushing across the border from Kuwait. It was far from welcome news that kit had been captured by the enemy, and particularly when it included such sensitive gear. But above all, it was extremely worrying to have so many elite operators from M Squadron still missing or potentially killed in action, as there were right then.

The day of their extraction, the men of M Squadron were shown photos taken from a series of air recces flown over the LUP where they had first been attacked. These showed that the area was criss-crossed with tank tracks, demonstrating that it had been comprehensively overrun by Iraqi armour. Without any Milans or similar heavy-armour-killing capability, the Squadron would have faced

Iraqi T-72s at close range with no way of fighting back, had they not abandoned the LUP when they did.

In an extraordinary turn of events, the third force was finally pulled out of Iraq late that day. With one Pinkie, three surviving quads and twenty-one blokes, their group had been horribly overloaded and lacking in mobility. Fortunately for them, it was the remnant of Six Troop at the southern end of the wadi of death that had drawn the main enemy force.

As the Iraqis had pursued the Six Troop remnant east and south, this third group had been able to sneak away into the dark at a slow crawl, which was all their vehicles could manage. Being barely mobile and low on fuel, they had no option but to find a location in which to go to ground. They'd stumbled on a ravine, which made a decent hideaway. By the time the extraction Chinook was able to get in to lift them out, they'd been lying low for many hours, during which time the battle had been moving south and west and away from their location. They were forced to blow their Pinkie, just before being extracted, for there was no room on the Chinook for the vehicle.

The twenty-one men thus rescued included Mucker, the quad driver on Grey's team. He had been one of the first into the wadi of death, following Gunner as quad leader. He'd made the decision to keep going through the soft ground, and he was nearly through when his quad bike had sunk to its axles. He'd rigged the bike with explosives, set it to blow, and joined the group gathering at the far end of the wadi.

Now that the third force was reunited with the rest of M Squadron, they were all but complete. Miraculously, there had been no loss of life. There were injuries, but nothing life-threatening. The story put out by the Iraqis that ten British Special Forces had been killed had to be a tissue of lies – although the two men on the quad were still missing. Nothing had been heard of Gunner and the officer perched on the rear of his machine. The two men were listed as 'missing in action'.

From the *G2* airfield the men of the Squadron were ferried back to their forward mounting base. There, the initial debriefs took place, during which the bigger picture began to emerge.

The major revelation resulting from their mission into northern Iraq was how woefully inaccurate the intelligence had proved to be. At this stage in the conflict, and contrary to what the Squadron had been led to believe, the Iraqi 5th Corps were far from ready to surrender, not to mention the Fedayeen. If nothing else, M Squadron's epic mission had secured ground truth in northern Iraq, proving that the Coalition were going to have to fight for every last inch of territory.

CSAR (combat search-and-rescue) flights overflew Iraq, plus the Combat RV point in Syria, as they tried to find the elusive two-man quad force. A good week after the rest of the Squadron had been pulled out, these repeated Chinook flights over Syrian territory forced the Syrians finally to admit that they had captured Gunner and his passenger, and were holding them. During all this time the two men had remained listed as missing in action.

It wasn't until 14 April – the day that the war in Iraq effectively ended, with the fall of Tikrit – that Gunner and his passenger were finally released. They'd been held for approaching three full weeks by the Syrians.

It turned out that they had made it well into Syrian territory and were a good four hours into 'safe' terrain and making for the Combat RV, when the quad had hit a ditch. They'd up-ended it, and were attempting to drag the machine out of the ditch when the Syrian forces had overrun them. Because dress was down to personal choice in the Squadron, Gunner had been wearing US-style combats, which have better rip-stop qualities. As a result, the Syrians had at first mistaken him for an American elite operator.

It had taken personal intervention from the then Prime Minister Tony Blair, who sent the Foreign Office minister Mike O'Brien to Damascus, Syria's capital, to win the men's release. He managed to convince the Syrians that the two soldiers were British Special Forces and not Americans, and to persuade them to let the men go.

They'd suffered the usual kind of interrogation at the hands of the Syrian authorities, but they had survived it all remarkably well. Gunner's biggest gripe seemed to be that the Syrians had dressed him in a cheap black nylon suit to prepare him for release, complete with black winkle-picker shoes. He'd have preferred to look the part of the man who was first in and last out, on what was without doubt the mission of a lifetime.

When Gunner and his pillion passenger were flown out of Syria, they were the last men of the Squadron to be heading home. Incredibly, the entire body of M Squadron had escaped from the fire of that mission without the loss of one single man. Gunner's escape and evasion to Syria had taken more than a hundred miles to achieve, and it was hailed by the British media as 'one of the most stirring escape stories yet to emerge from the Iraq War'.

The *Times* newspaper spoke about their achievement as an epic 'triumph over adversity'. Charles Heyman, editor of the definitive *Jane's World Armies*, commented: 'There's no doubt whatsoever that this is the sort of high standard of evasion of the enemy on the ground that we've come to expect of our Special Forces. It's still pretty remarkable.'

As with the Bravo Two Zero patrol of the First Gulf War, M Squadron had been given a mission that they doubted was doable from the get-go. Even so, when they set out to achieve that mission they little realized the extent to which the intelligence they had been given would prove faulty. The reality they drove into on the ground in northern Iraq proved almost the complete opposite to what the intel had suggested, rendering their objective largely unachievable.

In the immediate aftermath of the mission, M Squadron was pilloried in the media, especially when the captured Land Rovers were paraded on Iraqi TV and the story was picked up by the international press. Headlines appeared in the British newspapers declaring that the men of the Squadron had 'run away from the Iraqis', and there were even accusations that they had 'panicked and fled'. They were given almost no opportunity to respond to such criticism, which rankled. They had been largely vilified, and undeservedly so. Sadly, some of the men depicted in this book went on to be killed on future operations or exercises, so they will not have the opportunity to read the full story as told in these pages.

The truth is that M Squadron had been ordered to undertake a mission that was unprecedented in terms of geographic scope and goals, as well as being next to impossible in view of the faulty intelligence provided. Nonetheless, they went ahead to the best of their ability to achieve that mission, in keeping with the ethos of UK Special Forces whereby small groups of elite operators are sent in to achieve the seemingly impossible.

The Squadron penetrated some seven hundred kilometres into Iraq – amounting to over one thousand kilometres driving – without being compromised. When it was eventually hit in a deliberate attack by a combined force of Fedayeen, Iraqi infantry and heavy armour, the Squadron managed to extract with no loss of life – despite being trapped so far behind enemy lines, facing a vastly superior enemy force, and despite the fact that the limited air power provided was unable to mount any air strikes because of the confused battle situation on the ground.

The longest-ever British Special Forces mission behind enemy lines was one of David Stirling's operations with the SAS and the Long Range Desert Group during the North Africa campaign of the Second World War. In September 1942 the LRDG undertook Operation Caravan (mentioned in the main body of this book), penetrating some 1,859 kilometres across the desert, to attack airfields and barracks at the Italian-held Libyan town of Barce, and destroying many enemy aircraft on the ground.

Covering well over a thousand kilometres all told, M Squadron's mission into northern Iraq was certainly up there with the most epic undertakings by British Special Forces.

Ten days after the Squadron were pulled out of Iraq, a unit from Delta Force went into the same area, tasked with a similar mission. They had armour attached to their patrol and 24/7 dedicated air cover. They were hit by the Fedayeen in pretty much the same location as M Squadron. They ended up taking casualties, and although they inflicted heavy losses on the Fedayeen via air strikes, they too had to pull out and abandon their mission.

It wasn't until 11 April 2003 – approaching three weeks after the ground war proper had begun in Iraq – that the Iraqi 5th

Corps chose to surrender. By that time Saddam's regime had fallen, Basra, Baghdad and the northern city of Kirkuk were in Coalition hands, and the rump of Saddam's regime had retreated to the Tikrit–Bayji area and were surrounded. Supported by thousands of Kurdish Peshmerga guerrilla fighters, one thousand elite operators from the US 10th Special Operations Group, plus two thousand soldiers from the elite 173rd Airborne Brigade, took the Iraqi city of Salah, and accepted the surrender of the 5th Corps commander. However, only some fifteen thousand 5th Corps troops – a fraction of the suspected strength of the Corps – actually surrendered, and they were mostly sent back to their villages.

Most of the 5th Corps soldiers were believed to have simply 'melted away', discarding their uniforms for civilian clothing and mixing with the civilian population. This was a recurring feature of the war in Iraq, once Saddam's regime had fallen, and it contributed to the mass of weapons sloshing around the country in the aftermath of the conflict.

Thus it was that M Squadron's mission, the surrender of the Iraqi 5th Corps, had finally been achieved – but only by using three thousand crack US forces, with many battle-hardened Kurdish guerrilla fighters in support, in contrast to one squadron of sixty elite British operators. The US force was also backed by comprehensive and overwhelming air power.

Perhaps most importantly, the surrender of the Iraqi 5th Corps was taken only several weeks into the war and *after* the fall of Saddam Hussein's regime, when it was patently obvious that the Iraqi leader was never going to return to power. By that stage the Corps' commanders would have known they had nothing to lose – and potentially everything to gain – by agreeing to surrender.

When Saddam Hussein was eventually captured in Iraq in

December 2003, he was discovered hiding in the town of ad-Dawr, not far from Bayji and nearby Tikrit, his hometown. The city of Bayji and its inhabitants had indeed been a stronghold of support for the Iraqi leader, and subsequent months would prove it to be a scene of numerous insurgent attacks against US and allied forces.

To this day, Steve Grayling is convinced that M Squadron came out of the cauldron of northern Iraq without loss of life for one simple reason – because he let the Iraqi goat-herder live, the boy who had stumbled on their first LUP. Not normally one to be superstitious, Grayling has no doubt that the men of M Squadron had the gods looking after them when they found themselves centre-stage in the mother of all battles. Only the good karma of his earlier action, when he let his human instinct of compassion override his killer instincts – instincts that it might have made more sense to indulge at the time – earned the men of the Squadron the right to survive. To this day, this is his firm belief.

Whatever the truth of this, the Squadron's achievement against such overwhelming odds is extraodinary, and one that remains unparalleled in the modern history of Special Forces soldiering.

# GLOSSARY

**AFV** Armoured fighting vehicle. A blanket term used by the military that encompasses tanks, armoured cars and armoured troop carriers

**Black light** Vehicle operations conducted at night without using lights

**C130** Lockheed C-130 Hercules. A four-engine turboprop military aircraft employed primarily for transporting troops and supplies

**Chinook** Boeing CH-47 Chinook. A twin-engine, tandem rotor heavy-lift helicopter employed primarily for transporting troops and supplies

**Cyalumes** chemical light sticks

**Dicker** a phrase first used by British soldiers in Northern Ireland to describe lookouts posing as civilians who conducted reconnaissance on behalf of the iRA

**Diemaco** The Colt C7 7.62mm assault rifle is a variation of the popular M16 rifle and has become the weapon of choice for the UK Special Forces

**DPV** Desert Patrol Vehicle. Open-topped Land-Rovers designed for penetration missions deep behind enemy lines

**DShK** A 12.7mm Russian-designed anti-aircraft gun that can churn out 600 12.7mm rounds per minute. Known as the 'Dushka', meaning 'sweetie' in Russian, it can only fire on automatic, and it is a devastating weapon when targeting low-level aircraft

**ERV** Emergency rendezvous. An important element of SOP when on covert operations, ERVs are a series of locations committed to memory that allow a dispersed force to regroup securely

**Fedayeen** A combat militia under Saddam Hussein's direct control

**GPMG** General Purpose Machine Gun. Also known, affectionately, as the 'gimpy' the GPMG is a belt-fed medium machine gun, usually operated from a stationary position or mounted on a vehicle

**Humint** A source of human intelligence on the ground

**JTAC** Joint terminal attack controller. The soldier responsible for co-ordinating air strikes in support of ground troops

**Kraz 225s** A Soviet-era six-wheeled steel truck with strong off-road capabilities in widespread use with the Iraqi military

**Lion of Babylon** (Asad Babil) The Iraqi-manufactured version of the Russian T-72 main battle tank

**LRDG** Long Range Desert Group. A Second World War precursor to David Stirling's SAS

**LUP** Lying up point. A location chosen to allow a unit to occupy it undetected

**M72 LAW**. Light anti-tank weapon. A one-use 66mm rocket-launcher designed to employed against armoured vehicles.

**Milan** The Milan anti-armour missile packs a 7.1 kg wire-guided warhead that can defeat most armour, and is the most powerful and accurate piece of kit that can be operated by a light vehicle or foot patrol

**Millilux** A unit of illumination

**NBC** Nuclear, biological or chemical weapons.

**NEP** Night enhancement package. Specialist night-vision technology that shows a pilot the terrain over which they are flying in glowing near-daylight, on laptop-like computer screens mounted in the cockpit

**NVG** Night-vision goggles

**OPSEC** Operational Security

**Pinkie** Affectionate term for the open-topped, desert-adapted Land Rovers used by UKSF

**RPG** Rocket-propelled grenade

**SAM** Surface-to-air missile

**Satcom** An encrypted radio satellite communications system

*Shemagh* An Arab headscarf popular with UKSF engaged in desert operations

**SLAR** Shoulder-launched assault rocket. An 85mm rocket launcher that fires an enhanced blast warhead, more commonly known as a thermobaric device

**Terp** Military slang for interpreter

# INDEX